Basic Quality Management Systems

Essentials for Quality Management in the Medical Laboratory

James O. Westgard, PhD
Sten A. Westgard, MS

with contributions from
Leo Serrano MS, FACHE, DLM
Cheryl Wildermuth, MS, MT(ASCP)
Gabriel Migliarino, PhD
Evangelina Fernandez, MS

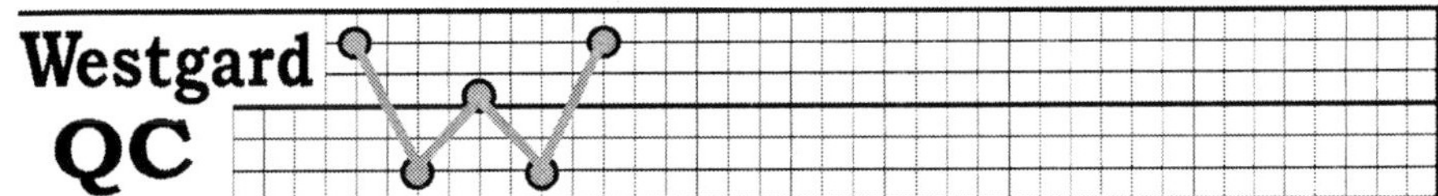

Library of Congress Control Number: 2014903024

ISBN 1-886958-28-9
ISBN-13 978-1-886958-28-9
Published by Westgard QC, Inc.
7614 Gray Fox Trail
Madison, WI 53717

Phone 608-833-4718

Preface: Managing the Quality of Laboratory Testing Processes

In 1986, Patricia Barry and I authored a book titled *Cost-Effective Quality Control: Managing the Quality and Productivity of Analytical Processes* [1]. That book introduced industrial principles of Total Quality Management (TQM) and demonstrated their application to analytical testing in Medical Laboratories. We paid particular attention to optimizing the quality and productivity (or cost) through optimization of Statistical QC procedures. We outlined the principles and approach that has guided our work on analytical quality management ever since. The foundation of TQM, together with enhancements from Six Sigma Quality Management, still provides the basis for ongoing improvement of quality in the Medical Laboratory.

This book also begins with the principles of quality management, as described in the ISO 15189 global standard for medical laboratories [2]. ISO 15189 represents the adaptation of industrial quality management for the particular application in medical laboratories. ISO standards, by their nature, provide *general* advice on what needs to be done, but the standards do not provide the details on *how* to do it. The ISO approach provides flexibility for implementing the guidance and permits adaptation for the particular operating conditions in a medical laboratory and the economic and legal environment in different countries. The difficulty for many laboratories is figuring out the "how to do it" part, which has become a crucial issue now that ISO 15189 is being adopted as the laboratory accreditation model in many countries. It is the purpose of this book to provide some practical guidance on "how to do it".

In today's vernacular, the principles of quality management are embodied in a Quality Management System (QMS). "How to do it" involves the implementing a QMS that includes both management and technical requirements, as described in ISO 15189. In this context, the first part of this book focuses on the "management" requirements and the second part on the "technical" requirements.

James O. Westgard, Ph.D. Madison, Wisconsin, 2014

How this book is structured

Part I – Basic Quality Management Systems for Regulation and Accreditation – reviews management requirements and outlines the steps for QMS implementation. Chapters 1 through 3 provide a description of QMS, review QMS essentials, and discuss the specific ISO 15189 management requirements. Guidance for implementation is provided in chapter 4 through 6. Deming's Plan-Do-Check-Act cycle (PDCA) provides the basic organization for the implementation plan. Chapter 7, written by Leo Serrano and Cheryl Wildermuth, describes a real world application in the first laboratory to be accredited by the College of American Pathologists CAP-ISO 15189 program.

Part II – Six Sigma Quality Management Systems for Examination Procedures – focuses on the technical requirements, particularly those for the assurance of quality in the analytic or examination procedures. Chapters 8 through 15 provide guidance for developing a scientific QMS, defining quality for intended use, selecting examination procedures, validating the performance of examination procedures, designing SQC procedures, formulating a Total Quality Control plan, monitoring nonconformities, and determining the uncertainty of measurements. These chapters provide the "how to do it" guidance for some of the most difficult technical requirements. They feature Sigma-metric tools to support quantitative assessments of laboratory tests and scientific guidance for managing and improving the quality of those tests.

Acknowledgements

A special thank you to Leo Seranno and Cheryl Wildermuth for authoring chapter 7 and providing a real world example of the implementation of the CAP-ISO 15189 guidelines.

The Wallace H. Coulter Foundation stimulated the development of this book with their support for Spanish translations of our books on *Basic Method Validation* and *Basic QC Practices* (as well as this book). We thank Dr. Gabriel Migliarino and Evangelina Hernandez for providing the Spanish translations and also for providing their insights on ISO 15189 accreditation in chapter 17.

It has been a privilege to author this book together with my son Sten, who has provided the motivation for Westgard QC to move forward in this area, as well as providing the technical support for converting my drafts into a finished product. It has been one of the great pleasures in my career to work with Sten on the development of the books and training materials and to have his support and participation in our educational programs. This is the tenth book published by Westgard QC! Few scientists have the resources to promote their ideas with minimum "editorial" oversight. I am one of those lucky few, thanks to Sten.

About the authors and contributors

James O. Westgard, PhD is an Emeritus Professor in the Department of Pathology and Laboratory Medicine at the University of Wisconsin Medical School. He is also the President of Westgard QC, Inc. His complete bio can be found at http://www.westgard.com/jimbio.htm

Sten Westgard, MS, is Director of Client Services and Technology for Westgard QC, where (among other duties) he manages the website and online training portal... and nags his father to write more books.

Leo Serrano, MS, FACHE, DLM Lean/Six Sigma Black Belt, is the Corporate Director of Laboratory Systems for Broward Health in Florida.

Cheryl Wildermuth, MS, MT(ASCP), Lean Green Belt, is the Quality Systems Manager at the Laboratory of Avera McKennan Hospital and University Health Center in Sioux Falls, South Dakota.

Gabriel Migliarino, Ph.D. is the president of GMigliarino Consultores. He provided the Spanish translation of three Westgard manuals, including the Spanish edition of this book, *Basic QC Practices* and *Basic Method Validation*.

Evangelina Hernandez, MS, is a Quality Assurance and Quality Control consultant at GMigliarino Consultores.

References

1. Westgard JO, Barry PL. Cost-Effective Quality Control: Managing the Quality and Productivity of Analytical Processes. Washington DC: AACC Press, 1986.

2. ISO 15189. Medical laboratories – Requirements for quality and competence. ISO, Geneva, 2012.

A Note on ISO standards and CLSI guidelines

This book discusses many different standards and guidelines related to Quality Management Systems, including ISO 15189 and CLSI EP23A. We should note that CLSI has *trademarked* EP23, and that they are extremely careful in their commercial use of that guideline.

In that spirit, readers should note that each standard, guideline, and regulation is inevitably a moving target. ISO and CLSI continuously review and attempt to improve their documents, issuing an update or revision every few years. The regulatory and accreditation bodies (CLIA, CAP, JC, A2LA, COLA, etc.) do the same. Thus, the specific language of some of these standards will change. However, as you are probably well aware, major changes in regulatory policy are infrequent. It is unlikely that significant changes will occur that change the goals of these organizations and their recommendations.

It is also important to note that this book is NOT meant to replace or substitute for ISO standards or CLSI guidelines. Laboratories are strongly encouraged to purchase the specific documents that they intend to implement in their operations. For a laboratory that intends to implement a Quality Management System, it will not be sufficient to read this book alone.

Where this book can be helpful is to give an overview and a comparison of ISO and CLSI (and other) recommendations. Laboratories may be able to decide *which* documents to purchase, as well as how to reconcile the differences between the different standards and guidelines.

The unique feature of this book is the Sigma-metric approach. While the other recommendations tend to be vague on how to implement and monitor the specifics of a quality management system, this book is very quantitative and data-driven. Assessing your processes on the sigma scale will give you a concrete estimate of the performance of your QMS. The combination of the Six Sigma approach with Quality Management System concepts can provide powerful tools and techniques to your laboratory.

Table of Contents

Part One: Basic Quality Management Systems for Regulation and Accreditation

Part Two: Six Sigma Quality Management Systems for Examination Procedures

But Wait, That's Not All!

Readers who visit Westgard Web can gain access to online extras, such as a full reference list, glossary of terms, links to spreadsheets, checklists, worksheets, and other downloads related to this book.

Go to **http://www.westgard.com/qmsextras.htm**

Part I. Basic Quality Management Systems for Regulation and Accreditation

The first part of this book presents a broad perspective of management and technical requirements for laboratory accreditation, with a focus on the plan and process for implementing a Quality Management System. It emphasizes the management responsibility to make a commitment to quality and implement a quality system that supports all laboratory personnel in their efforts to produce quality test results and continually improve production processes.

Chapter 1 – Understanding Quality Management Systems – introduces Deming's Plan-Do-Check-Act cycle (PDCA) as the fundamental building block for a QMS.

Chapter 2 – Reviewing QMS Essentials – compares and contrasts the principles and approaches of Total Quality Management, the US CLIA regulations for laboratories, the WHO/CLSI/CDC quality system essentials, and the ISO 15189 guidance.

Chapter 3 – Focusing on ISO 15189 – enumerates the list of management and technical requirements to provide an overview of the complete QMS for a medical laboratory.

Chapter 4 – Preparing for QMS Implementation – reviews Deming's principles for Total Quality Management and his requirements for implementation, along with other more specific guidance for implementation in medical laboratories.

Chapter 5 – Implementing Management Requirements – provides a step-by-step description of a PDCA plan for addressing the ISO 15189 management requirements.

Chapter 6 – Implementing Technical Requirements – provides a step-by-step description of a PDCA plan for addressing the ISO 15189 technical requirements.

Chapter 7 – A Lab's Journey to CAP-ISO 15189 Accreditation – presents the real world experience of one laboratory's effort to achieve accreditation.

1. Understanding Quality Management Systems

There is extensive literature about quality management in medical laboratories. Topics frequently include Quality Control, Quality Assurance, Quality Assessment, Quality Improvement, and Quality Planning, which are all part of Quality Management today. In addition, there is discussion of Quality Indicators, Lean Management, Six Sigma, Risk Analysis, ISO standards, and CLSI guidelines. For laboratory scientists, it's a challenge to integrate all these programs, guidelines, standards, and tools into a cohesive Quality Management System, whose purpose is to define the organizational structure and essential activities that are necessary to achieve quality in routine laboratory services.

W. Edwards Deming, who is often considered the father of Quality Management, described a "system" as a "series of functions or activities within an organization that work together for the aim of the organization" [1]. The parts of the system are interdependent and therefore require management to keep them in balance. Deming often referred to "optimization of the system" as the responsibility of management. He suggested that an orchestra was a good example of a system and that the conductor was a manager responsible for optimizing quality and performance.

Today there is a new emphasis on Quality Management Systems in medical laboratories and an increased recognition that management leadership and commitment are essential to guarantee the quality in all activities and processes in the laboratory. In effect, this is the second coming (or re-discovery) of the Total Quality Management principles and lessons learned back the 1990s when healthcare organizations began to adopt industrial models for Quality Management. The ISO 15189 standard adapts industrial principles and concepts specifically for application in the medical laboratory, creating a global standard for quality and competence in medical laboratories [2]. In addition, CLSI has developed detailed guidance for development of QMS in healthcare organizations [3] and medical laboratories [4]. CLSI's Quality System Essentials (QSEs) emphasize organization, customer focus, facilities and safety, personnel, equipment, process management, documents and records, information management, nonconforming event management, assessments, and continual improvement.

All of these activities are part of current management practices and are already included in regulatory and accreditation requirements. So what is new and different about a Quality Management System?

ISO/CLSI definitions of terms

The language of quality today is defined by ISO (International Organization for Standardization) in an effort to standardize terminology for world-wide commerce. Because of that focus on commerce, business and industry are the main drivers and contributors to ISO standard development. CLSI functions as an agent of ISO for development of standards of practice for medical laboratories. In that role, CLSI provides a "harmonized terminology database" that is accessible at www.clsi.org.

Here are the ISO/CLSI definitions of some of the common terms in quality management:

- **Quality management** – *coordinated activities to direct and control an organization with regard to quality. Note (GP29): Direction and control with regard to quality usually includes establishment of the quality policy and quality objectives, quality planning, quality control, quality assurance, and quality improvement.*
  - **Quality** – *degree to which a set of inherent characteristics fulfills requirements.*
  - **Quality policy** – *overall intentions and direction of an organization related to quality as formally expressed by top management*
  - **Quality objective** – *something sought, or aimed for, related to quality*

- **Quality planning** – *part of quality management focused on setting quality objectives and specifying necessary operational processes and related resources to fulfill the quality objectives.*

- **Quality control** – *part of quality management focused on fulfilling quality requirements.... Note 2. In health care testing, the set of procedures designed to monitor the test method and the results to ensure appropriate test system performance.... Note 8. The purpose of quality control is to ensure that all quality requirements are being met. Note 9: The set of mechanisms, processes, and procedures designed to monitor the measuring system to ensure the results are reliable for the intended clinical use.* [see CLSI database for complete definition and all the notes, which run more than a page]

- **Quality assurance** – *part of quality management focused on providing confidence that quality requirements will be fulfilled. Note 1: The practice that encompasses all procedures and activities directed toward ensuring that a specified quality of product is achieved and maintained. In the testing environment, this includes monitoring all the raw materials, supplies, instruments, procedures, sample collection/transportation/storage/processing, recordkeeping, calibrating and maintenance of equipment, quality control, proficiency testing, training of personnel, and all else involved in the production of the data reported.*

- **Quality improvement** – *part of quality management focused on increasing the ability to fulfill quality requirements.*

- **Quality management system** – *management system to direct and control an organization with regard to quality. Note 1: Systematic and process-oriented efforts are essential to meet quality objectives. Note 2: For the purposes of ISO 15189, the "quality" referred to in this definition relates to matters of both management and technical competence; Note 3: A quality management system typically includes the organizational structure, resources, processes, and procedures* *needed to implement quality management; Note 4: These principles include the following categories: documents and records, organization, personnel, equipment, purchasing and inventory, process management, information management, nonconforming event management, assessments, continual improvement, customer focus, and facilities and safety.*

- **Quality system** – *the organizational structure, resources, processes, and procedures needed to implement quality management.* [same as note 3 above]
- **Quality System Essentials** – *coordinated management activities to direct and control an organization with regard to quality.* [the activities defined in note 4 above]

Practical Purpose of QMS

Quality objectives and requirements must be defined if quality is to be measurable and manageable.

Quality Management describes the activities that are necessary to achieve quality objectives and requirements.

A **Quality Management System** provides the organizational structure, processes, procedures, and tools for implementing the activities necessary to achieve the quality objectives and requirements.

Defining Quality Objectives and Requirements

Given the importance of defining quality objectives and requirements, the ISO definition of quality may need some additional explanation. Other definitions are helpful to supplement and expand its meaning, such as the following:

- Juran – *Quality is fitness for use.* [5]
- Deming – *Quality should be aimed at the needs of the customer.* [6]
- Crosby – *Quality is conformance to requirements.* [7]
- CDC 1986 – *Quality of a laboratory testing service depends on providing the totality of features and characteristics that conform to the stated or implied needs of users or customers.* [8]

Important points are (a) the focus on needs of users and customers to define requirements; (b) the phrase "totality of features and characteristics" which reveals that quality is multi-dimensional, e.g., right patient, right specimen, right turnaround time, right test result, right report format, right patient record, etc.; (c) recognition that needs may be stated or implied, e.g., turnaround time will be a *stated* need that can be defined by the user, whereas analytical quality is an *implied* need that must be defined by the laboratory based on the intended clinical use of the test results; (d) "conformance to requirements" reveals how quality itself can be measured by identifying non-conformities or defects.

Developing a QMS

The fundamental model for a quality management system is Deming's Plan-Do-Check-Act cycle, which embodies the principles of scientific investigation and objective decision-making. The PDCA cycle is commonly presented as shown in Figure 1-1.

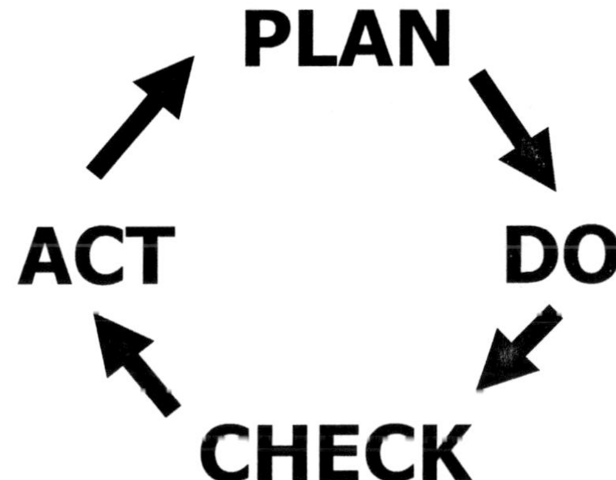

Figure 1-1. Deming's Plan-Do-Check-Act (PDCA) cycle.

- PLAN clearly aligns with quality planning.
- DO describes the policies, procedures, and processes for laboratory testing.

- CHECK involves quality control of the laboratory production processes.
- ACT relates to actions based on results obtained, such as decisions on the acceptability of production, root cause identification, quality improvement, etc.

Westgard TQM model. In adapting the Deming model for application in medical laboratories [9], the PDCA cycle can be expanded to include a component for quality assessment (QA) and also to provide a central focus on quality goals and objectives, as shown in Figure 1-2.

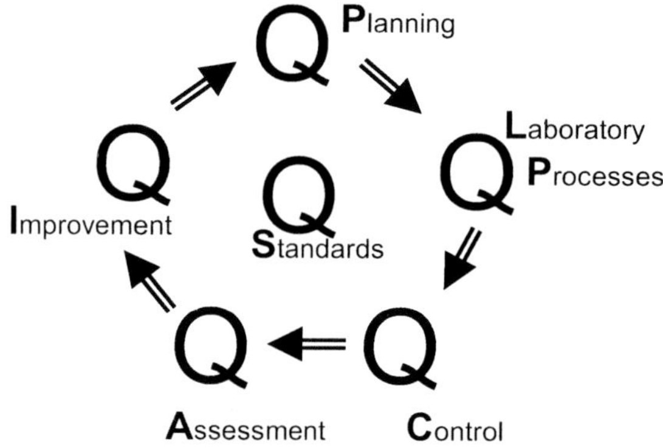

Figure 1-2. Total Quality Management Laboratory Process.

QP refers to Quality Planning; QLP to Quality Laboratory Processes; QC to Quality Control; QA to Quality Assessment; QI to Quality Improvement; and QS to Quality Standards, which represent the quality policy, goals, objectives, and requirements that need to be achieved. It bears repeating that the term QA here refers to quality *assessment*, not quality *assurance*. Quality assessment provides for measuring and monitoring the "*totality of features and characteristics*," whereas quality control is focused on monitoring the analytical quality of the test results. In the CLIA regulations, QA always means quality assessment, rather that quality assurance. Quality assurance is the outcome of the entire quality management system.

Six Sigma DMAIC model. Another well-known version of the Deming model is found in Six Sigma Quality Management and is called DMAIC [9]. As shown in Figure 1-3, the steps or components start at the top with Define, then complete the cycle with Measure, Analyze, Improve, and Control. In this adaptation, the Define step relates to quality-planning and includes definition of quality objectives and requirements, the Measure step applies to determining the performance of a procedure, process, or product; the Analyze step involves evaluation of the observed quality, which naturally leads to the Improve step of the process; finally, Control here means maintaining the quality of the improved procedure, process, or product so that it continues to meet the quality objectives and requirements.

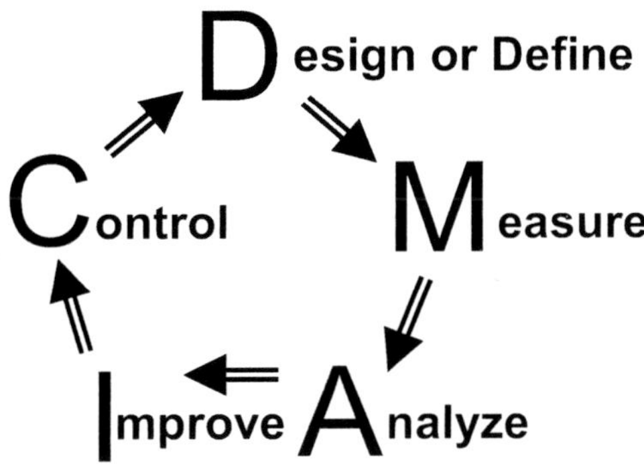

Figure 1-3. Six Sigma DMAIC Model for Process Improvement.

ISO 15189 PDCA model. The Deming cycle can also be applied to the ISO 15189 management and technical requirements, as described by Dr. David Burnett, who chaired the committee that developed the latest 2012 standard. Figure 1-4 represents Burnett's view of ISO as a process, rather than as a list of activities [Note that in the figure shown here, the PDCA cycle is presented as a clockwise rotation to have the same orientation as the other models.] This process perspective is not presented in the ISO standard itself, but Dr. Burnett features it in his public lectures about ISO 15189 and it is also presented in his book on ISO 15189 implementation[10].

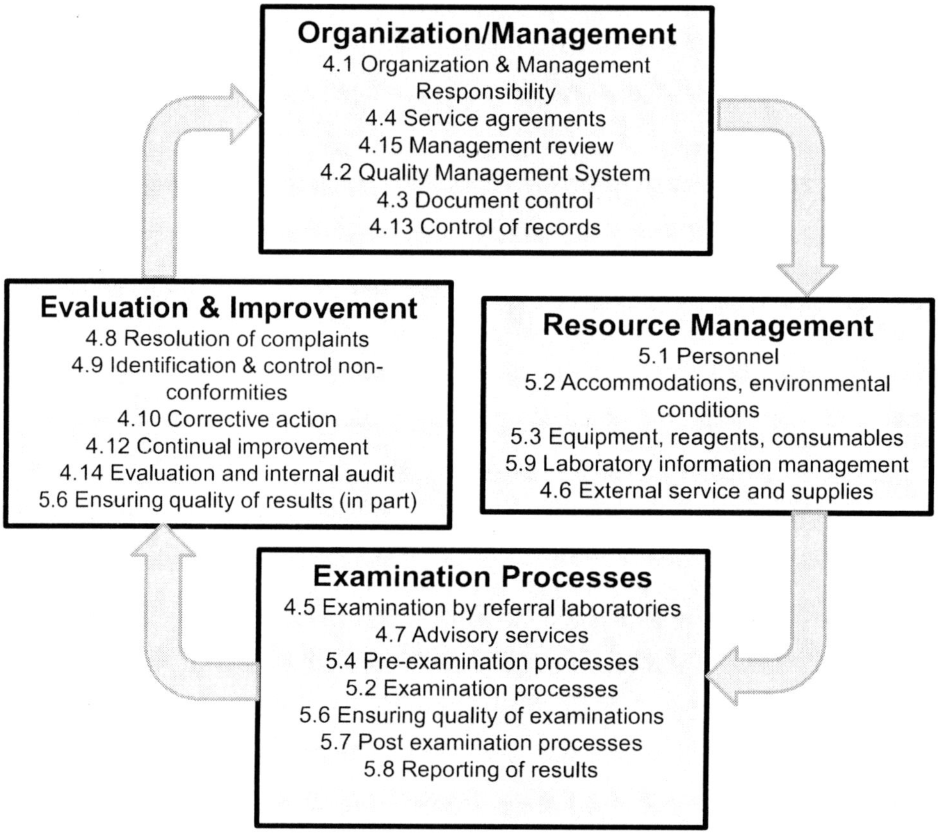

Figure 1-4. Burnett's PDCA Process model for ISO 15189 QMS.

ISO Requirements versus QMS

The ISO 15189 management and technical requirements, as well as the US CLIA regulatory requirements, are often presented as items in checklists in order to facilitate inspection and accreditation. However, for practical applications in the laboratory, those activities must be organized to support the daily management of testing processes. That organization, along with support for implementation, defines the Quality Management System.

Given the inherent differences between laboratories based on their resources, skills, and missions, it is expected that Quality Management Systems will vary from one laboratory to another, yet they should all be designed to guarantee that the laboratory fulfills its quality objectives and requirements. Certain principles guide the formulation of all Quality Management Systems, certain approaches may prove to be useful in many laboratories (such as Six Sigma), and certain tools are almost universally needed (method validation protocols, SQC, PT/EQA), yet the organization and deployment in individual laboratories will depend on the available resources and skills.

What is different about QMS is not the activities or requirements necessary to guarantee the quality of laboratory tests, but how to organize and embed those activities to ensure quality in the daily management and production of laboratory tests. Deming's PDCA model provides the fundamental guidance for structuring Quality Management Systems, but needs to be adapted, expanded, and detailed for efficient and effective management of laboratory testing processes.

What's the point?

On the road to quality, there is an itinerary for the journey. That itinerary details the important landmarks along the way that contribute to the success of the journey. The implementation of that journey requires a map to effectively organize the trip and to identify the correct path. Quality management identifies the itinerary of activities; a quality system provides a plan or map for organizing and implementing those activities. There is a basic structure for maps (North is up, rivers are blue, interstate highways are bold, etc.) and likewise, there is a basic structure for a QMS in the form of Deming's PDCA model. The maps for individual states and the QMSs from one laboratory to another may differ, but they should maintain a commonality of structure and purpose even though there may be unique paths for each laboratory's journey.

References

1 Nillson Orsini J. The Essential Deming: Leadership Principles from the Father of Quality W. Edwards Deming. Mc-Graw Hill, 2013.

2 ISO 15189. Medical laboratories – Requirements for quality and competence. ISO, Geneva, 2012.

3 CLSI HS1. A Quality Management System Model for Health Care. Clinical and Laboratory Standards Institute, Wayne, PA.

4 CLSI GP26. Application of a Quality Management System Model for Laboratory Services. Clinical and Laboratory Standards Institute, Wayne PA.

5 Juran JM. The Quality Trilogy. Quality Progress. 1986;August:19-24.

6 Deming WE. Out of the Crisis. Cambridge MA:MIT Center for Advanced Engineering Study, 1986.

7 Crosby PB. Quality is Free. New York:New American Press, 1979.

8 Centers for Disease Control. Proceedings of the 1986 Institute – Managing the quality of laboratory test results in a changing health care environment. DuPont Company, 1987.

9 Westgard JO, Burnett RW, Bowers GN. Quality management science in clinical chemistry: a dynamic framework for continuous improvement of quality. Clin Chem 1990;36:1712-1716.

10 Burnett D. A Practical Guide to Accreditation, 2nd ed. London:Association of Clinical Biochemists, 2013.

2. Reviewing QMS Essentials

Regulatory and accreditation requirements differ from country to country, but they typically include management responsibilities and technical competencies that are to be achieved through a Quality Management System (QMS). The US CLIA regulations [1] provide a regulatory model that focuses on specific quality systems for pre-analytic, analytic, and post-analytic processes, with some coverage of management requirements. ISO 15189 [2] provides the global model for a QMS with its description of management requirements plus specific technical requirements for pre-examination, examination, and post-examination processes. The World Health Organization (WHO) in collaboration with the Clinical Laboratory Standards Institute (CLSI) and the Centers for Disease Control (CDC) provides education and training for quality management that focuses on "Quality System Essentials", which describe the general requirements for a QMS [3-6]. In addition, there are professional organizations and consulting businesses that offer specific guidance for developing and implementing QMS that satisfy particular accreditation requirements. For example, the College of American Pathology (CAP) provides both a CLIA accreditation based on technical requirements [7] and a CAP 15189 accreditation based on ISO 15189 management requirements [8]. The A2LA also has a QMS focus.

This wealth of information and guidance may be confusing for the personnel in busy medical laboratories where there is limited time to study, select, plan, and develop a QMS. To help summarize the various guidelines, a Total Quality Management model is presented here to compare the organization and information content of the various recommendations. The purpose in this chapter is to consider the common elements and describe the "essentials" that should be part of any QMS.

Total Quality Management Model for a Medical Laboratory

Figure 2-1 provides a TQM model of a medical laboratory, where top of the figure focuses on technical requirements for the pre-analytic, analytic, and analytic phases of the laboratory testing and the bottom focuses on management requirements. This "upside-down" organizational diagram is intentional and embodies the TQM principles that (a) quality is dependent on processes, (b) management is responsible for the design and implementation of those processes, and (c) problems with quality at the bench level are due to imperfect processes, rather than the fault of the analysts. In this model, management requirements are the structure that supports the production processes. Because problems with quality are attributed to the processes, not the people, this means management is responsible for resolving any and all problems with quality. This requires management to lead and commit to quality and plan, implement, monitor, and improve those processes. The Quality Management System is the structure and organization for assuring the quality of the laboratory processes and the testing services.

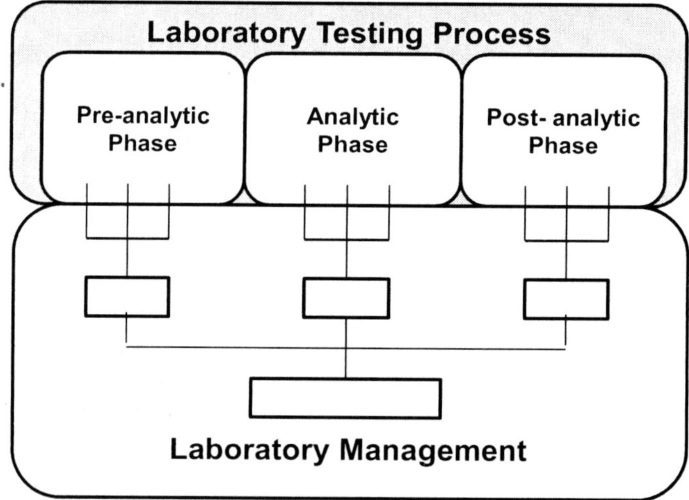

Figure 2-1. Total Quality Management model for a Medical Laboratory

CLIA Quality Systems for the Total Testing Process

The CLIA rules were first released in 1992, in response to a 1988 law of Congress, which is to say that the "rules" are the mechanism for implementing the law. The CLIA rules were updated in 2003 with the intent of integrating QMS concepts and principles in the Final Rule [2], but it is difficult to recognize some of the elements because the regulatory intent and organizational structure pre-date the ideas of Quality Management Systems. That means that some important principles such as assessment of quality, correction of problems, and continuous improvement have been squeezed in where possible in the periodic revisions that led to the CLIA Final Rule in 2003, often without sufficient context to help laboratories understand the full meaning of Quality Systems. More practical guidance is provided in a separate document known as the State Operations Manual (SOM).

Figure 2-2 describes the CLIA model for quality management. The "Total Testing Process" is comprised of Pre-analytic, Analytic and Post-analytic Systems. The General Laboratory System considers management requirements to support the total testing process.

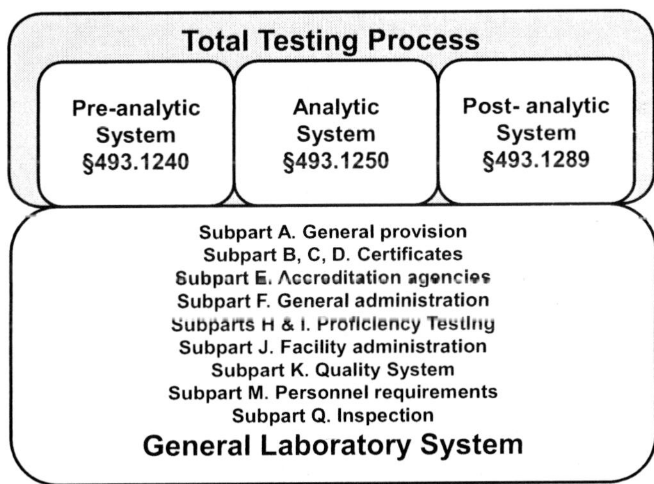

Figure 2-2. CLIA Guidance for Quality Systems (Part 493)

The structure of the CLIA document makes it difficult to maintain a focus on quality systems, but Subpart K clearly contains essential information about the desired Quality Management Systems for Nonwaived Testing, which refers to moderate and highly complex methods according to the CLIA classifications of methods. Nonwaived methods generally are those found in a central laboratory, in contrast to "waived" methods that may be employed in Physician Office Laboratories. Proficiency testing requirements are found in Subparts H & I, facility administration in Subpart J, and personnel qualifications are found in Subpart M. Thus the organizational structure of the CLIA document makes it difficult to separate the management and technical responsibilities. Nonetheless, CLIA places a strong emphasis on the Total Testing Process and the quality systems for pre-analytic, analytic, and post-analytic parts of that process. It provides some of the elements for management responsibilities and competencies, but it is not as thorough and specific in that area as ISO 15189.

WHO/CLSI/CDC Quality System Essentials

The World Health Organization (WHO), in collaboration with the Clinical Laboratory and Standards Institute (CLSI) and the Centers Disease Control (CDC), provides a Laboratory Quality Management System Handbook [5] and Training Toolkit [6]. These materials were developed to provide education on quality management to all laboratory personnel, from managers and administrators to bench-level analysts. The materials describe 12 "Quality System Essentials" (QSEs), which are the generic elements of a QMS in any medical laboratory. The materials are also intended to support the application of ISO 15189, but they are organized differently and combine the 25 ISO requirements into 12 essentials.

These QSEs are building blocks, all of which are required, but without any dictated order of development and implementation. The WHO materials present the essentials in the following order: facilities and safety; equipment; purchasing and inventory; sample management; introduction to quality control, quantitative quality control, and quality control for qualitative and semi-quantitative procedures; audits; external quality assessment; personnel; customer service; occurrence management; process improvement, documents and records; information management; and organization.

CLSI GP26 provides a different organization and numbering, as shown in Figure 2-3. Lucia Berte has been a key leader in the development of the CLSI documents on QMS. In a paper titled *Laboratory Quality Management: A Roadmap*, she provides an excellent historical perspective on the development of QMS, a thorough overview of the essentials, and a discussion of their relationship to quality management tools and practices [9]. For those who do not have ready access to the CLSI guidelines, Berte's paper is an excellent reference. She also provides a wide variety of training courses and services to support QMS implementation [10].

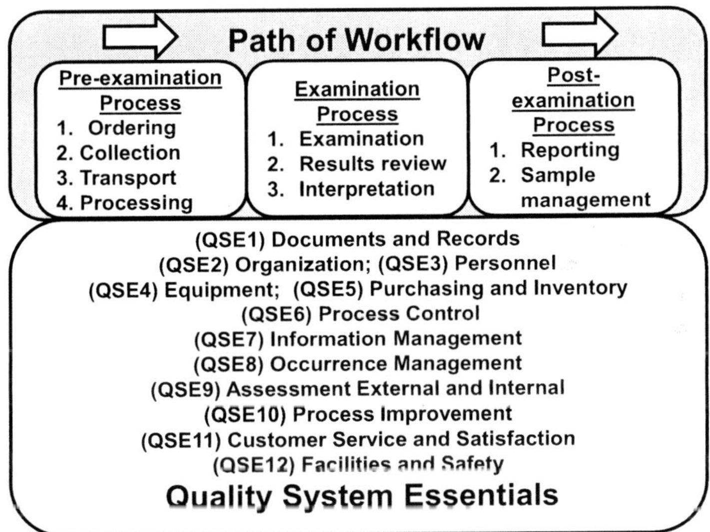

Figure 2-3. WHO/CLSI/CDC Quality System Essentials

One element in common with CLIA's "Total Testing Process" is the "Path of Workflow." While the terminology is different, there is a consistent emphasis on the three phases of the laboratory testing process. Whereas CLIA separates the pre-analytic, analytic, and post-analytic quality systems, the three are combined under "process control" in the CLSI essentials. ISO 15189 also provides a more distinct separation of the technical requirements from the management requirements.

Here's a brief description of the WHO Quality System Essentials:

- **Organization.** Top management in the laboratory must make a commitment to quality and provide the leadership to plan, develop, and implement a QMS. A Quality Steering Team is essential for planning and developing the QMS. A Quality Manager is needed to manage the implementation. A Quality Policy must be issued and Quality Goals and Objectives developed to guide the process.

- **Customer focus.** Requirements for laboratory services need to be defined with the intent of satisfying the clinical intended use of those services. The focus must be to understand the needs of customers, consumers, clients, and users (whatever terms are preferred in referring to patients, physicians, nurses, and medical staff, including laboratory staff). Management must develop planning procedures that focus on fulfillment of customer needs, then monitor performance, quality, customer satisfaction, and complaints.

- **Facilities and safety.** A laboratory needs adequate space that is appropriately designed for services to be provided. Safety programs are an important part of the basic structure of a laboratory to protect patients from any harm from the laboratory testing process and protect hospital and laboratory staff from any harm from laboratory operations.

- **Personnel.** Qualifications for technical personnel are critical for quality services. In-service training and continuing education are necessary to maintain and update technical skills and scientific knowledge. A system for periodic assessment of competency is integral for maintaining a skilled workforce.

- **Purchasing and inventory.** Requirements for supplies, materials, and services must be specified by the laboratory to ensure achievement of quality goals and objectives. The purchasing process will often involve other parties in the healthcare organization, but the laboratory must participate to make sure technical specifications are considered along with costs. Control of incoming materials may likewise involve parties outside the laboratory, but the laboratory must take responsibility for any testing and qualification that is necessary to assure quality. The laboratory must also consider processes for inventory and tracking, monitoring of storage, and re-ordering.

- **Equipment**. Acquisition of analytic equipment and systems is a critical activity because the quality of testing is primarily determined by the quality of the testing processes provided in the analytic systems that are purchased from industry. Development of specifications is critical, followed by review of performance of available systems, selection based on quality and cost, qualification and validation of performance in the laboratory, and ongoing maintenance.

- **Process management.** This single essential covers the pre-examination, examination, and post-examination processes, including design of those processes, verification or validation of performance, ongoing process control, monitoring via EQA and quality indicators, managing events or changes, and initiating corrective and preventive actions.

- **Documents and records.** There are content requirements for documents and records, as well as a need for standardized formats. A document management system is essential for identifying documents and assuring each policy, process, procedure, and form is the current version for use. A record management system is likewise needed to monitor the creation, identification, change, review, retention, and storage.

- **Information management.** Distribution of test results and summary reports is critical for effective service and most often will be achieved through an electronic information system. Security of access and confidentiality of information must be assured, along with accuracy of reports and storage and retention of records.

- **Nonconforming event management.** This essential is often discussed as occurrence management, i.e., occurrence of events of nonconformance to requirements. In simple terms, this means mistakes, problems, device failures, critical incident reports, and complaints that identify errors that have occurred. Known events should lead to corrective actions, preventive actions, and continual improvement. Unknown events, i.e., potential process failures that might occur, should be addressed using risk management techniques.
- **Assessments.** There are many techniques that can be employed to assess the state of quality and performance in the laboratory. Ongoing assessments are an essential part of any QMS. Internal assessments include process controls and quality indicators selected by the laboratory to monitor quality and performance. Periodic audits and management review are also essential. External assessments include PT or EQA programs, benchmarking programs, inspection, and accreditation.
- **Continual improvement.** Information on nonconformities, internal and external assessments and audits, and management review should identify needs for improvement and lead to action plans that target specific tests and services for improvement. In contrast to corrective and preventive actions, continual improvement should aim at eliminating problems and achieving new levels of quality and performance.

Much more detailed descriptions of these essentials are found in the WHO Handbook [5], which is nearly 250 pages, and the CLSI G26 document [4], which is over 100 pages. In contrast, ISO 15189 is only about 50 pages long.

ISO 15189 Requirements for Quality and Competence

Management requirements are identified in Figure 2-4 and can be seen to be consistent, though not identical, with the WHO/CLSI/CDC essentials. Technical requirements include 5.1 Personnel, 5.2 Accommodations and environmental conditions, 5.3 Laboratory equipment, reagents, and consumables, 5.4 Pre-examination processes, 5.5 Examination processes, 5.6 Ensuring the quality of examination processes, 5.7 Post-examination processes, 5.8 Reporting of results, 5.9 Release of results, and 5.10 Laboratory information management. All these management and technical requirements will be reviewed in more detail in the next chapter. The objective here is to again to illustrate how various guidance documents differ in their contents and organization.

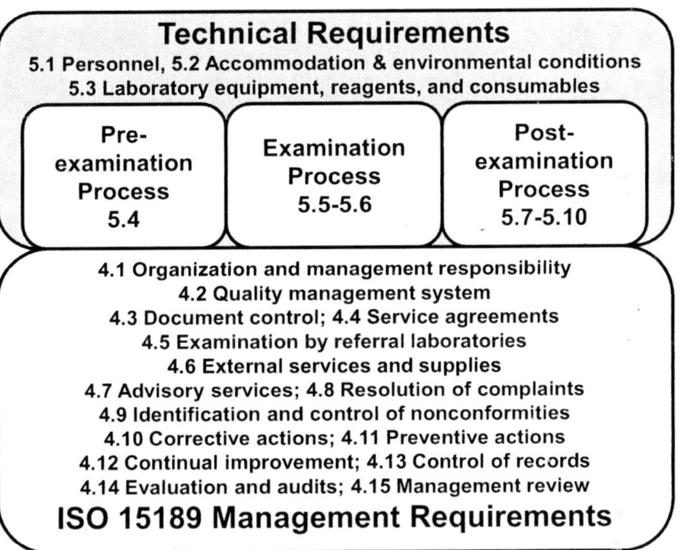

Figure 2-4. ISO 15189 Technical and Management Requirements

ISO 15189 provide a particularly good "definition" of QMS in section 4.2.1, which reads as follows:

> *The laboratory shall establish, document, implement and maintain a quality management system and continually improve its effectiveness in accordance with the requirements in this International Standard. The quality management system shall provide for the integration of all processes required to fulfill its quality policy and objectives and meet the needs and requirements of the users. The laboratory shall:*

- *Determine the processes needed for the quality management system and ensure their application throughout the laboratory.*
- *Determine the sequence and interaction of these processes,*
- *Determine criteria and methods needed to ensure that both the operation and control of these processes are effective;*
- *Ensure the availability of resources and information necessary to support the operation and monitoring of these processes;*
- *Monitor and evaluate these processes;*
- *Implement actions necessary to achieve planned results and continual improvement of these processes.*

This QMS requirement itself illustrates the structure of the PDCA cycle. PLAN involves determination of processes, sequences and interaction, and criteria and methods; DO involves ensuring the resources and information to implement and operate the processes; CHECK involves monitoring and evaluation; and ACT requires actions and continual improvement.

What's the point?

It's a jungle out there and you have to find your own path through all the available guidance and other educational materials. Based on your background and experience, you have to select the materials that will help you move forward. The WHO/CLSI/CDC Quality Management System Handbook provides a good introduction to quality management, as well as an overview of Quality System Essentials. In addition, there are detailed training materials available online in the "Training Kit." If you already have a good understanding of quality management and are comfortable with this background material, then you are ready to tackle the ISO 15189 standard itself and utilize the CLSI G26 guideline for specific details about ISO management requirements. The next chapter will provide an overview of the ISO 15189 requirements and the following chapters some guidance on implementing QMS. The second half of this book will provide in-depth guidance for the technical requirements.

References

1. US Centers for Medicare & Medicaid Services (CMS). Medicare, Medicaid, and CLIA Programs. Laboratory Requirements Relating to Quality Systems and Certain Personnel Qualifications. Final Rule. Fed Regist Jan 24 2003;16:3640-3714.

2. ISO 15189. Medical laboratories – Requirements for quality and competence. ISO, Geneva, 2012.

3. CLSI HS1. A Quality Management System Model for Health Care. Clinical and Laboratory Standards Institute, Wayne, PA 2011.

4. CLSI GP26A4. Quality Management System: A model for laboratory services. Clinical and Laboratory Standards Institute, Wayne, PA 2011.

5. WHO Laboratory Quality Management System Handbook. World Health Organizations, Geneva, Switzerland; 2011. Available from WHO website, www.who.int/ihr/publications/lqms/en/index.html, accessed August 22, 2013.

6. WHO Laboratory Quality Management System Training Toolkit. World Health Organization, Geneva, Switzerland. Available from WHO websiste, www.who.int/ihr/training_quality/en/index.html, accessed August 22, 2013.

7. CAP Laboratory Accreditation Program

8. CAP 15189 Management Accreditation.

9. Berte LM. Laboratory Quality Management: A roadmap. Clin Lab Med 2007;27:771-790.

10. Better Quality Management Implementation. www.laboratoriesmadebetter.com, accessed 8/28/2013.

3. Focusing on ISO 15189 QMS Requirements

The ISO 15189 standard [1] provides a concise description of both management and technical requirements. Management requirements are listed in section 4 and technical requirements in section 5. This is a well-organized description of the requirements for a QMS in a medical laboratory. But while ISO 15189 identifies *what* needs to be done, *it is not prescriptive in how to do it.* Professionals in the field will need to supply their own "how" for implementation, or solicit support from other organizations such as WHO, CLSI, or global, national, or regional accrediting bodies.

Management requirements are described first, followed by technical requirements. These requirements were identified earlier in Chapter 2 and are discussed in more detail here. First, however, let's consider how the ISO 15189 requirements themselves fit into the Deming Plan-Do-Check-Act cycle for a QMS.

Process Model for ISO 15189

For many laboratory scientists, it is difficult to see how this list of 25 requirements can be integrated into a comprehensive quality management system. Here's where Deming's Plan-Do-Check-Act cycle provides a basic structure for organizing and implementing a QMS. One good example of this perspective is provided by the Canadian Institute for Quality Management in Healthcare (IQMH) [2], which organizes the requirements, as shown in Figure 3-1, under four components: (1) management responsibility, (2) resource management, (3) service realization, and (4) measurement, analysis, and improvement.

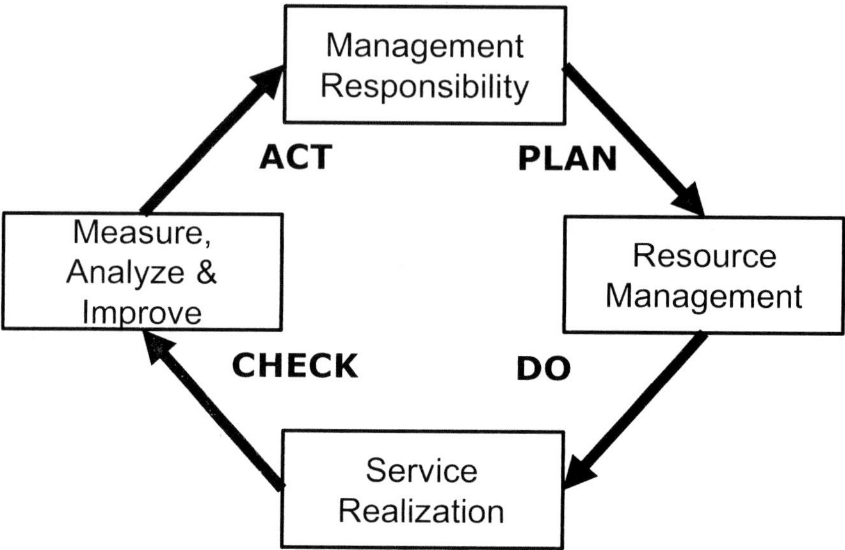

Figure 3-1. General process model for deployment of ISO 15189 requirements. From GJ Flynn, J Coffey. ISO 15189 Medical Laboratories: Understanding the four components of a quality management system. www.darkdaily.com (2011 White Paper)

The IQMH PDCA model can be expanded to identify all the management and technical requirements as shown in Figure 3-2.

Management responsibility. Implementation requires management leadership and commitment, which should be first documented through the laboratory Quality Policy. Implementation begins with the appointment of a Quality Manager and the formation of a quality management steering committee that creates the infrastructure to develop and document policies, processes, procedures, and records. This includes 4.1 Organization and management responsibility, 4.2 Quality management system, 4.3 Document control, 4.4 Service agreements, 4.5 Examination by referral laboratories, 4.6 External services and supplies, 4.7 Advisory services, and 4.13 Control of records.

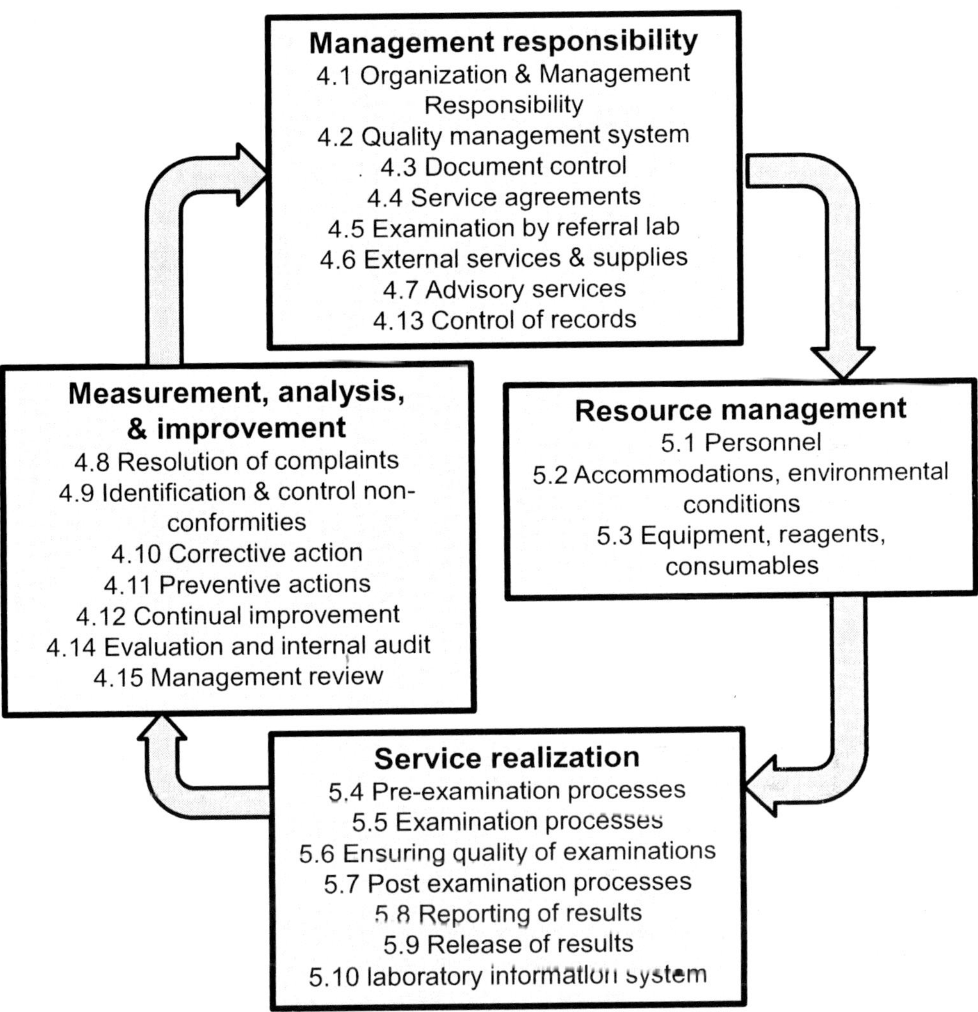

Figure 3-2. Detailed model for deployment of ISO 15189 requirements. From GJ Flynn, J Coffey. ISO 15189 Medical Laboratories: Understanding the four components of a quality management system. www.darkdaily.com (2011 White Paper)

Resource management. The laboratory must develop a plan for acquiring equipment and supplies, employing and managing personnel who have the appropriate technical competencies, providing adequate space and a safe environment for operations, and developing processes that provide the desired services. This includes 5.1 Personnel, 5.2 Accommodation and environmental conditions, 5.3 Laboratory equipment, reagents, and consumables.

Service realization. This component represents the implementation of laboratory services in the form of the pre-examination, examination, and post-examination processes. This includes 5.4 Pre-examination processes, 5.5 Examination processes, 5.6 Ensuring the quality of examination results, 5.7 Post-examination processes, 5.8 Reporting of results, 5.9 Release of results, and 5.10 Laboratory information system.

Measurement, analysis and improvement. This represents the monitoring of quality and performance, the identification of problems, and the corrective and preventive actions that must be planned and implemented to provide continual improvement of the laboratory services. This includes 4.8 Resolution of complaints, 4.9 Identification and control of nonconformities, 4.10 Corrective actions, 4.11 Preventive actions, 4.12 Continual improvement, 4.14 Evaluation and audits, and 4.15 Management review.

This process plan for QMS considers management requirements as part of the components of "Management responsibility" and "Measurement, analysis, and improvement," whereas technical requirements are considered in "Resource management" and "Service realization." Note that this model does not map exactly to Burnett's PDCA model, which was described earlier in Figure 1-3. The differences are minor, but they illustrate that different people have different interpretations of the requirements and how they should be implemented. In both examples, it is clear that the 25 ISO requirements are not expected to be implemented in the order they are numbered in the standard, but rather they should be considered in the context of the PDCA process model. Depending on the status of the particular laboratory, it is expected that some requirements may already have been implemented and need only be documented, whereas other requirements may require extensive development to meet the ISO standard. Again, this implies that a particular laboratory should make a careful assessment and provide an appropriate plan for development and deployment.

Management Requirements

4.1 Organization and management responsibility. Includes qualifications for the laboratory director, management responsibility for implementing a QMS, a focus on needs of users, and requirement for a Quality Policy that includes quality objectives and planning, organizational authority and responsibility for implementing QMS, and appointment of a Quality Manager to ensure implementation, review by management, and ongoing awareness of users' needs and requirements.

4.2 Quality management system. *The laboratory shall establish, document, implement and maintain a quality management system and continually improve its effectiveness in accordance with the requirements in this International Standard. The quality management system shall provide for the integration of all processes required to fulfill its quality policy and objectives and meet the needs and requirements of the users. The laboratory shall:*

- *Determine the processes needed for the quality management system and ensure their application throughout the laboratory;*
- *Determine the sequence and interaction of these processes;*
- *Determine criteria and methods needed to ensure that both the operation and control of these processes are effective;*
- *Ensure the availability of resources and information necessary to support the operation and monitoring of these processes;*
- *Monitor and evaluate these processes;*
- *Implement actions necessary to achieve planned results and continual improvement of these processes.*

This QMS requirement itself illustrates the structure of the PDCA cycle. PLAN involves determination of processes, sequences and interaction, and criteria and methods; DO involves ensuring the resources and information to implement and operate the processes; CHECK involves monitoring and evaluation; and ACT requires actions and continual improvement.

Documentation of the QMS should include the laboratory quality policy, a Quality Manual, procedures that describe implementation, records that document policies, processes, and procedures, and copies of regulatory and accreditation standards. Specific guidance states that *the quality manual should include: (a) the quality policy; (b) a description of the scope of the quality management system, (c) a presentation of the organization and management structure of the laboratory..., (d) description of the roles and responsibilities of laboratory management, particularly the laboratory director and the quality manager, (e) structure and relationships of the documentation in the QMS, (f) policies established by the QMS and the managerial and technical activities that support them.*

4.3 Document control. *The laboratory shall control documents required by the quality management system and shall ensure that unintended use of any obsolete document is prevented.* ISO takes the issue of document control very seriously in order to assure there is only one set of policies, processes, and procedures that governs how laboratory tests are performed. Documents must be authorized and approved, properly identified to assure only the current edition is available for use, registered in a document list, updated when changes are made, and periodically reviewed to assure currency and appropriateness.

4.4 Service agreements. *The laboratory shall have documented procedures for the establishment and review of agreements for providing medical laboratory services.* Such agreement should define the requirements of the users and customers, identify the examination procedures that are appropriate to fulfill those requirements, and assure the laboratory has the necessary skills, expertise, and resources to fulfill those requirements and services.

4.5 Examination by referral laboratories. *The laboratory shall have a documented procedure for selecting and evaluating referral laboratories and consultants who provide opinions as well as interpretation for complex testing in any discipline.* In cases where the laboratory refers samples to outside laboratories for testing, the laboratory is still responsible to manage the flow of specimens and return of test results to the ordering party. The laboratory is responsible for overseeing the quality of the referral laboratory to assure appropriate report formats, reference values, turnaround time, and test interpretation.

4.6 External services and supplies. *The laboratory shall have a documented procedure for the selection and purchasing of external services, equipment, reagents and consumable supplies that affect the quality of its service.* There shall be requirements and specifications for materials and services, review of receipt of materials and services, and monitoring the satisfaction with those materials and services. The laboratory shall maintain a list of approved suppliers.

4.7 Advisory services. *The laboratory shall provide consultation services for users and customers on the choice of examinations, usefulness for clinical situations, professional interpretation of results, effective utilization of services, and issues with sample acceptance criteria.*

4.8 Resolution of complaints. *The laboratory shall have a documented procedure for the management of complaints or other feedback received from clinicians, patients, laboratory staff or other parties.* Records must be kept of all complaints and their resolution.

4.9 Identification and control of nonconformities. *The laboratory shall have a documented procedure to identify and manage nonconformities in any aspect of the quality management system, including pre-examination, examination or post-examination processes.* Nonconformity is defined as the *"nonfulfillment of a requirement."* More commonly, a nonconformity means an error, an adverse event, an incident, or an occurrence where a customer's requirement for quality is not achieved. The industrial term is defect or defective result. The laboratory shall identify such nonconformities and take actions to control their consequences. The laboratory should identify the responsibility and authority for handling nonconformities, the actions to be taken particularly to halt analytic testing and deal with erroneous test reports when necessary.

4.10 Corrective actions. *The laboratory should take corrective action to eliminate causes of nonconformities.* The laboratory should have a procedure for reviewing nonconformities, determining root causes, implementing corrective actions, recording such actions, and monitoring their effectiveness.

4.11 Preventive actions. *The laboratory should take preventive action to eliminate the causes of potential nonconformities in order to prevent their occurrence.* While corrective actions are a response to observed nonconformities, preventive actions are based on a review of data and information with the objective of identifying potential causes of nonconformities. This may involve trend analysis of Quality Indicators as well as formal risk analysis to identify possible failure-modes.

4.12 Continual improvement. *The laboratory should continually improve the effectiveness of the quality management system, including the pre-examination, examination and post-examination processes...* The laboratory shall monitor the effectiveness of its QMS with the objectives of making improvements in its testing processes as well as the QMS itself. Improvement activities should be prioritized based on risk assessment, action plans should be developed and implemented, and the effectiveness of improvements should be monitored and controlled. *Laboratory management shall ensure that the laboratory participates in continual improvement activities that encompass relevant areas and outcomes of patient care. When the continual improvement programme identifies opportunities for improvement, laboratory management shall address them regardless of where they occur. Laboratory management shall communicate to staff improvement plans and related goals.*

4.13 Control of records. *The laboratory shall have a documented procedure for identification, collection, indexing, access, storage, maintenance, amendment and safe disposal of quality and technical records.* The laboratory should define the time periods necessary for different records on basis of legal, regulatory, and medical requirements. Records include virtually all documents that pertain to the performance of laboratory testing services.

4.14 Evaluation and audits. *The laboratory should plan and implement the evaluation and internal audit processes to (a) demonstrate that the pre-examination, examination, and post-examination and supporting processes are being conducted in a manner that meets the needs and requirements of users; (b) ensure conformity to the quality management system; (c) continually improve the effectiveness of the quality management system.* These include periodic review of requests for examination, suitability of examination procedures, and sample requirements. There should also be periodic assessment of user feedback, staff suggestions, results of internal audits, risk analysis, assessment of Quality Indicators, and reviews by external organizations.

4.15 Management review. *Laboratory management shall review the quality management system at planned intervals to ensure its continuing suitability, adequacy and effectiveness and support of patient care.* This review should encompass all information in 4.14 above, as well as changes expected in the volume and scope of work and the ongoing requirements to support that work. Management is responsible for assessing weaknesses in the QMS and for prioritizing opportunities for improvement. The output of the management review should be a record that documents decisions made and an action plan to improve the effectiveness of the QMS and the quality of services, as well as addressing resource needs.

Technical Requirements

5.1 Personnel. *The laboratory shall have a documented procedure for personnel management and maintain records for all personnel to indicate compliance with requirements.* This includes documenting personnel qualifications, job descriptions, orientation for new employees, training in the QMS and work processes and procedures, periodic competence assessment, reviews of staff performance, and continuing education and development.

5.2 Accommodation and environmental conditions. *The laboratory shall have space allocated for the performance of its work that is designed to ensure the quality, safety and efficacy of the service provided to the users and the health and safety of laboratory personnel, patients and visitors.* This includes laboratory and office facilities, storage facilities, staff facilities, patient sample collection facilities, and facility maintenance and environmental conditions.

5.3 Laboratory equipment, reagents, and consumables. *The laboratory shall have a documented procedure for selection, purchasing, and management of equipment.* This shall include equipment acceptance testing, instructions for use, calibration and metrological traceability, maintenance and repair, reporting of adverse incidence, and detailed records of use, maintenance, and operation. *The laboratory shall have a documented procedure for the reception, storage, acceptance testing and inventory management of reagents and consumables.* This shall also include instructions for use and reporting of adverse events.

5.4 Pre-examination processes. *The laboratory shall have documented procedures and information for pre-examination activities to ensure the validity of the results of examinations.* This shall include information for patients and users, forms for requesting laboratory service, procedures for sample collection and transportation, specimen processing procedures, and facilities for proper storage of samples.

5.5 Examination processes. *The laboratory shall select examination procedures which have been validated for their intended use. The identity of persons performing activities in examination processes shall be recorded. The specified requirements (performance specifications) for each examination procedure shall relate to the intended use of that examination.*

Specific guidance for verification and validation of examination procedures is provided in sections 5.5.1.2 and 5.5.1.3, respectively. **Verification** refers to the confirmation of a manufacturer's claims for performance, whereas **validation** refers to the assessment that performance is adequate for the intended use of test results. Verification assumes that manufacturers have performed extensive validation studies, thus allowing the laboratory to simply confirm the manufacturer's performance claims. Validation is applicable when the laboratory wants to evaluate performance relative to requirements for intended use. This is required for methods modified or developed by the laboratory.

In addition or verification or validation, section 5.5.1.4 requires that *the laboratory shall determine measurement uncertainty (MU) for each measurement procedure in the examination phase used to report measured quantity values on patients' samples. The laboratory shall define the performance requirements for the measurement uncertainty of each measurement procedure and regularly review estimates of measurement uncertainty.* This recommendation on MU has evolved from an **option** (*where practical and useful*) in the 2007 version of ISO 15189 to a **Requirement** in the 2012 version. The past issue was that the recommended methodology for determining MU (GUM, Guidelines for estimated of the Uncertainty of Measurements) was not practical in medical laboratories. The 2012 version includes a recommendation *that measurement uncertainties may be calculated using quantity values obtained by the measurement of quality control materials under intermediate precision conditions that include as many routine changes as reasonable possible in the standard operation of a measurement procedure, e.g., changes of reagent and calibrator batches, different operators, scheduled instrument maintenance.* This change in methodology makes it practical to determine MU for any test where stable control materials are available.

Biologic reference intervals or clinical decision cutoff values should be defined by the laboratory to support use and interpretation of test results (Section 5.5.2). Detailed documented should be kept on examination procedures (section 5.5.3).

5.6 Ensuring the quality of examination results. *The laboratory shall ensure the quality of examinations by performing them under defined conditions. Appropriate pre and post-examination processes shall be implemented. The laboratory shall not fabricate any results.*

Section 5.6.2.1 considers quality control and states that ***the laboratory shall design quality control procedures that verify the attainment of the intended quality of results.*** It is recommended that quality control materials be examined at a frequency that reflects the stability of the examination procedure and the patients' consequence of harm if erroneous results are produced. The laboratory should apply statistical control rules to make decisions on the acceptability of analytical results and the need to reject runs and repeat patient testing.

The laboratory shall participate in an interlaboratory comparison programme(s) (such as an external quality assessment programme or proficiency testing programme) appropriate to the examination and interpretations of examination results. If an interlaboratory comparison program is not available, the laboratory should utilize alternative mechanisms, such as use of certified reference materials, previously examined samples, exchange of samples with other laboratories, or control materials that are tested daily in interlaboratory comparison programmes.

There is also a need for comparison of results by methods used within the laboratory to ensure the comparability of examination results.

5.7 Post-examination processes. *The laboratory shall have procedures to ensure that authorized personnel review the results of examinations before release and evaluate them against internal quality control and, as appropriate, available clinical information and previous examination results. The laboratory shall have a documented procedure for the identification, collection, retention, indexing, access, storage, maintenance and safe disposal of clinical samples.*

5.8 Reporting of results. *The results of each examination shall be reported accurately, clearly, unambiguously and in accordance with any specific instructions in the examination procedures. The laboratory shall define the format and medium of the report and the manner in which it is to be communicated from the laboratory.* Important attributes of reports include comments on sample quality, sample suitability, critical results, and interpretative comments on results. There is also a detailed description of the appropriate contents of a report.

5.9 Release of results. *The laboratory shall establish documented procedures for the release of examination results, including details of who may release results and to whom.* This should include procedures for notifying physicians about critical or alert values and assuring that test results are distributed only to authorized personnel. When there is automated selection and reporting of results, e.g., autoverification programs, the criteria for such reporting should be carefully defined and validated for use. Information about sample interferences should be included, as well as instrument warning or alert signals. The laboratory should also have a documented procedure for revised or corrected reports to clearly notify the user of changes in test results.

5.10 Laboratory information system. *The laboratory shall have access to the data and information needed to provide a service which meets the needs and requirements of the user. The laboratory shall have a documented procedure to ensure that the confidentiality of patient information is maintained at all times.* The laboratory shall define the authorities and responsibilities for the entry, access, change, and release of test results. The laboratory information system must be validated by the supplier and verified by the laboratory as operating under appropriate conditions.

What's the point?

It's helpful to understand the organization of the ISO 15189 management and technical requirements in terms of a PDCA cycle. One advantage of this "process" perspective is to observe that "service realization" depends heavily on achieving the technical requirements for a laboratory testing process. Yes, that assumes adequate resource management, which in turn depends on "management responsibility," but the "measurement, analysis, and improvement" phase will highlight technical shortcomings in service realization and will make improvements in that area a high priority. It is also clear that "management responsibility" for developing and implementing a QMS will be a pre-requisite to development of the "measurement, analysis, and improvement" phase, as well as supporting technical improvements.

Implementation of a QMS requires detailed planning, with consideration of the state of quality practices and the priorities for improvement in the particular laboratory. Top management needs to understand the complexity of the issues, the potential difficulties in the process, and, ultimately, management's responsibility for commitment and leadership to make it happen.

References

1. ISO 15189. Medical laboratories – Requirements for quality and competence. ISO, Geneva, 2012.
2. GJ Flynn, J Coffey. ISO 15189 Medical Laboratories: Understanding the four components of a quality management system. www.darkdaily.com (2011 White Paper)

4. Preparing for QMS Implementation

Implementation of a Quality Management System is a serious undertaking. It begins with an understanding of the principles of quality management, a deep knowledge of quality, and a serious commitment by management to make quality a priority. The plan for implementing a QMS will vary from laboratory to laboratory depending on the laboratory's readiness to implement the management and technical requirements, the state of the laboratory's current quality management practices, the priorities from strategic planning, the education and training available to support implementation, and the guidance provided by registrars or accreditation organizations.

Principles of Quality Management

Experience in industry, beginning with the re-development of Japanese industries after World War II and a resurgence of interest in quality in American industries in the 1980s, provides the background for today's quality management practices. We discussed these influences in a 1986 book, *Cost-Effective Quality Control: Managing the quality and productivity of analytical processes* [1] and provided the following summary of the principles for quality management:

- Quality should take priority over production and cost. Achieving satisfactory quality is more important than getting the product out the door.
- Quality improvement begins with management. Management commitment, leadership, and active participation are required.
- Top management must give quality equal consideration with finance, marketing, etc.
- Quality is related to customer needs. Achieving quality means satisfying customers needs.
- Quality problems are process problems, not people problems. Problems occur when processes go wrong, not because people want to make mistakes.

- Cost must be understood in broad terms that include the costs of prevention, appraisal, and failure. Failure costs are the cost of not having adequate quality and show up internally as scrap and rework, and externally as customer complaints and need for service.
- Quality improvement leads to reduced costs because the cost of unsatisfactory or poor quality is high, money that is already being expended. Increases in productivity are possible by improving quality and eliminating rework. With increases in productivity come lower costs of production.
- Extensive education and continuing in-service training are required for everyone in the organization, including top managers.
- Quality improvement occurs only when specific problems in the process or system are identified and corrected on a permanent basis.
- Quality is everyone's job and requires teamwork. Project teams are the mechanism for solving problems with quality.
- Quality is a continually improving target. Quality improvement must be an ongoing process. The goal is perfection, nothing less, and is to be pursued relentlessly.
- Quality is a way of managing the organization. It is a way of life to be firmly ingrained in all operations of the organization.

Everyone who is interested in improving quality in an organization would benefit from reading about the ideas and experiences of W. Edwards Deming [2]. Deming was an American statistician who worked with Walter Shewhart, the developer of statistical process control in the 1930s. In the 1940s, Deming worked with American industries to introduce statistical control for production of armaments. Following the War, Deming was invited to Japan to help revive industrial production, where he introduced statistical principles and statistical quality control in Japanese industries. In the 1970s and 80s, Deming was at the center of the revitalization of quality in American industries and the development of principles of Total Quality Management, which was first introduced in healthcare organizations in the 1990s [3].

Deming was very clear that there is no quick fix for quality, or "no instant pudding" in his words. Unfortunately, Deming has been largely forgotten in the last few decades and many industries, particularly healthcare organizations, seem destined to repeat the mistakes of the past. Historically, a major stumbling block has been the lack of management commitment and leadership. The responsibilities of management go well beyond the formulation of a quality policy and the initiation of a Quality Management System. Management often underestimates the efforts and leadership required to truly commit an organization to quality and make quality improvement an integral part of the management process!

Management commitment and leadership

While management requirements are carefully delineated in ISO 15189, it is difficult to understand the meaning of management commitment and leadership without understanding past experiences in other industries. Deming's "14 points" provide guidance for the philosophy and culture that are needed to make quality the focus of an organization [4].

1. ***Create constancy of purpose for improvement of product and service.*** This means putting quality first in all the activities of the organization.

2. ***Adopt the new philosophy.*** Deming uses the term "philosophy" to emphasize that quality is not just a characteristic of a product and service, but must also permeate all the thinking and all the people in the organization. Quality is a way of doing business.

3. ***Cease dependence on mass inspection.*** This point is aimed at industrial quality management practices and more broadly means the development of processes that operate in a state of statistical quality and can therefore be monitored by periodic testing of the production process.

4. ***End the practice of awarding business on price tag alone.*** Quality is more important that price when acquiring goods and materials because poor quality will require pre-testing of materials, rejection of some lots, re-order, or re-work to maintain quality. This is a tough sell in healthcare organizations, but laboratory analysts

know that their work would be easier if they could avoid acquiring equipment, supplies, and services based on the lowest price.

5. ***Constantly and forever improve the system of production and service.*** Here's the source of the idea of continuous quality improvement which is now prevalent in laboratory regulations and accreditation guidelines.

6. ***Institute modern methods of training on the job.*** Training should not simply be one operator training the next operator, but rather a formalized in-service training process where the trainer is an expert in the process. In addition, Deming emphasizes the need for training to support the use of statistical methods in all phases of management and production.

7. ***Institute modern methods of supervision.*** This requires management and supervisors to support the needs of production workers, rather than act as controllers. Deming opposed management by objectives, performance evaluations, and merit pay because workers performance is mainly attributable to the performance of work processes that have been designed and controlled by management.

8. ***Drive out fear.*** Deming is very strong about the need for workers to feel secure in their jobs and be able to discuss all issues that hinder them from doing their jobs right.

9. ***Break down barriers between staff areas.*** Anyone who works in a healthcare organization is well aware of the difficulties that occur between departments. Communication and cooperation are critical because many of the chronic problems occur at the borders between departments. Chronic problems continue because of the difficulties in resolving issues between departments (e.g., Emergency Room vs laboratory) and between different personnel in the healthcare "team" (e.g., administrators vs doctors vs nurses vs laboratorians).

10. ***Eliminate material goals for the work force.*** Deming believed that many goals just amount to slogans. They may sound good, but they don't take into account that most of the problems with production are due to processes, not people. People should not

be responsible for goals that depend on processes controlled by management.

11. ***Eliminate work standards and numerical quotas.*** Deming goes an additional step to clarify that production quotas and incentive pay only penalize the people for failures of processes. This is why he opposed "pay for performance" programs, which are a current trend in US healthcare. Who gets the money in such programs – the doctors, most likely? How will that build teamwork and patient focus for other professionals and workers in the healthcare organization?

12. ***Remove barriers that hinder the hourly worker.*** Management must create a culture and environment that allows workers to take pride in their work. Were Deming alive today, he would agonize over the current attitudes towards workers, management actions against workers rights, and the increasing inequity from the top to bottom of our business and healthcare organizations.

13. ***Institute a vigorous program of education and training.*** Deming recognized that jobs would change as technology improved and that workers needed ongoing education and training to adapt to new jobs and new technology.

14. ***Create a structure in top management that will push every day on the implementation of the above 13 points.*** Management is responsible for quality. Management must be committed to make quality happen. Management commitment to quality means adhering to Deming's 14 points.

Deming's words may seem dated because these 14 points were published in the early 1980s and the language is oriented to manufacturing organizations. The principles apply to quality management in all organizations and are as relevant today as they were over 30 years ago. For example of current relevancy, see the 2013 report on "Improving the safety of patients in England" [5], where the executive summary recommends the following solutions:

1. ***Recognise with clarity and courage the need for wide systemic change.***

2. ***Abandon blame as a tool.***

3. ***Reassert the primacy of working with patients and carers to set and achieve health care goals.***
4. ***Use quantitative targets with caution.***
5. ***Recognize that transparency is essential and expect and insist on it at all levels and with regard to all types of information.***
6. ***Ensure that responsibility for functions related to safety and improvement are vested clearly and simply in a comprehensible set of agencies...***
7. ***Give the people of the NHS – top to bottom – career-long help to learn, master and apply modern methods for quality control, quality improvement and quality planning.***
8. ***Make sure pride and joy in work, not fear, infuse the NHS.***

There is no mistaking that these recommendations reflect Deming's approach for quality management, particularly those points that emphasize the need for systemic change, abandon blame, limit use of quantitative targets, career-long help to learn, and making sure that pride and joy in work, not fear, becomes the organizational culture. The principles, philosophy, and values that Deming outlined are still important for implementing Quality Management Systems and improving quality and patient safety in healthcare organizations.

Evolution of laboratory quality practices

Industrial quality practices evolved from inspection of products, standardization of production processes to statistical control of processes, then to broader quality assurance, formal quality improvement, and quality planning. Juran described the "triology" of quality control, quality improvement, and quality planning in the 1980s as Total Quality Management was being implemented in industry [6]. He recognized that production processes are established and operations standardized, then they are inspected and controlled to maintain consistent quality, which leads to identification of problems (nonconformities) and the need for quality improvement, which in turn leads to the need to re-plan those production processes to eliminate problems in the future. Quality management practices evolve from technical processes through management processes to become a quality management system [7].

In this context, laboratories should assess the state of their quality management practices in relation to the Total Quality Management process model that was discussed earlier and is shown with additional detail in Figure 4-1.

Figure 4-1. TQM Process Model. QLP represents Quality Laboratory

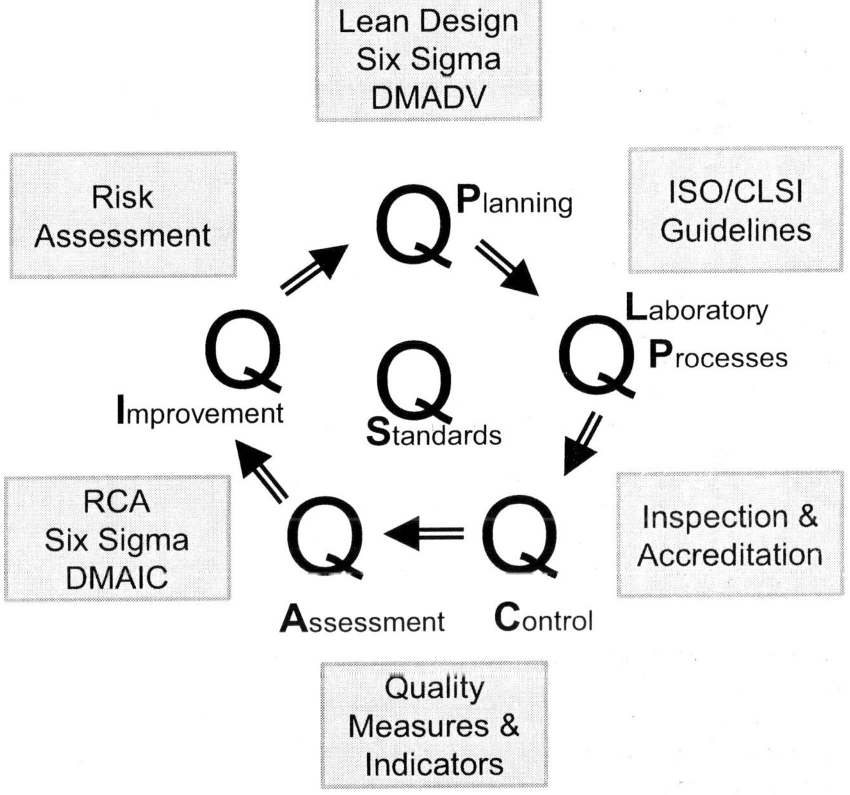

Processes; QC, Quality Control; QA, Quality Assessment; QI, Quality Improvement; QP, Quality Planning; QC, Quality Standards. Boxes represent tools, techniques, and programs that are employed in the TQM process.

1. Does the laboratory have existing documentation of Standardized

operating procedures (SOPs) or Quality Laboratory Practices (QLPs)?

2. Has the laboratory established quality control procedures, including method validation protocols?
3. Does the laboratory assess quality with broad measures and quality indicators, such as turnaround time, proficiency testing performance, uncertainty of measurements, customer surveys and complaints, etc.?
4. Has the laboratory a formalized Root Cause Analysis (RCA) methodology and a Quality improvement (QI) team problem-solving methodology, such as Six Sigma DMAIC?
5. Does the laboratory utilize planning methodologies such as Lean and Design for Six Sigma? Does the laboratory perform quantitative quality planning (QP) for analytical processes that accounts for quality required for tests and the precision and accuracy observed for methods?
6. Has the laboratory defined quality standards (QS) that include specific quality requirements for individual tests, as well as general quality policies, priorities, and plans for improvement?

Virtually all laboratories have established SOPs for their testing processes. Most laboratories have established QC procedures, but fewer have well-established method validation protocols. Many laboratories have implemented broader measures of quality, but may still have technical deficiencies related to the determination of measurement uncertainty. Some laboratories have implemented a formal team problem-solving methodology for quality improvement [8], but many lack the capabilities to work across departments within the laboratory and through the healthcare organization. Relatively few laboratories have defined quality goals and requirements for each of their testing processes, though they may have a formal quality policy that implies they strive to meet customer needs. Many laboratories will need to pay attention to the ISO technical requirements and make sure they are properly implemented, rather than assume that only the management requirements will need to be addressed to implement a QMS.

It may also be helpful for laboratories to review the quality programs and tools that have been implemented, such as use of ISO and CLSI guidelines, laboratory inspection and accreditation, quality measures and indicators, Six Sigma problem solving methodology (DMAIC, Define-Measure-Analyze-Improve-Control), root cause analysis (RCA), risk assessment (FMEA, Failure Modes and Effects Analysis), Lean/Six Sigma and Design for Six Sigma (DMADV, Define-Measure-Analyze-Design-Verify). These programs/tools are typically applied as shown in Figure 4-1 and therefore also relate to the evolution of quality practices in the laboratory. Many laboratories have applied Lean design to improve efficiency; some have also applied Six Sigma, but often in a limited way without defining "tolerance specifications" for the important quality characteristics ("Critical to Quality, CTQ" in Lean terminology). Quantitative quality management requires that these "tolerance specifications" be defined and thus Six Sigma is advantageous for bringing a quantitative focus and understanding of customer needs and requirements for the intended clinical use of laboratory test results.

CLSI recommends a "gap analysis" that compares current quality practices directly to the CLSI Quality Essentials [9,10] or the ISO 15189 requirements [11]. This kind of assessment will suffer if there are inadequacies in the comparative requirements. For example, the ISO 15189 guidelines have statements that relate to "intended use" but there is no recommendation on how to define quantitative quality goals and requirements for analytical performance.

- *5.5.1.1. The laboratory shall select examination procedures which have been validated for their intended use... The specified requirements (performance specifications) for each examination procedure shall relate to the* <u>*intended use*</u> *of that examination.*
- *5.5.1.4 The laboratory shall determine measurement uncertainty for each measurement procedure in the examination phase used to report measured quantity values on patients' samples. The laboratory shall define the* <u>*performance requirements*</u> *for the measurement uncertainty of each measurement procedure and regularly review estimates of measurement uncertainty.*
- *5.6.2.1. The laboratory shall design quality control*

procedures that verify the attainment of the intended quality of results.[10]

Similarly, the CLSI Quality Essentials are vague on how to define customer expectations and intent for use:

- *5.2.1.3 The laboratory needs to understand the expectations of each type of customer... The laboratory should refrain from trying to predict its customers' expectations and instead collect the specific expectations and desires from individual customers.*
- *5.7.2 Processes critical to the quality of the laboratory's product (with 'product' defined as the reports that contain examination results and information) need either validation or verification as meeting the laboratory's intent for use before implementation...*
- *5.7.2.1 Validation consists of a plan for personnel to challenge and record the results of any new or modified process to ensure that the process works as intended before actual implementation. In addition, the process needs to meet customer expectations...*

CLSI uses the term "expectations" rather than requirements, which relates more to "wants" than to "needs." This is an unfortunate choice of terminology because expectations do NOT necessarily equate to requirements for intended use. CLSI also assumes that customers can communicate their expectations and cautions the laboratory not to try and predict customer expectations. That may work for a requirement such as turnaround time where the customer and the laboratory have a common understanding of performance in units of time. But, that does not work for analytical requirements such as precision and accuracy because those characteristics are NOT understood by customers. Here's where the laboratory must take responsibility to understand the intended clinical use of a test, then translate that intended use into performance specifications for allowable Total Error (TE_a), imprecision (SD, CV), and inaccuracy (bias).

Specific goals and quality requirements should be defined for each laboratory test in order to guide the validation, control, and improvement in relation to the intended clinical use of each test.

That need will not be identified in any gap analysis referenced to ISO 15189 or CLSI QSEs because of the shortcomings of those guidelines.

Strategic planning

Laboratory management typically carries out a strategic planning exercise every year or two. That exercise typically focuses on issues such as the following:

- Who are our customers and what are their needs?
  - Summary of services and requirements that must be planned
- What future issues and trends will affect us?
  - Assumptions for planning
- What are our strengths, weaknesses, opportunities, and threats (SWOT analysis)?
  - Important issues for planning
- What do we want to become?
  - Mission statement
- What are the priorities for change and improvement?
  - Strategic goals
- What specifically needs to be accomplished?
  - Strategic objectives

Strategic planning can be combined with a quality improvement to provide the methodology and mechanisms for improvement. The quality improvement process focuses on the following:

- How will the goals and objectives be implemented?
  - Project by project quality improvement
- Who will coordinate the implementation?
  - Quality Planning Team

- What will be implemented first?
    - Action plan to prioritize projects
- Who will develop the implementation strategies?
    - Individuals and project teams
- What resources must be provided?
    - Training for team leaders, members, facilitators
- How will the project teams do their work?
    - Structured problem-solving methodology, such as Six Sigma DMAIC process (Define-Measure-Act-Improve-Control, see Figure 1-3)

An example of this combined strategic planning and quality improvement process was described for implementing Total Quality Management in the 1990s [18]. Another example described the implementation of a core laboratory service following a similar approach that combined strategic planning with reengineering [19]. This combined strategic planning and process improvement approach can be adapted to focus on the current interests and the needs for a Quality Management System. Implementation of a QMS then becomes a priority outcome from strategic planning and provides a natural way for management to incorporate the implementation of QMS as a management responsibility for planning and improvement.

Education, training, and guidance

From the above discussion, it should be clear that management must study the principles of quality management, recognize the seriousness of management commitment to quality, recognize the state of quality practices and the evolutionary process that leads to a Quality Management System, and integrate the development of QMS in the laboratory's strategic plan. A deep knowledge of quality management is needed to implement a QMS. Education and training will be needed, first for top management and later for the rest of the laboratory. This may be obtained from professional organizations, registrar and accreditation organizations, and consulting services.

Some illustrative sources that provide training and support (in English) are the World Health Organizations (WHO), the Clinical and Laboratory Standards Institute (CLSI), the Canadian Institute for Quality Management in Healthcare (IQMH), and the College of American Pathologists (CAP).

World Health Organization (WHO)

WHO provides an excellent educational resource with its Laboratory Quality Management System Handbook, which can be downloaded from the WHO website [14]. Its 250 pages are divided into 18 chapters, plus a glossary, summary of acronyms, and references for each chapter. The contents include: (1) Introduction to quality; (2) Facilities and safety; (3) Equipment; (4) Purchasing and inventory; (5) Process control – sample management; (6) Process control – introduction to quality control; (7) Process control – quality control for quantitative tests; (8) Process control – quality control for qualitative and semi-quantitative procedures; (9) Assessment – audits; (10) Assessment – external quality assessment; (11) Assessment – norms and accreditation; (12) Personnel; (13) Customer service; (14) Occurrence management; (15) Process improvement; (16) Documents and records; (17) Information management; (18) Organization.

This WHO handbook should be considered essential reading for top management! It provides a thorough, but very readable, introduction to Quality Management Systems. The focus is on what needs to be accomplished to provide reliable testing services. The recommendations are based on both the ISO 15189 standard for accreditation and the CLSI Quality System Essentials. Chapter 18 discusses QMS implementation, identifying "the principal element for a successful quality management system is managerial commitment." Important requirements for success include leadership, organizational structure, planning process, implementation, and monitoring. It advises that all laboratories need a quality manager and large laboratories may need more than one, perhaps one per section. It recommends a phased plan of implementation, but does not provide any specific guidance except to prioritize implementation based on a "gap analysis."

The related WHO "Training Toolkit" [15] provides extensive resources that can be adapted for workshops and in-service training for laboratory staff. The contents follow the handbook's organization for 18 modules or lessons. Trainers are provided a module overview including purpose, learning objectives, materials, instructional plan, presentation slides, and test questions. Participants are provided with content sheets that summarize the main points, forms and examples as handouts, and a glossary and list of references. All these materials are available online and can be downloaded from the WHO website.

Clinical Laboratory and Standards Institute (CLSI).

CLSI's main business is the development of guidelines. CLSI also administratively facilitates the ISO 212 Technical Committee that is responsible for development of ISO standards for medical laboratories.

CLSI began to develop guidelines for QMS in the 1990s and several are now in their fourth and fifth editions. In continuing to promote QMS, CLSI initiated a training program that leads to a certificate in Laboratory Quality Management Systems (LQMS) [16]. This program focuses on the CLSI Quality System Essentials (QSEs), which represent a comprehensive set of requirements based on regulatory and accreditation requirements. This training is not specific for ISO 15189, but these "essentials" are consistent with the ISO requirements and certainly provide a comprehensive study of current quality practices and guidelines on how to organize and structure both management and technical activities. Training materials include "The Key to Quality" that describes the 12 QSEs, the requirements for policies, processes, and procedures for each QSE, and how to apply the QSEs in individual laboratories. The LQMS certificate is an online training program that provides continuing education credits.

Institute for Quality Management in Healthcare (IQMH).

This is a Canadian non-profit organization that is associated with the Ontario Medical Association. Its origin was in the Ontario Quality Management Program for Medical Laboratories, which has a long history of accrediting medical laboratories. IQMH was organized to provide proficiency testing services, education and training, and accreditation services to a wider audience.

Their training program "Decoding ISO 15189" provides online education on ISO 15189 and includes the following 15 modules:

1. Introduction to ISO 15189: World class excellence
2. Quality management: The essential cycle
3. Setting the stage for change: The paradigm shift
4. Document control: Say what you do
5. The quality manual: Your system roadmap
6. Process maps and procedures: Get your picture and develop it
7. Occurrence management: The heart of quality
8. Internal audit and management review: Take a close look at yourself
9. Quality indicators: Measuring success
10. Managing personnel: The precious resource
11. Laboratory equipment : The tools of our trade
12. Referrals and contracts: Refer onto others
13. Pre-examination process. You get what they give
14. Examination process: It's what we do
15. Post-examination process: They get what we give

A more complete description with objectives and expected outcomes can be found on the IQMH website [17].

American Association for Laboratory Accreditation (A2LA)

In 2014, A2LA was approved by CMS for inspection of laboratories under the US CLIA rules. A2LA has a long history of inspecting other types of laboratories for accreditation by ISO, for example, testing and calibration laboratories under ISO 17025. It is a natural evolution for A2LA to also accredit medical laboratories because ISO 15189 represents the adaptation of ISO 17025 for the particular competencies required in medical laboratories. With "deemed status" for inspection of CLIA laboratories, A2LA is able to offer accreditation for both CLIA and ISO 15189 in a single inspection. One other advantage is that A2LA itself is accredited by ILAC (International Laboratory Accreditation Cooperation), which means that A2LA accreditation is accepted worldwide. For education and training, A2LA has partnered with IQMH to utilize their "Decoding ISO 15189" training program.

College of American Pathologists

CAP offers 15189 accreditation for the ISO management requirements as an addition to its CLIA oriented accreditation for technical requirements. CAP has a long history of accrediting laboratories on the basis of technical requirements and is a "deemed accreditor" for the US CLIA requirements. CAP 15189 requires that laboratories have already been accredited for technical requirements by the CAP Laboratory Accreditation Program (LAP).

The CAP 15189 process involves the following stages [18]:

1. Application by the laboratory. Once complete, CAP assigns a lead assessor who will guide the laboratory through the process.
2. Desk assessment by CAP. Documents submitted by the laboratory are reviewed to assess readiness and identify potential issues.
3. Gap assessment by the laboratory and CAP. CAP performs an on-site assessment of the laboratory's current quality practices and technical competency in order to develop a plan of action to prepare for 15189 accreditation.
4. Optional pre-assessment may be performed by CAP if requested by the laboratory.

5. Internal audit is performed by the laboratory to assess compliance with the 15189 requirements.
6. On-site accreditation inspection is performed by CAP to provide a review of the laboratory's QMS, technical competency, document control system, and management of records.
7. Accreditation for a 3 year period based on conformance to requirements in the accreditation visit.
8. Surveillance review of the laboratory's QMS management requirements after 1 year.
9. Surveillance review of the laboratory's technical requirements after 2 years.
10. Re-accreditation after 3 years.

CAP provides guidance and educational support throughout the accreditation process. Online training modules are provided, as well as guidance from the lead assessor.

Additional guidance

There are many businesses that support the implementation of ISO 15189. These organizations often offer templates for quality manuals, policies, processes, and procedures that can be adapted to the particulars of an individual medical laboratory. They may also offer consulting services to guide a laboratory through the process, identify deficiencies that need to be corrected, and provide pre-audits or pre-inspections in preparation for accreditation.

You should identify the accreditation organization that will inspect your laboratory, review their application process, and become familiar with their inspection requirements. This information is not necessarily available publicly unless and until you contact the organization with the intention of making an application. However, one good example of the process can be found on the A2LA website [19]. This is a 19 page application form that requires an organization chart, documentation of credentials of key staff, proficiency testing plan, current quality manual, list of all equipment, laboratory floor plan, plus completion of additional forms, such as a

36 page "Medical Testing Scope Selection List" (Form F622) which requires identification of all tests performed by the laboratory for which accreditation is sought. There is also a General Checklist for ISO 15189 that must be completed, but that form C650 is not available to the public.

Getting started – steps and phases

By now, you realize that there isn't a "one size fits all" Quality Management System, just like there isn't a "one size fits all" QC procedure. There are principles that guide your application, existing practices that influence how you develop your QMS, and priorities for improvement in your laboratory.

CLSI recommends a phased implementation. The initial phase should confirm management commitment to quality, then begin development of a quality manual (which involves quality policies and processes, the management analogs to SOPs and QLPs), implementation of occurrence management (complaints, incidents, problems), analysis and verification of work processes (method verification/validation), and implementation of process controls (QC, PT, etc.). In the context of the ISO 15189 requirements, this means starting with certain management requirements and then focusing on the technical requirements, particularly process control. It is noteworthy that the implementation of process controls should occur in the early stage of development of a QMS. The CLSI guidance affirms that quality management practices evolve from standardizing production processes (which should include validation of performance) to monitoring production via quality control, then to more advanced practices that depend on management support and commitment. In the implementation guidance presented in this book, three phases will be considered: the first for implementing management requirements, the second for implementing technical requirements, and the third for audit and review for inspection and accreditation.

In summary, here's a short plan for getting started with the implementation of a Quality Management System in your laboratory:

- Ensure management commitment to quality in the beginning as the first step in any implementation plan for a Quality

Management System. This will require serious study of quality management principles to understand management's responsibility.

- Take advantage of strategic planning activities to establish the need for implementing a QMS as a natural part of management responsibilities for planning and improvement.
- Decide whether the objective is improvement of quality and/or accreditation. For example, in US laboratories, there may be a desire to improve the management aspects of their QMS without any need or desire to apply for ISO 15189 accreditation.
- Establish a quality policy, a QMS implementation steering committee, and a quality manager who is tasked with managing the development and implementation process.
- Provide initial training to understand the importance of a QMS, the broad construct of management and technical competencies that are needed, and the process for development and implementation.
- Assess the state of current quality management practices, or perform a "gap analysis", to identify the strengths and weaknesses of your current situation.
- Prioritize your activities in relation to management and technical requirements where improvement is needed. Clarify the extent of tests and service for which the QMS will be applied.
- Obtain additional training, as necessary, to support the development of new capabilities that are required for QMS implementation.
- Acquire the necessary resources, e.g., a document control system, possible templates for the quality manual and processes and procedures, consider whether consultants are needed for QMS implementation, assess the need for additional training for specific competencies.

- Identify "implementation phases" for your plan, e.g., initial management requirements, then technical requirements for pre-analytic, analytic, and post-analytic systems, and finally specific needs and issues based on the requirements of your accrediting organization.

This brief overview will start you on the right road to quality. These initial steps will help you understand what to do and how to proceed with implementation. With each of these initial steps, you will gain more knowledge of the process and predict what is needed for the implementation and expansion of your QMS.

References

1. Westgard JO, Barry PL. Cost-Effective Quality Control: Managing the Quality and Productive of Analytical Process. Washington DC:AACC Press, 1986.
2. Nillson Orsini J. The Essential Deming: Leadership Principles from the Father of Quality W. Edwards Deming. McGraw Hill, 2013.
3. Berwick DM, Godfrey AB, Roessner J. Curing health care: new strategies for quality improvement. San Francisco:Jossey-Bass Publishers, 1990.
4. Deming WE. Quality, Productivity, and Competitive Position. Massachusetts Institute of Technology, Center for Advanced Engineering Study, 1982.
5. Berwick D. A promise to learn – a commitment to act: Improving the safety of patients in England. National Advisory Group on the Safety of Patients in England. August, 2013.
6. Juran JM. The quality triology. Quality Progress 1986(Aug);19-24.
7. Westgard JO, Barry PL. Total quality control: Evolution of quality management systems. Lab Med 1989;20:377-384.
8. Westgard JO, Barry PL. Beyond quality assurance: Committing to quality improvement. Lab Med 1989;20:241-247.

9. CLSI HS1. A quality management system model for health care. Clinical and Laboratory Standards Institute, Clinical Laboratory and Standards Institute, Wayne PA, 2011.

10. CLSI GP26A4. Quality Management System: A Model for Laboratory Services. Clinical Laboratory and Standards Institute, Wayne PA, 2011.

11. ISO 15189. Medical laboratories – Requirements for quality and competence. ISO, Geneva, 2012.

12. Westgard JO, Barry PL, Tomar RH. Implementing total quality management (TQM) in healthcare laboratories. CLMR 1991;5:353-370.

13. Tomar R, Westgard J, Eggert A. Quality Reengineering in Health Care: A case study from the clinical laboratories at the University of Wisconsin. Chicago:ASCP Press, 1999.

14. WHO Laboratory Quality Management System Handbook. World Health Organizations, Geneva, Switzerland; 2011. Available from WHO website, www.who.int/ihr/publications/lqms/en/index.html, accessed August 22, 2013.

15. WHO Laboratory Quality Management System Training Toolkit. World Health Organization, Geneva, Switzerland. Available from WHO website, www.who.int/ihr/training_quality/en/index.html, accessed August 22, 2013.

16. Clinical Laboratory and Standards Institute, www.clsi.org, accessed August 8, 2013.

17. Institute for Quality Management in Healthcare website, www. iqmh, accessed August 8, 2013.

18. College of American Pathologist's website, www.cap.org, accessed August 8, 2013.

19. American Association for Laboratory Accreditation, F651 – Application for Accreditation: ISO 15189 Medical Testing Laboratories. www.a2la.org/forms/15189_Application.doc, accessed August 12, 2013.

5. Implementing Management Requirements

The purpose of this chapter is to describe the typical implementation steps of the ISO 15189 management requirements. That process will vary from laboratory to laboratory, as discussed earlier, but the first phase of implementation must consider the management requirements. In our recommended approach, there will be a second phase that focuses on technical requirements and a third phase that deals with the inspection and accreditation process.

Keep in mind that the implementation of a QMS should be initiated by the top management in your laboratory. Given your position in the organization, you may be heavily involved in the implementation of the management requirements if you are a director, manager, or supervisor, or you may mainly participate in the implementation of the technical requirements if you are a supervisor or bench level analyst.

The laboratory needs to develop a QMS plan, begin implementing that plan, monitor progress of the implementation, and periodically review the accomplishments with the intent of updating the plan and improving implementation. The general nature of this process is shown in Figure 5-1 in the form of Deming's Plan-Do-Check-Act cycle. Note that the steps will not necessarily occur in the exact order shown here and that the steps in different stages may overlap and occur simultaneously. For example, the implementation of a document control system and the development of a Quality Manual must begin early. The documentation supports all of the management policies, processes, procedures, and forms for records. That work may even begin before the action plan is finished.

PLAN and DO Stages of Implementation

The discussion here will focus on the Plan and Do stages, with more limited discussion of the Check and Act stages. The reason is that each laboratory will need to adapt the general approach to the specifics of their own circumstances. The initial steps for getting started may be the same, but then the strengths and weaknesses of a

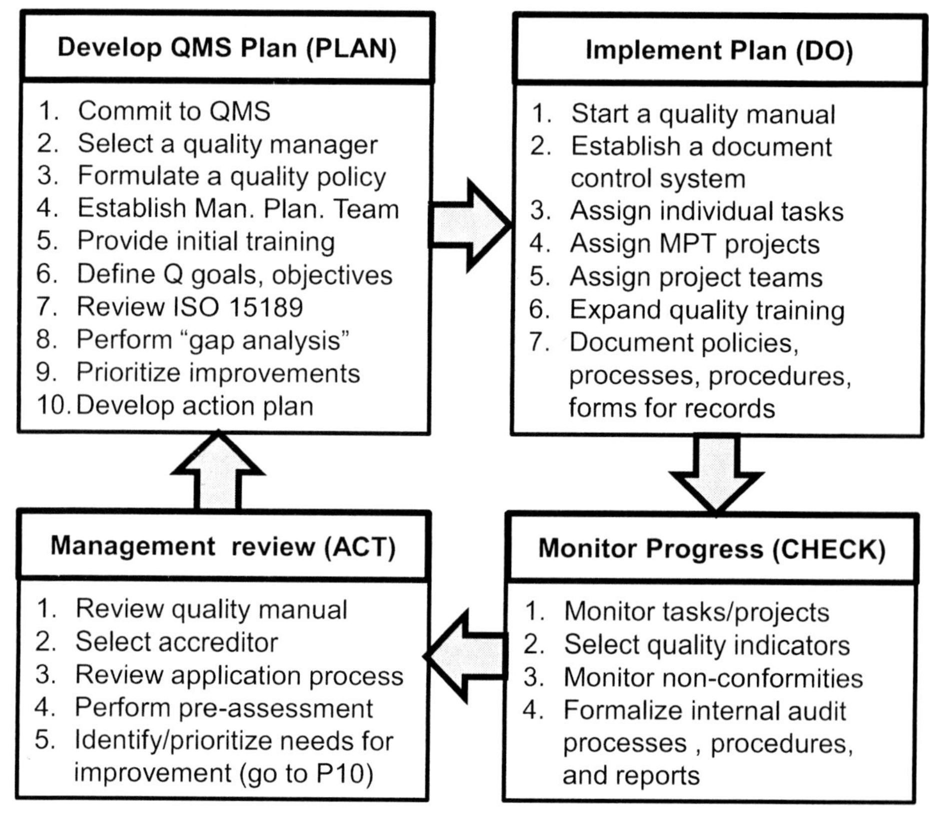

Figure 5-1. Plan for implementing a Quality Management System

laboratory's existing quality management practices will determine the direction and priorities for implementation of the management requirements for a QMS. It is useful to have a general picture of the implementation process, but it should be recognized that each laboratory's action plan is likely to be different and their process will change and evolve during implementation.

P1. Commit to Quality and QMS

It is the first responsibility of top management to communicate their commitment to quality and their strategic goal of implementing of a Quality Management System. Top management in a medical laboratory may refer to one or a few people, for example, a medical director will likely be involved, but there may also be an administrative manager and a technical supervisor. In small laboratories, top management may be only one of these individuals. In large laboratories, there may be associate directors for quality and informatics, assistant directors for various sections of the laboratory, as well as managers and supervisors with laboratory-wide or section-specific responsibilities. Top management should study the issues related to providing quality testing services and develop an understanding of the principles and their responsibility to lead the improvements.

Management responsibilities were discussed in the previous chapter, based on Deming's perspective and industrial principles of quality management. Another statement of these ideas is provided by Levett and Burney in their book [1] on "Using ISO 9001 in Healthcare." Note that ISO 9001 is the *generic* form of management requirements for a quality system that can be applied to any business or industry. ISO 15189 adapts these requirements *specifically* for a medical laboratory [2]. Levett and Burney, who are both physicians involved in patient care, emphasize that *"commitment must be conveyed to the employees throughout the organization in order to set the goals and expectations..."* by communication of the following quality management principles:

1. *Customer focus – seeking to understand customer needs, meet their requirements, and exceed their expectations*
2. *Leadership – setting direction and developing a strategy in order to achieve the goals and objectives of the organization*
3. *Involvement of people – involving everyone in the organization and equipping each employee with the resources necessary to achieve the goals that are set*
4. *Process approach – achieving the desired results (outputs) by managing resources and services (inputs) as a process*
5. *Systems approach to management – improving an organization's effectiveness by understanding and managing interrelated processes for a given objective*

6. *Continual improvement – focusing on improvement as a permanent objective of the organization*
7. *Factual approach to decision making – using data and information to make effective and informed decisions*
8. *Mutually beneficial supplier relationships – developing relationships that are mutually beneficial and create value for everyone involved*

Points 1 through 6 clearly align with Deming's principles. Point 7 – factual approach to decision making – relates to Deming's emphasis on application of statistical principles for measuring and monitoring performance. Point 8 extends Deming's idea that purchases of materials and supplies should not be based solely on price, but rather on value. That idea is extended here to "mutually beneficial supplier relationships."

It is critical that this meaning of management commitment is understood. The failure of many quality initiatives comes back to the lack of true commitment by management. Commitment means that management understands the principles and responsibilities and also recognizes their consequences for the organization, its operations, and its culture. Management must communicate the intent of the laboratory to move forward with a focus on quality and the implementation of a QMS.

P2. Select a Quality Manager

At least one Quality Manager will be needed, but larger organizations may need more than one. The Quality Manager has responsibility for moving the process forward and actively managing the processes and procedures necessary for QMS implementation. In many laboratories, this requires a full time commitment. In small laboratories, it will still require a large share of one person's time. Sharing the Quality Manager responsibilities between two or more positions is not recommended because of the need for accountability.

An early decision to commit resources to a Quality Manager position is advantageous because this individual will need extensive education and training to organize, facilitate, and support the implementation process. Previous experience in supervision and expertise in technical operations provide a good background, along with dedication to improving the quality of laboratory services.

P3. Formulate a Quality Policy

One of the first responsibilities to communicate management's intent is the formulation of a Quality Policy. This signals to the laboratory personnel and the healthcare organization that management is serious about improving quality and that QMS implementation is the mechanism and process for accomplishing this. The Quality Policy should emphasize the organization's commitment to deliver the quality of services necessary for good patient care. For example:

- The medical laboratory at General Hospital will deliver the quality and diversity of services to satisfy the changing clinical needs and assure the safety of our patients, physicians, and staff.

Some Quality Managers and consultants recommend keeping the policy statement simple to facilitate conformance during inspection and accreditation. While a simple policy statement may satisfy accreditation requirements, a more detailed set of Quality Goals and objectives will be helpful to guide the personnel in the laboratory. Other mechanisms for providing additional guidance to laboratory personnel include organizational statements for vision, mission, and values.

P4. Establish a Management Planning Team (MPT)

Following top management's decision and commitment to improving quality, other key personnel must be brought into the process to guide the implementation. The establishment of a steering committee is the next step for developing the concepts and ideas about how to implement a QMS in a particular laboratory. The number of members will depend on the size and complexity of the laboratory. It is generally recognized that small committees are optimal for purposes of efficiency, whereas large committees are both difficult to schedule and difficult to manage. However, a laboratory's current organization will often guide the selection of members. Key people must buy into the QMS process in order for it to succeed. Those people will often need to be part of the steering team. In addition, the steering team will need a chairperson, a recorder, and often a facilitator who can integrate group problem-solving tools into the discussions and deliberations of the team and help manage group dynamics. The Quality Manager is a logical choice to lead this team.

P5. Provide initial training

For the MPT to do its job, it will need to understand the principles of quality management, the meaning of quality as conformance to customer requirements, the idea that quality problems are process problems that must be solved by management, and the organization, development, and implementation of a Quality Management System. If accreditation is the objective for developing a QMS, then the accreditation guidelines should be introduced. In addition, the Quality System Essentials from CLSI will provide resource documents for further study and application. This training should ideally be led by top management in order to provide evidence of their commitment to quality and its improvement in the laboratory.

P6. Define Quality Goals and Objectives

The MPT should discuss and refine the laboratory Quality Policy, then provide a more detailed explanation of its meaning in the form of Quality Goals and Objectives. Those goals and objectives will reflect the mission of the laboratory, for example, a University laboratory will have goals that relate to service, education, and research [3]:

- Maintain excellence in service to patients and healthcare providers, including physicians, nurses, and other health care professionals.
- Provide high quality and creative academic programs for health care providers.
- Generate new knowledge to provide a foundation for meeting the healthcare needs of the future.

Each of these goals will then have more detailed objectives, such as the following service Quality Objectives:

- Provide management leadership that focuses on the changing needs of internal and external users and consumers and the improvement of services to meet those needs.
- Implement a Quality Management System that provides effective monitoring of services and ensures that quality requirements are met.
- Maintain a highly skilled work force to meet the changing needs of users and consumers.
- Define quality requirements based on the needs of users and consumers to clearly specify the quality that needs to be achieved by the laboratory.
- Establish a quality improvement process to support continuous improvement of laboratory services.
- Improve the cost-effectiveness, productivity, and appropriate utilization of testing services to satisfy the changing reimbursement policies.
- Optimize the use of information technology to facilitate appropriate test ordering, specimen tracking, interpretation of test results, and result reporting.

P7. Review ISO 15189 management requirements

All members of the MPT need to understand the management responsibilities and requirements for implementing a QMS. The MPT should review the ISO 15189 standard if the purpose is to obtain accreditation from ISO. Alternatively, they may review the CLSI Quality System Essentials if the purpose is to improve quality through implementation of a QMS, but not necessarily to obtain accreditation. An important part of this review is to identify the requirements and essentials that must be implemented. Implementation will require policies, processes, procedures, and forms for records.

Of particular importance in the beginning are the requirements for a Quality Manual and a document control system. The responsibility for the Quality Manual may be assigned to the Quality Manager. The responsibility for a document control system may be assigned to a subgroup of the MPT. These two requirements must be addressed upfront because documentation is a critical issue in developing a QMS.

D1. Start a Quality Manual

The Quality Manual will become the source of the policies, processes, procedures, and records that are needed to document and manage how the work gets done in the laboratory. This particular form of documentation – policies, process, procedures, and records – is the methodology necessary for ISO accreditation.

The Quality Policy and Quality Goals and Objectives should become part of the laboratory Quality Manual. The Quality Manager should take the initial responsibility for developing the Quality Manual to document progress in implementing the QMS. Others on the MPT may be assigned the development of certain polices and processes, for example, a system for document control.

Organization of the Quality Manual can follow the ISO 15189 presentation of management and technical requirements. This provides a table of contents such as shown in Table 5-2.

D2. Establish a document control system

An essential part of documentation is a document control system that identifies the currently applicable policies, processes, procedures, and forms for records. According to Levett and Burney [1], "the biggest change in your organization will come under the heading of document control." CLSI GP26 [4] describes the elements of a document management system as including (a) document identification and control, (b) new document creation, review, and approval process, (c) document change process, (d) periodic review of documents, and (e) archival, storage, and retention. The objective is to ensure that the documents in use – policies, processes, procedures, and forms for records – are current and up-to-date throughout the laboratory.

Number	Section	Page
1.0	Introduction and purpose of this Quality Manual	
	Laboratory Quality Policy	
	Laboratory Quality Goals and Objectives	
2.0	Laboratory organization	
3.0	Extent of services	
	MANAGEMENT REQUIREMENTS	
4.1	Organization and management responsibilities	
4.2	Quality management system	
4.3	Document control	
4.4	Service agreements	
4.5	Examination by referral laboratories	
4.6	External services and supplies	
4.7	Advisory services	
4.8	Resolution of complaints	
4.9	Identification and control of nonconformities	
4.10	Corrective action	
4.11	Preventive action	
4.12	Continual improvement	
4.13	Control of records	
4.14	Evaluation and audits	
4.15	Management review	
	TECHNICAL REQUIREMENTS	
5.1	Personnel	
5.2	Accommodations and environmental conditions	
5.3	Equipment	
5.4	Pre-examination processes	
5.5	Examination processes	
5.6	Ensuring quality of examination results	
5.7	Post-examination processes	
5.8	Reporting of results	
5.9	Release of results	
5.10	Laboratory information management	

Table 5-2. Outline of the contents of a Quality Manual following ISO 15189 organization of management and technical requirements.

Documents require a unique identification number, version number, name of author, name of reviewing authority, and date of issue. A master index or log of documents should be maintained to identify current documents and their location of all copies.

A manual system for document control is acceptable, but an electronic system is ideal. Resources to develop and implement an electronic document control system should be a high priority for the MPT. Acquiring a document control system will provide real evidence of management commitment. Electronic templates are available for the Quality Manual and for many of the policies, processes, and procedures that must be documented. Given that documentation is the heart of a QMS, this issue must be addressed early on in the implementation process.

P8. Perform a gap assessment

A generic form of gap analysis that is commonly used in strategic planning in business and industry is to assess the "strengths, weaknesses, opportunities, and risks," or SWOT analysis. It may be advantageous to employ this approach first to provide a general perspective of the laboratory's strategic position, then follow with a specific gap assessment based on the ISO 15189 requirements or CLSI QSEs. Or, the laboratory's current strategic plan should have this information and can become part of the initial assessment. In fact, a laboratory's strategic plan is a natural way to launch a QMS as an integral part of management activities [5].

With an understanding of the ISO 15189 requirements and/or the CLSI QSEs, the shortcomings or limitations of the current quality management practices can be assessed by comparison with the QMS requirements. This is the "gap analysis" or "gap assessment" that is recommended in many QMS implementation guidelines

Here are some examples of the gap analysis process:

- ISO 15189 requirement 4.4 relates to the establishment of service agreements. Does the laboratory have documented service agreements? If so, do the policy, process, procedures, and records meet the documentation requirements? If not, how serious is this gap in quality practices? Are there service relationships that need to be better documented? For example, does the laboratory provide reference services to clinics and doctors' offices?

- Requirement 4.5 relates to examinations by referral laboratories. Does the laboratory have in place policies, processes, procedures, and records that document each of the reference laboratories that are used for referral of patient specimens?
- Requirement 4.9 relates to nonconformities. This is a high priority in many QMS implementation plans in order to obtain metrics of the quality of services. A good example is the laboratory practice when an analytic run is out-of-control. What immediate actions should be taken? What is the extent of the nonconformities? Are examinations halted and reports withheld? What happens to results that were already reported? What actions are taken to eliminate the problem? Who is authorized to resume the testing process? Is the problem properly documented?
- Requirement 4.10 relates to corrective actions. Does the laboratory have procedures for reviewing nonconformities, determining root causes, implementing corrective actions, reviewing the effectiveness of corrective actions, and documenting the process? If this is a weakness, the laboratory may need to implement a more rigorous problem-solving process for Root Cause Analysis (RCA), which may require additional training and support.

P9. Prioritize improvements

The gaps in practice should be identified and prioritized for improvement. Factors to consider are activities that are prerequisites to other management requirements (e.g., a document control system), requirements that are considered high priority in QMS implementation plans (e.g., management of nonconformities), requirements upon which higher quality management activities are built (e.g., process control), clear weaknesses in present quality practices (e.g., policies for corrective actions, procedure manuals but no Quality Manual), and new management activities that must be implemented (e.g., audits, risk management, management review).

P10. Develop an action plan

Based on the priorities for improvement and other strategic considerations, action must now be initiated. The action plan can be implemented by assignments to individual members of the laboratory or the MPT, subgroups of the MPT, and other laboratory staff via "project teams" or problem-solving teams, as illustrated in Figure 5-3.

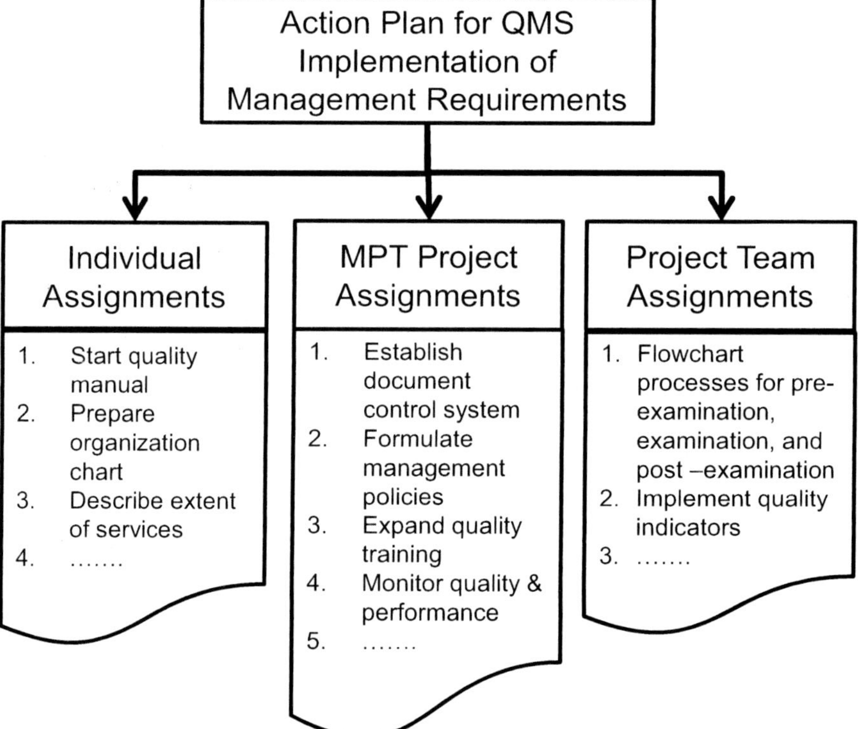

Figure 5-3. Mechanisms for implementing changes and improvements

D3. Assign individual tasks

Assignments to individuals are an effective mechanism when the problem is small and the improvement can be identified by someone with the proper administrative or technical skills. For example, the legal entity that the laboratory is part of must be properly defined, the organizational chart must be up-to-date, and the extent of services must be defined. Someone in top management can be assigned the responsibilities for these activities. Others may be asked to contribute, but an individual can be responsible to see these activities are completed.

D4. Assign MPT projects

Assignments to subgroups of the MPT are important for problems and issues that require different perspectives to understand the problem and develop remedies. For example, development of a document control system may require a high level manager, a technical leader, and an information specialist. Formulation of other management policies can be delegated to MPT subgroups.

D5. Assign project teams

Assignments to project teams will be effective for processes and problems that cross the boundaries between laboratory sections and/or other departments. As an example of an cross-section and inter-departmental process, consider the technical requirements for pre-examination processes. The project team will need to involve several people who understand the procedures for test ordering, patient preparation, patient identification, specimen collection, specimen transport, specimen processing, and sample distribution. Initial projects to flowchart the pre-examination, examination, and post-examination phases of the Total Testing Process will provide critical information about the state of practice in the laboratory.

D6. Expand quality training

Because the action plan will involve more laboratory personnel in the implementation of improvements, there will be a broader need for quality training. This training should be aimed at supporting project teams in their use of tools such as brain storming, nominal group, flowcharts, cause and effect diagrams (or "fishbone" diagrams), data collection, Pareto analysis, and force field analysis. These skills will be particularly important in the implementation of the technical requirements and uniform practices throughout the laboratory.

D7. Document policies, processes, procedures, and forms for records

All these assignments should lead to properly documented laboratory practices. For ISO 15189, this specifically means policies, processes, procedures, and forms for records. Cooper and Gillions [6] provide the following definitions of these terms:

- A **policy** specifies intent and direction. Some polices should be developed by the Quality Steering Team and others by working groups. There may be multiple processes for a given management requirement.
- A **process** describes activities that transform the intent of a policy into action (or inputs into outputs). Processes should be developed by working groups. Processes provide general instructions, assign responsibility for activities required to meet the intent of the policy, and are not prescriptive. There may be multiple processes for each policy.
- A **procedure** is a step-by-step instruction that defines "how to" perform a single specific task. Procedures are usually developed by staff familiar with the task itself, and can be product inserts or instrument manuals that describe how to perform specific examination procedures, activities, or functions. There may be multiple procedures for each process.
- **Forms and records** are controlled documents that provide the framework on which to build and operate a quality system. [Records provide the documentation of what has been done to comply with every policy, process, and procedure.]

Cooper and Gillions provide detailed examples for the ISO requirements for assuring the quality of laboratory examination procedures, specifically for internal quality control procedures. CLSI provides many examples in their extensive series of documents on Quality Management Systems, starting with GP26 [4]. Standard formats should be defined in each laboratory as part of the development of a document control system. Thereafter, the implementation of each management requirement should be documented in the laboratory's standard formats.

CHECK Stage of Implementation

Activities in the Check phase will be both formal and informal and will occur both as scheduled and unscheduled activities. The Quality Manager and the MPT will need to be heavily involved in promoting quality improvement activities, participating in MPT subgroups and project teams, and checking on the progress of all the assigned activities. While these activities will occur informally and unscheduled in the early work, they will need to become more formal and scheduled as the QMS implementation proceeds.

C1. Monitor tasks and projects

At this point, there will be many improvement activities and it is important that the MPT monitor their progress. This oversight should assess the state of development of the policies, processes, procedures, and forms for records for each of the management requirements. Individual assignments will probably be completed faster than group or team assignments, which often tackle the more difficult and complex issues. Lack of progress may require assistance by the Quality Manager or intervention by the MPT.

C2. Select Quality Indicators

Another critical requirement is to develop measures of quality and performance, or Quality Indicators, which ISO 15189 defines as "*measures of the degree to which a set of inherent characteristics fulfills requirements.*" ISO further suggests that "*measures can be expressed, for example, as % yield (% within specified requirements), % defects (% outside specified requirements), defects per million occasions (DPMO) or on the Six Sigma scale.*" The important idea here is to focus on defects, or nonconformities, which inherently requires the laboratory to define "good quality" in the form of tolerance limits for acceptable performance. Six Sigma provides concepts, principles, metrics, and tools that are advantageous for measuring quality, therefore the MPT should also consider training and support for Six Sigma applications, particularly for implementing technical requirements.

C3. Monitor nonconformities

The CLSI guideline for implementing a QMS in a medical laboratory [4] recommends that the management of nonconformities, also called occurrence management, be part of the initial phase of implementation. This is important to provide some measures of the current performance of the laboratory, benchmark the level of quality, and provide a baseline for assessing improvements.

C4. Formalize internal audit processes, procedures, and reports

Information collected via various monitoring procedures should be reviewed by the MPT on a regular basis – daily, weekly, or monthly, depending on the particular monitor. In addition, periodic audits and inspections should be scheduled to assess compliance with the laboratory's documented policies, processes, procedures, and records. Periodic review by top management should occur frequently during implementation of the QMS, at least monthly, then perhaps quarterly after implementation is complete. There should be a yearly report that summarizes changes and improvements, evaluates the measures of performance and quality, identifies areas for improvement, prioritizes the needs for improvement, and provides a plan and schedule for those improvements.

ACT Stage of Implementation

Monitoring and assessing the progress of QMS implementation will naturally require decisions on how to move forward, changes that are needed in the process and activities, and updates of the action plan as different management requirements are implemented. The Quality Manager and the MPT will be involved and should further involve top management when necessary. In addition, top management must monitor progress and initiate new phases of development, for example, a decision to move forward with a second phase of implementation for technical requirements, and ultimately for the decision to apply for accreditation. The second phase may be advanced by authorizing a Technical Planning Team to oversee the implementation of the technical requirements.

A1. Review Quality Manual

Top management should review the Quality Manual to assess the status of the implementation plan. Appropriate documentation must be in place for all the policies, processes, procedures, and forms for records for all the management and technical requirements. One implementation strategy is to make a first pass through the PDCA cycle with attention to the management requirements, then a second pass through the cycle with emphasis on the technical requirements (which will be described in the next chapter), and finally a third pass to prepare for accreditation, as described below.

A2. Select the accreditor

Selection of an accreditor will be based on those organizations that serve your area and particularly share your language. While there are global accreditors, or registrars, there are also regional and national organizations that may provide better services in your region. One issue is whether the accreditor itself is in compliance with the practice guidelines of the International Laboratory Accreditation Cooperation (ILAC, www.ilac.org). There are around 45 accreditation bodies that participate in the ILAC arrangement, which ensures consistency and recognition worldwide. Not all accreditors belong to ILAC (e.g., CAP 15189 maintains independence from ILAC).

A3. Review application process

You will have to contact the accreditor to obtain detailed information about their accreditation process. An initial step is to review their application form and identify all the information and documentation that is initially required, which will be extensive. As noted earlier, a good example of the application process is available on the website of the American Association for Laboratory Accreditation (A2LA) [7]. This is a 19 page application form that requires an organizational chart, documentation of credentials of key staff, proficiency testing plan, current Quality Manual, list of all equipment, laboratory floor plan, plus completion of additional forms, such as a 36 page "Medical Testing Scope Selection List" (Form F622) which requires identification of all tests performed by the laboratory for which accreditation is sought. There is also a General Checklist for ISO 15189 that must be completed, but that form C650 is only available once the laboratory applies for accreditation.

A4. Perform pre-assessment

An essential step is to compare your QMS with the requirements of your accrediting organization. Some organizations offer a pre-assessment as part of their services. Others may provide a checklist that can be used for an internal audit. One way or another, this pre-assessment will be necessary and will provide a new gap analysis.

A5. Identify needs for improvement

The pre-assessment gaps must be prioritized for improvement, much like what was done earlier in step P9. This will then lead to a new action plan, which brings you back to step P10 and initiates another cycle of activities for improvement.

Staying organized – Phases and Stages

Here's a short summary of the guidance in this chapter:

- Adopt the Deming Plan-Do-Check-Act Cycle for developing and implementing your Quality Management System. Ultimately, that's the structure needed for a QMS. It makes sense; use the same structure to develop and implement a QMS.
- Begin implementing the management requirements first because they bring together the organization, structure, and capabilities needed to implement a QMS. A document control system is a key building block for documentation of the policies, processes, procedures, and forms for records that are essential for implementing all management and technical requirements.
- Plan for three phases of implementation – the first for management requirements, the second for technical requirements, and the third for accreditation. These phases will probably overlap and you will complete some work simultaneously. In particular, a Management Planning

Team could begin the implementation of the management requirements and launch a Technical Planning Team to focus on the technical requirements, working in parallel on the implementation. Then the Management Steering Team could move forward to start the accreditation phase.

- Keep in mind that the steps outlined here for the PDCA stages are for initial guidance. As your laboratory proceeds, its unique characteristics and capabilities will require adjustments and customization of the implementation plan.

References

1. Levett JM, Burney RG. Using ISO 9001 in Healthcare: Applications for quality systems, performance improvement, clinical integration, and accreditation. Milwaukee, WI:ASQ Press, 2011.

2. ISO 15189. Medical laboratories – Requirements for quality and competence. ISO, Geneva, 2012.

3. Tomar R, Westgard J, Eggert A. Quality Reengineering in Health Care: A case study from the Clinical Laboratory at the University of Wisconsin. Chicago:ASCP Press, 1999.

4. CLSI GP26A4. Quality Management System: A model for laboratory services. Clinical and Laboratory Standards Institute, Wayne, PA 2011.

5. Westgard JO, Barry PL, Tomar RH. Implementing total quality management (TQM) in healthcare laboratories. CLMR 1991;5:353-370.

6. Cooper G, Gillions T. Producing Reliable Test Results in the Medical Laboratory: Using a quality system approach and ISO 15189 to assure the quality of laboratory examination procedures. Irvine CA;Bio-Rad Laboratories, 2007.

7. American Association for Laboratory Accreditation, F651 – Application for Accreditation: ISO 15189 Medical Testing Laboratories. www.a2la.org/forms/15189_Application.doc, accessed August 12, 2013.

6. Implementing Technical Requirements

Establishing a QMS begins with the implementation of management requirements as the first phase and the implementation of technical requirements as the second phase. This doesn't necessarily mean the two phases have to be entirely sequential, only that management requirements must be considered first to ensure top level commitment and leadership and the availability of necessary resources. Top management and/or the Management Planning Team (MPT) could authorize a second Technical Planning Team (TPT) that would work in parallel to implement the technical requirements. That would help minimize the time for implementation, utilizing the scientific expertise of the laboratory analysts and supervisors, and achieving more widespread buy-in throughout the laboratory.

The implementation model recommended here follows Deming's Plan-Do-Check-Act cycle, is similar to the PDCA cycle for implementing management requirements, but focuses on the technical requirements found in section 5 of ISO 15189 [1] and the Process Control essentials in the WHO/CLSI/CDC methodology [2-4]. Figure 6-1 summarizes the implementation process.

PLAN stage of implementation

Top management must consider how and when to begin the implementation of technical requirements. The priorities are first to deal with management requirements for organization of the QMS, designation of a Quality Manager, formation of a Management Planning Team, definition of quality goals and objectives, analysis of gaps in quality practices, development of an action plan, and implementation of a document control system. The MPT should also consider how to share the responsibilities for the technical requirements (5.1) personnel, (5.2) accommodations and environmental conditions, and (5.3) laboratory equipment, reagents, and consumables.

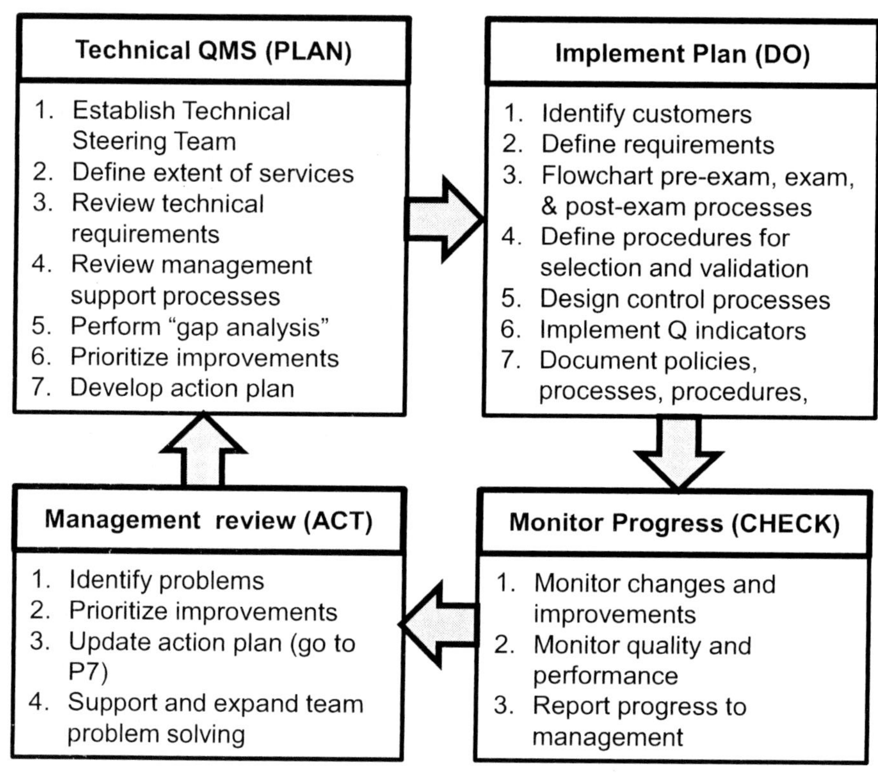

Figure 6-1. Plan for implementing QMS technical requirements.

P1. Establish a Technical Planning Team

In a small to moderate size laboratory, the Management Planning Team could also function as the Technical Planning Team. In a large laboratory, separate teams would be better to keep the sizes of the teams small and to provide specific focus for the management and technical planning activities. The Quality Manager must be a part of the TPT in order to coordinate the activities of the two teams. Other members should represent the pre-examination, examination, and post-examination phases of the testing process, along with the various laboratory disciplines, e.g., hematology, clinical chemistry, microbiology, blood bank, molecular diagnostics, etc. In a large laboratory, the TPT will also include Quality Specialists (those with special responsibilities for Method Validation, design and review of QC, monitoring of EQA/PT and other Quality Indicators, and auditing.

P2. Define priorities of services

An important consideration is the scope of testing that will be included in the application of technical requirements. It may be easier to start with clinical chemistry and hematology than with microbiology and molecular diagnostics. Blood banks may already be subject to stricter requirements for QMS, or if not, may be a high priority. It is possible to have additional phases of implementation related to the particular laboratory disciplines. The MPT and TPT should discuss and agree on the priorities for implementation of the technical requirements.

P3. Review technical requirements

All members of the TMT must understand the technical requirements. If necessary, they should review the ISO 15189 standard and undertake training about certain requirements, such as definition of quality requirements, meaning of traceability, validation and verification studies, design of control procedures, and determination of the uncertainty of measurements.

P4. Review management technical requirements

There is overlap of management responsibilities for certain technical requirements, particularly for (5.1) personnel, (5.2) accommodations and environmental conditions, and (5.3) laboratory equipment, reagents, and consumables. The Management Planning Team should take responsibility for most of the required activities, but the Technical Planning Team should review those requirements and deal with provisions related to laboratory equipment, reagents, and consumables. For example, technical expertise is required for acceptance testing, equipment instructions for use, equipment calibration and metrological traceability, etc.

P5. Perform a gap analysis

The existing quality practices of the laboratory must be compared to the technical requirements, in order to identify any deficiencies.

Here are some possible examples of potential gaps:

- ***5.3.1.4 Equipment calibration and metrological traceability.***
  The laboratory shall have a documented procedure for the calibration of equipment that directly or indirectly affects examination results. This procedure includes: (b) recording the metrological traceability of the calibration standard and the traceable calibration of the item of equipment... Metrological traceability shall be to a reference materials or reference procedure of the higher metrological order available. Note: Documentation of calibration traceability to a higher order reference material or reference procedure may be provided by an examination system manufacturer. Such documentation is acceptable as long as the manufacturer's examination system and calibration procedure are used without modification. Where this is not possible or relevant, other means for providing confidence in the results shall be applied, including by not limited to the following: use of certified reference materials; examination or calibration by another procedure; mutual consent standards or methods which are clearly established, specified, characterized and mutually agreed upon by all parties concerned.

All laboratories need to examine this requirement. A wide range of policies and procedures are possible among the different laboratory disciplines, e.g., clinical chemistry versus microbiology versus molecular diagnostics. The availability of reference materials and reference methods varies considerably from discipline to discipline.

- ***5.3.2.3 Reagents and consumables – Acceptance testing.***
  Each new formulation of examination kits with changes in reagents or procedure, or a new lot or shipment, shall be verified for performance before use in examinations.

There is increasing concern about the uniformity of reagents and materials from different manufacturing lots. Does the laboratory have a policy for acceptance testing? What level of testing is required to verify a new lot? Can you depend on testing with your existing quality control materials? Is it necessary to test patient samples to verify performance? Does the laboratory have a standard process? What is the protocol – numbers of samples, data to be collected, how to analyze statistically, how to judge acceptability?

- ***5.5.1 Selection, verification and validation of examination procedures.*** *The laboratory shall select examination procedures which have been validated for their intended use... The specified requirements (performance specifications) for each examination procedure shall relate to the intended uses of that examination.*

There may be several possible gaps here. What is the selection process for analytic systems and measurement procedures? How are "purchase specifications" established? How are manufacturer's performance claims evaluated before and after purchase? What is the difference between verification and validation? Does the laboratory have well-defined protocols for verification and validation? Has the laboratory defined the performance specification on the basis of the intended use of each examination? Does the laboratory perform its own verification studies or depend on the manufacturer to provide that service? How does the laboratory make its own decision on the acceptability of the performance based on the experimental results? How do the laboratory practices for validation different from those for verification?

- ***5.5.1.4 Measurement uncertainty of measured quantity values.*** *The laboratory shall determine measurement uncertainty for each measurement procedure in the examination phase used to report measured quantity values on patients' samples. The laboratory shall define the performance requirements for the measurement uncertainty of each measurement procedure and regularly review estimates of measurement uncertainty.*

This requirement has been strengthened in the 2012 version of ISO 15189 compared to the 2007 version, where measurement uncertainty was to be estimated "where practical and useful". This earlier qualification – *where practical and useful* – allowed laboratories considerable flexibility in whether or not they needed to determine measurement uncertainty (MU). That flexibility has now been eliminated; laboratories ***must*** determine MU. However, the methodology for determining MU has been simplified to allow use of routine QC data obtained *under intermediate precision conditions,* rather than the formidable GUM methodology. What is the meaning of "intermediate precision" conditions? How should the laboratory define a procedure for determining MU? Where does determination of MU fit – initial verification/validation or ongoing monitor of performance?

- ***5.6.2 Quality control.*** *The laboratory shall design quality control procedures that verify the attainment of the intended quality of results.*

Note the term "intended quality of results". How should the laboratory design its QC procedures on the basis of intended quality? How does the laboratory take into account the observed precision and bias of the method and the quality required for the intended use of the test? How does the laboratory select its control rules and number of control measurements to verify the attainment of the intended quality of results? Even more basic, how does the laboratory define "intended quality"? This is a common weakness in many laboratories – the lack of definition of the requirements for quality in quantitative terms.

- ***5.6.2.3 Quality control data.*** *The laboratory shall have a procedure to prevent the release of patient results in the event of a quality control failure. When the control rules are violated and indicate that examination results are likely to contain clinically significant errors, the results shall be rejected and relevant patient samples re-examined after the error condition has been corrected and within-specification performance is verified. The laboratory shall also evaluate the results from patient samples that were examined after the last successful quality control event.*

This requirement gets to the heart of quality control. How does the laboratory determine if an analytical run provides within-specification performance? That depends on a properly designed QC procedure that takes into account the intended quality of results (which is required in 5.6.2). Given a proper design that identifies the control rules and the numbers of control measurements, what is the policy for handling out-of-control runs? What corrective action is required? How is corrective action documented to demonstrate or verify within-specification performance? What patient samples are repeated? What patient results are reported?

- ***5.6.4 Comparability of examination results.*** *There shall be a defined means of comparing procedures, equipment and methods used and establishing the comparability of results for patient samples throughout the clinically appropriate intervals. This is applicable to the same or different procedures, equipment, different sites, or all of these.*

There may be two or more measurement procedures in use in the same laboratory, for example, one for emergency service, perhaps in a stat laboratory or a point-of-care application, and another for central service. How does the laboratory ensure that different measurement procedures for the same measurand provide comparable results? What data is collected and how is it analyzed to demonstrate comparability? What actions are to be taken when there is a lack of comparability?

- ***5.9.2 Automated selection and reporting of results.*** *If the laboratory implements a system for automated selection and reporting of results, it shall establish a documented procedure to ensure that: (a) the criteria for automated selection and reporting are defined, approved, readily available and understood by the staff; (b) the criteria are validated for proper function before use and verified after changes to the system that might affect their functioning; (c) there is a process for indicating the presence of sample interferences (e.g., haemolysis, icterus, lipaemia) that may alter the results of the examination; (d) there is a process for incorporating analytical warning messages from instruments into the automated selection and reporting criteria, when appropriate; (e) results selected for automated reporting shall be identifiable at the time of review before release and include date and time of selection; (f) there is a process for rapid suspension of automated selection and reporting.*

This requirement addresses a practice sometimes called "autoverification", which typically is a software feature that examines test results and automatically releases or reports patient results when certain data check "autoverification rules" have been satisfied. Does the laboratory use autoverification? If so, what are the rules that have been implemented? Has the laboratory validated that those rules work as intended? Are samples with hemolysis, icterus, and lipaemia appropriately identified? How are the test results that would be affected by those conditions reported? What conditions would lead to suspension of automated reporting of results? What is the procedure for recovery and return to autoverification?

P6. Prioritize improvements

There will first be a need to clarify current laboratory policies, processes, and procedures. This may involve a high level overview of the total testing process as a flowchart, then a detailed mapping of the pre-examination, examination, and post-examination processes. This review of current practices will naturally identify needs for improvement, similar to the gap analysis. From the examples of gaps discussed here, it is probable that one high priority will be the definition of quality requirements. These need to be defined early, since they will be used to validate process performance, judge the acceptability of method performance, guide the design of QC procedures, and assess the acceptability of measurement uncertainty.

P7. Develop action plan

The mechanisms for developing improvements include referral to the Management Planning Team, assignment to individuals on the Technical Planning Team, assignment to subgroups of the TPT, and assignments to project teams that are formed to resolve specific issues. Ideally, these project teams should be chaired by a person from the TPT in order to closely coordinate those activities with other assignments.

DO phase of implementation

The PLAN and DO phases will probably overlap. Once the need for improvement is identified, actions are taken to implement the necessary changes. As more gaps are identified, an organized plan for action is needed. In general, the lab must consider the identification of customers, definition of requirements for pre-examination, examination, and post-examination processes, then assessment of the capabilities of all these processes. Figure 6-2 provides some ideas for an action plan.

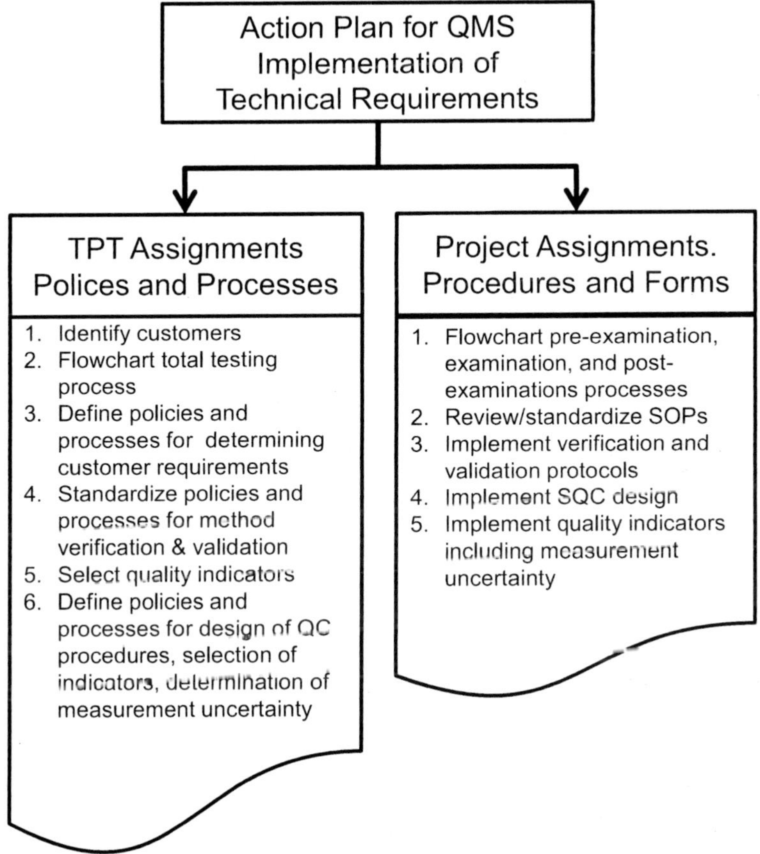

Figure 6-2. Action plan for implementing technical requirements through assignments to the Technical Planning Team and to Project Teams

The TPT should focus on the policies and processes related to the technical requirements and then assign responsibilities for the detailed procedures and forms for records to project teams that involve bench level personnel who know the reality of routine operations.

D1. Identify customers

The purpose here is to gain a clear understanding of your customers, consumers, clients, and end users, whatever you prefer to call them. Of particular importance are those customers who may have the highest demands for service, e.g., emergency room physicians, intensive care units, transplant programs, and specialized clinics.

D2. Define requirements

The laboratory will typically define the specimen requirements, patient preparation directions, collection procedures, and transport, processing, and distribution procedures as part of the laboratory's pre-examination processes. Examination requirements should address the quality required for intended clinical use in terms of analytical performance, e.g., the allowable total error or allowable imprecision and allowable bias. Post-examination processes must consider report formats, delivery, and documentation. Turnaround time is a critical requirement for the total examination process and must be defined for different levels of service, such as emergency orders, routine orders, and reference laboratory orders.

D3. Flowchart processes

A good mechanism for assessing pre-examination, examination, and post-examination processes is to develop a flowchart of the important steps. Initially, a broad "top-down" flowchart can provide an overview of the total testing process, from physician order to patient report back to the physician. More detailed flowcharts can then be constructed for the pre-examination, examination, and post-examination processes. An important outcome will be that all people on the TPT develop a common understanding of the core work processes. Once the work processes are uniformly understood, the TPT can systematize and standardize them across disciplines and across different types of service laboratories, e.g., clinic, central, emergency, reference, etc.

D4. Define procedures for validation of processes

Knowing the quality requirements and having standardized processes, the evaluation of process performance is critical to determine the capability of achieving the required quality. Evaluation is often described in terms of verification and validation. Verification refers to assessing performance relative to a *manufacturer's* claimed performance. Validation should assess performance relative to the defined *customer* requirements. Detailed protocols are required for verification and validation of examination procedures, along with scientific expertise. Reliance on the manufacturers to provide verification data is not sufficient; the laboratory must be able to assess the suitability of experimental design, adequacy of data collection, plus independently interpret the results to judge acceptability of performance.

D5. Design control procedures

ISO 15189 specifically requires the laboratory to design control procedure to verify the attainment of the intended quality of test results. The definition of analytical quality requirements is the starting point, along with the observed precision and bias from method performance studies. Statistical control rules and the number of control measurements must be selected to provide adequate detection of medically important errors. Optimal Statistical QC procedures (SQC) can be designed in accordance with the ISO requirement to verify attainment of intended quality.

D6. Implement Quality Indicators

The laboratory must be able to measure performance in order to manage, control, evaluate, and improve the quality of testing services. Recall that ISO 15189 defines a Quality Indicator as a "measure of the degree to which a set of inherent characteristics fulfills requirements" and recommends that the measure can be expressed in terms of the number of defects per million opportunities or occasions (DPMO) or on the Six Sigma scale. An important consideration for the laboratory is the adoption of Six Sigma concepts and metrics as part of the implementation strategy for quantitative quality management.

The MPT can provide guidance for the selection of Quality Indicators, but it is likely they will delegate or assign the implementation to another team, such as the TPT. Some indicators that are often in place and are useful in most laboratories include:

- Number of specimens (or % defects) rejected as inadequate in sample control;
  - Numbers incorrectly requested, incorrectly scheduled, improper patient preparation, inappropriate collection time; improper specimen type, hemolyzed, lipemic, insufficient volume, wrong container, unstable;
- Number of specimens (or % defects) incorrectly identified and/or incorrectly labeled;
- Number of specimens lost;
- Number of analytical runs (or % defects) rejected as "out-of-control" by SQC procedures properly designed to detect medically important errors;
- Number of patient results (% defects) repeated from "out-of-control" runs;
- 95th percentile of turnaround times for tests ordered as "stat" or emergency service;
- 95th percentile of turnaround times for tests ordered as routine service;
- Number of tests exceeding critical values that require special notification to physicians;
  - Number (or % defects) not called;
- Number of test results corrected after initial reporting;
- Number of external proficiency testing samples (or % defects) that do not satisfy criteria for acceptable performance;

- Number of cases of inadequate service documented by complaints and incident reports;
- Number of tests sent to reference laboratories;

D7. Document policies, processes, procedures and forms for records

Progress in implementing the technical requirements can be assessed from the documentation of laboratory policies, production processes, operational procedures, and records that demonstrate proper applications in the laboratory, as outlined in the previous chapter.

CHECK phase of implementation

Progress in implementing the technical requirements should be documented by the policies and processes added to the Quality Manual and the updated and improved procedures for routine operations of the pre-examination, examination, and post-examination processes. These procedures will appear as Standard Operation Procedures (SOPs) in the "method manuals" of the laboratory. They require signoff by managers and all reviews and updates should become part of a master log of documents.

C1. Monitor changes and improvements

Progress in implementing the technical requirements should be monitored first by reviewing progress in completing assignments and projects, and secondly, by reviewing progress in development of appropriate documents for policies, processes, procedures, forms and records.

C2. Monitor quality and performance

Measures of quality and performance should be obtained to provide a baseline from which to assess improvements. General indicators include performance in EQA or PT programs, comparison with peer groups in benchmarking programs, and determination of measurement uncertainty from intermediate QC data. Additional setting-specific indicators should be selected and implemented in the laboratory.

C3. Report progress to management

There is a need for ongoing communications with the MPT, as well as periodic reports that are part of management review. Minutes from meetings should be provided to document project activities. Periodic project reports should identify progress and problems. Policies, processes, and procedures should be available in the Quality Manual to document progress in addressing the technical requirements.

ACT phase of implementation

Management review and action must involve both the management and technical planning teams. The Quality Manager may be the key for communication, cooperation, and coordination between the two teams.

A1. Identify problems

Progress will be impeded by problems that require management attention for resolution. The authority of project teams to recommend changes and implement improvements may encounter resistance due to resource limitations, particularly the time and effort required to implement changes that affect a large number of people in the laboratory. There will often be a demand for information technology and assistance that may require additional personnel and software support.

A2. Prioritize problems for resolution

The TPT should prioritize their specific needs for improvements and work with the MPT to incorporate those improvements into the laboratory's action plans. Where resource limitations are not an issue, the TPT may prioritize the actions to improve implementation of technical requirements. When resources are an issue, it will be necessary for the MPT to include those improvements in the MPT action plan.

A3. Update action plans

Managing the changes involved in implementation of a QMS requires that action plans be living documents that reflect achievements in problems solved and improvements implemented, as well as the new priorities and new project activities.

A4. Support and expand team problem solving

Additional project teams may be authorized to analyze specific problems and address specific improvements. This will require additional training of personnel in a structured group problem-solving process and tools. Continued management support is necessary because of the time and resources that are required to implement improvements.

Increasing momentum – Phases and Cycles

The implementation plan presented here suggests 3 phases, the first to implement the management requirements, the second to implement technical requirements, and the third for inspection and accreditation. You should also understand that each phase may involve more than one cycle of the Plan-Do-Check-Act methodology. There are wheels inside of wheels, i.e., there are PDCA cycles within a PDCA methodology for implementing a PDCA Quality Management System.

The requirements for the third phase for accreditation will depend on the Accreditor selected by the laboratory. The Management Planning Team should coordinate this phase once it has completed implementation of the management requirements and the Technical Planning Team is well on its way to completing implementation of the technical requirements.

References

1. ISO 15189. Medical laboratories – Requirements for quality and competence. ISO, Geneva, 2012.

2. WHO Laboratory Quality Management System Handbook. World Health Organizations, Geneva, Switzerland; 2011. Available from WHO website, www.who.int/ihr/publications/lqms/en/index.html, accessed August 22, 2013.

3. WHO Laboratory Quality Management System Training Toolkit. World Health Organization, Geneva, Switzerland. Available from WHO websiste, www.who.int/ihr/training_quality/en/index.html, accessed August 22, 2013.

4. CLSI GP26A4. Quality Management System: A model for laboratory services. Clinical and Laboratory Standards Institute, Wayne, PA 2011.

7: A Community Hospital Laboratory's Journey To CAP-ISO 15189 Accreditation

Leo Serrano, MS, FACHE, Lean/Six Sigma Black Belt, Broward Medical Center

Cheryl Wildermuth, MS, MT(ASCP), Quality Manager, Avera McKennan Lab

A brief introduction

During Leo Serrano's tenure as laboratory director for the Avera McKenna Hospital and University Medical Center in Sioux Falls, South Dakota, the hospital was the first in the nation to achieve ISO 15189 accreditation through CAP. He has valuable insights into the accreditation process through uniquely American eyes.

Some of these observations were reported in the May 2009 issue of CAP Today, in the article by Anne Ford, *Making the Leap to ISO 15189 – What Lab Leaders Have Learned.*

Leo shared some of his experiences about the impact of achieving ISO 15189 on the hospital and its business:

"'We're already seeing the financial benefits pay off.... We have a very strong research arm, the Avera Research Institute, and they are using our ISO accreditation to help them garner grants.... We've also been able to use it to our advantage as we have discussions with payers. When you can show them that your laboratory is 15189-ac credited, that definitely gets their attention."

"'And then there are the non-financial rewards,' Leo continues, 'It gives us a significantly more powerful platform from which to tout the laboratory and its contributions to patient care and to quality. While we have consistently world-class turnaround times, world class error rates, we still had physicians who emphasized the outliers. This acheivement confirms what we had been telling them.'"

While Leo Serrano has since moved on to another institution, we are fortunate that he has agreed to share with us his past experiences with developing and implementing a Quality Management System.

Introduction

This is the true rendition of the journey to becoming the first hospital laboratory in the US to achieve CAP-ISO15189 accreditation. No names are used but otherwise the details are as they actually occurred. The basic layout of this chapter is following the PDCA format. As you take this journey, PDCA becomes second nature in helping you achieve success in any endeavor you choose to undertake. Our journey began when one of our senior pathologists approached us with the idea of being a "pilot site" for a new ISO based CAP Accreditation. A little investigation into the idea intrigued us and fit in to our organization's culture of excellence. The rest is history.

PLAN:

As you choose to undertake this journey, and it truly is a never-ending journey, the planning portion is critical to the success and smoothness of the process.

1. Obtaining Administrative Support

The first step of the journey was obtaining support from the hospital administration as well as from the pathologists. In order to obtain their support, it was important to demonstrate the advantages of obtaining a "world-class" internationally recognized accreditation. This required research into the ISO-15189:2007 standards and how they differed from our standard CAP accreditation standards. This was an interesting challenge since the laboratory was already widely recognized as a leading exponent of LEAN (Toyota Production System) and was accredited by the College of American Pathologists, the AABB and FDA (for our full service blood bank) and FACT (for our Stem Cell transplant processing lab). Why do we need another accreditation? What is the advantage? What is the burning platform?

2. Commitment to Quality Management

Because of our robust TPS/LEAN experience, we already had a strong and well-developed commitment to quality. Our MPT had several LEAN certified members. Many of the details that are important in

ISO-15189 were already in place; although in some areas, we had to expand or strengthen our efforts. Through planning and investigation, we were able to determine our strengths and weaknesses and work on those areas in need of shoring up.

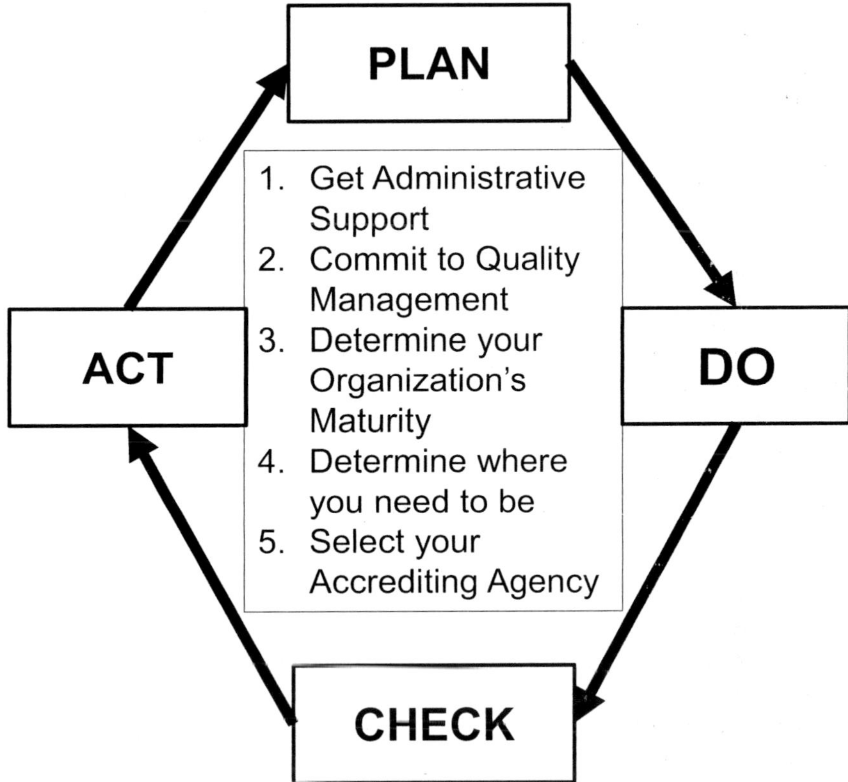

Figure 7-1. The CAP-15189 experience at Leo Serrano's hospital

3. Determining Your Organization's Maturity

This is the most emotionally demanding portion of the preparation. It is not an easy thing to critique an organization that you and your team have been developing over the years. It requires a willingness to look outside of the bounds and think out of the box. Because the QMS manager had been away from the laboratory for a while, hers were fresh eyes looking at our operation, culture and processes. This became an invaluable tool.

4. Determining Where You Need to Be

This occurs quasi-simultaneously with determining your organizational maturity. You look at where you are; compare it to the standard and identify those areas that require strengthening or further development. The ISO-15189 standards are somewhat dry reading. In our case, we were able to obtain much information from the CAP ISO team. While we had not officially completed the application process, we made our complete commitment known. Their help was invaluable as we performed our own "gap" analysis. This was an eye-opening experience. Using the ISO standard documents, we took a thorough look at our operation. We actually looked better than we had expected. We identified areas of need and began to prioritize the improvements necessary. The MPT under the direction of the QMS manager developed our action plan.

5. Selection of the Accrediting Agency

In order to be thorough, even though we had discussed the pilot program with CAP, we researched the other potential Accreditor. In this case, we found that they had not inspected or accredited any clinical laboratories in North America. There was a lab in the Caribbean which had undergone inspection. We were aware of the issues with being a signatory to ISO as well as the relationship between ISO and CLSI, we felt that regardless of which way we went, we were plowing new ground. Having a long history with the CAP and having been accredited under them for over 30 years, plus the fact that they were so helpful answering our questions; we decided to select the CAP ISO-15189 program.

DO

The "DO" part came naturally to our MPT. As a group of action-oriented individuals, this was the most natural part of PDCA. It was because of our natural predilection for action that we chose the PDCA model. Our LEAN training really helped us. The planning made sure we thought things out first. It helped that our MPT was composed of people with different personality traits. We had action-oriented people, cautious thinkers, and careful organizers on the team; all with the same goal.

1. Obtaining Administrative Support

The answer to obtaining the support lay in the competitive nature of healthcare in our particular region. With two very large, very competitive healthcare systems within three miles of each other; any opportunity to differentiate yourself becomes important. In the case of the laboratories, we had already begun that differentiation by adopting the Toyota Production System (LEAN) and developing a robust program. As we discussed the advantages, it was helpful that as a "pilot" we would be getting a break on the fees. After a short meeting detailing our plan, expected outcome and potential advantages, we received strong support from both the administration and the pathology group.

2. Commitment to Quality Management

At the beginning of our journey, quality oversight was up to the Laboratory Administrator. We had several individuals responsible for specific areas and coordinated by laboratory administration. While it worked well, we realized that in a QMS heavy accreditation such as ISO, this was not going to robust enough. So, the first step was to interview and select a Quality Manager. This meant developing a job description, revamping the laboratory organizational chart and adjusting the budget.

After reviewing several job descriptions (easily obtained from the internet as well as with help from ASQ); we formulated our job description and began our search. Fortunately, we were able to convince a former laboratory supervisor who had been part of the original Lab LEAN Team, to return to the lab. After the laboratory LEAN project reached its major milestone, she transferred to the newly formed HOSPITAL Process Improvement Department. This had allowed her to expand her understanding of the interrelationships between the lab and the other departments. It had also exposed her to a variety of Quality Plans; some stronger than others.

Having selected the manager, we now began to evaluate which policies were adequate and which needed strengthening. The formulation of policy was assigned to a small group. Led by the QMS Manager, it also included the Director of Laboratory Services, the

Director of Outreach (who had expertise in Compliance) and the Manager of Operations. Again, because of our past LEAN efforts, we had very strong and broad administrative policies. We reviewed them, compared them to the ISO 15189 Standards and edited/updated them as needed. This small group became the core of the Management Planning Team (MPT). The QMS manager and the Director took the lead in planning, with input from the other members as needed. As we completed the policy plan, it was shared with the Pathologist Medical Director for his review and input.

3. Determining Your Organization's Maturity

We began by looking at the culture of the lab. Because we had been a LEAN laboratory for several years, the LEAN culture was firmly entrenched. We had a number of key quality and performance indicators that were regularly and consistently monitored. However, LEAN and ISO, while complimentary, are not the same. We identified the areas that needed strengthening in our culture.

We now looked at the knowledge level of our staff when it came to Quality Management. They were strong in QC. However, QC is just a small part of QMS. However, we had a strong blood bank group and thanks to their AABB influence and experience, we were able to draw on some parallels. Training was going to be significant.

Our single largest challenge was the evaluation of our software and documentation. We had excellent documentation (LEAN makes you do that), which we strengthened selectively; however, our document control was in need of significant development. This became the primary focus of the QMS Manager. In many organizations, a simple solution is to acquire the software. Because of budget constraints, however, that was not an option for us.

The maturity of our QM plan was determined to be inadequate.

The development of the QMS fell to the MPT under the direction of the QMS manager. While members of the team would prepare rough drafts of their assigned sections, it was the QMS manager who would polish them and prepare them for review and editing by the Director and the Pathologist.

While this was underway; we began by assessing the level of knowledge of those selected as auditors. Additional audit training was implemented. It was understood that no one could audit an area for which they had responsibility. The MPT and the selected auditor candidates received audit training from the hospital education department and the hospital Compliance office all of whom had undergone formal audit training.

4. Determining Where You Need to Be

Using the ISO standard documents, we took a thorough look at our operation. We actually looked better than expected. We identified areas of need and began to prioritize the improvements necessary. The MPT under the direction of the QMS manager developed our action plan. Specific areas we targeted included improvements in our knowledge base when it came to a true QMS. Staff training in QMS was done through in-house training using a variety of methods including PowerPoint presentations.

Our QMS manager developed a very effective Document Control System using Microsoft Excel. To say she was creative would be an understatement. However, it was robust and worked very well. We were able to augment it by acquiring an SAAS application (Inspection Ready), which allowed us to download the CAP checklists and ISO standards and link them to our online documents in a seamless and efficient manner.

5. Selection of the Accrediting Agency

Having a long history with the CAP and having been accredited under them for over 30 years, we decided to select the CAP ISO 15189 program. Since neither agency had accredited a laboratory in the US, we felt comfortable with an agency we knew well and which had extensive clinical experience.

CHECK

1. Administrative Support

We found it critical to keep the administration and the pathology group constantly updated on our status and progress. This is a critical component of the CHECK aspect of PDCA. We wanted to make sure that there was consistency and oversight of our efforts. You can never communicate enough. We provided weekly updates to the pathologists at our weekly meeting and bi-weekly updates to the administration at our administrative one-on-one meetings.

2. Commitment to Quality Management

Keeping our fingers on the pulse as to the improvements on our journey from conventional QC to an all-encompassing QMS were the key CHECK aspect. The MPT met periodically to review where we stood on the various aspects. The open door policy allowed members to address issues as they arose and kept us on track for a very ambitious schedule.

3. Determining Your Organization's Maturity

Along with the evaluation of our QMS commitment, came the review and evaluation of our maturity in the other areas. Regular updates on the progress of the document control software and the implementation of the SAAS Inspection Ready software were the norm at our MPT meetings.

Additionally, we kept a close watch on the development of our audit staff.

4. Determining Where You Need to Be

We now began to perform our own gap analyses of our situation. A gap analysis is a thorough evaluation of where you are and where you need to be. By performing our own "informal" gap analysis, we felt we would be better prepared when the CAP-ISO 15189 group came to do the "real thing". The MPT and the Audit Team performed the gap analysis. By having several individuals look at our processes, we were able to get a cross-section of opinions and by having consensus on the strength of our processes, we felt more secure in our future success.

ACT

1. Post Gap Preparation

Once we had completed the CHECK portion, we acted on the findings, again re-strengthened any areas we found lacking and prepared for the visit from the CAP ISO assessors.

2. The CAP Process

With our preparations behind us, we took full advantage of the CAP pilot status. CAP assessors came and performed the "pre-assessment" inspection. This was reassuring to us since we corrected any "tweaks" that were suggested. A month later, they returned to do the "official" gap analysis over a two and a half day period. The technical assessor as well as the management assessor gave our lab a thorough going over. They missed little if anything. Any paper that wasn't "document controlled" was caught despite our best efforts. Their input, based on extensive ISO assessment experience, proved invaluable. The gap analysis provided the "tidying up" advice that we needed.

The MPT worked hard to close any loopholes that had been pointed out and in just four short weeks, the assessors returned to do the complete final inspection. This was to say the least, the most thorough and comprehensive assessment any of us had ever experienced. The proudest moment of this experience came when we were advised that the team of assessors had found NO major non-conformances and only five minor non-conformances. In January, a scant eight (8) months after we first decided that we wanted to undergo this journey, we were notified of our successful accreditation to the CAP-ISO 15189 standard, becoming the first hospital laboratory to become accredited not only in the clinical laboratory but also in the anatomic pathology laboratory.

Closing

This short chapter does not do justice to the hard work undertaken by the laboratory staff nor to the dedication of the individuals that comprised the laboratory MPT, audit team or LEAN team. As a result of the experience, we were recognized for our exceptional, world-class quality and performance by a third party organization. This resonated with the laboratory staff, the medical staff and the hospital as a whole.

The CAP-ISO 15189 accreditation is a 3 year cycle – Cycle 1 assesses the entire laboratory operation; both technical as well as management. It is a multi-day assessment by a team of experienced assessors. Cycle 2 occurs a year later and concentrates on the technical component of the assessment, however, the management and continuous quality improvement aspects are also evaluated. Cycle 3 occurs a year after Cycle 2 and concentrates on the Quality Management portion while still looking at the technical competence aspect. Once those are completed, it starts all over again.

Oh, and one other thing; every time they come back, the bar gets raised so that you must continually improve on your processes. What passed last visit may not be sufficiently strong to pass on the next visit. You don't just meet the standards; you continually improve on them.

In retrospect, one would ask the question: Was it worth it? Would you do it again? The answer to both questions would be a resounding and unqualified YES!!

Part II. Six Sigma QMSs for Examination Procedures

The first part of this book presents a broad perspective of management and technical requirements for laboratory accreditation. The second part provides a more detailed example of a QMS that is focused on the technical requirements, particularly the analytical quality of the examination procedure. Six Sigma concepts and metrics are applied to develop an objective, quantitative QMS, which we call a Six Sigma Quality Management System (***6σQMS***).

Our intention is to describe and develop this ***6σQMS*** as an extension of Deming's Plan-Do-Check-Act (PDCA) cycle. However, we do not provide a complete set of policies, processes, and procedures (that probably can't be done for all laboratories and all scenarios), but rather examples for specific technical requirements that require quantitative assessments and implementation guidance.

Chapter 8 – Developing a Scientific Quality System – provides an overview of the recommended Six Sigma Quality Management System, along with some illustrations of the tools and techniques that are applicable at different steps in the ***6σQMS***.

Chapter 9 – Defining Quality for Intended Use – focuses on the most critical step for making quality measurable. How good does an examination need to be?

Chapter 10 – Selecting an Examination Procedure – emphasizes the need to consider traceability as a critical characteristic in the choice of any examination procedure in order to achieve comparability of results across methods, laboratories, and countries.

Chapter 11 – Validating Performance of an Examination Procedure – describes how to assess quality on the Sigma Scale to provide a standard yardstick for measuring quality and making decisions about the acceptability of performance.

is inherently insufficiently robust to allow the achievement of a narrow analytical variation regardless of the effort to control the analytical process (i.e., creatinine Jaffe method). Second, there is sub-optimal control over the IQC process and a lack of defined limits."

The authors recognize the limitations of current analytical technology, as well as the IQC process itself. They acknowledge that the quality of the test system can only be improved by the manufacturer and that the laboratory must select appropriate methods, then apply properly designed IQC procedures. They describe the need for a scientifically-based quality control process to improve the comparability of laboratory tests.

"The implementation of national and international guidelines is beginning to standardize clinical practice. However, since many guidelines have decision limits based on laboratory tests, there is an urgent need to ensure that different laboratories obtain the same analytical results on any sample. A scientifically based quality control process will be a pre-requisite to provide this level of analytical performance which will support evidence-based guidelines and movement of patients across boundaries while maintaining standardized outcomes."

Developing a scientifically-based quality control process

Key concepts that must be adopted include the following:

- Six Sigma concept of measuring quality on a sigma scale;
- Definition of "tolerance limits" for analytical specifications for the intended clinical use in terms of an Allowable Total Error (TE_a) as the quality requirement for analytical performance;
- Calculation of a Sigma-metric from the tolerance limits (TE_a) for the process and the centering (bias) and distribution (SD) observed for the measurement procedure, i.e., Sigma = $[(TE_a - bias)/SD]$;
- Utilization of the Sigma-metric in the selection and validation of examination procedures, selection and design of statistical QC procedures (control rules, number of control measurements), formulation of a Total QC strategy and a Total QC plan;

- Monitoring nonconformities in terms of Defects Per Million (DPM) and expressing quality on the sigma scale;
- Measuring the uncertainty and bias of examination procedures and comparing to requirements for intended use by calculation of Sigma-metrics.

Implementing Six Sigma concepts and principles

Figure 8-1 provides initial guidance for implementing a Six Sigma Quality System that follows Deming's Plan-Do-Check-Act cycle.

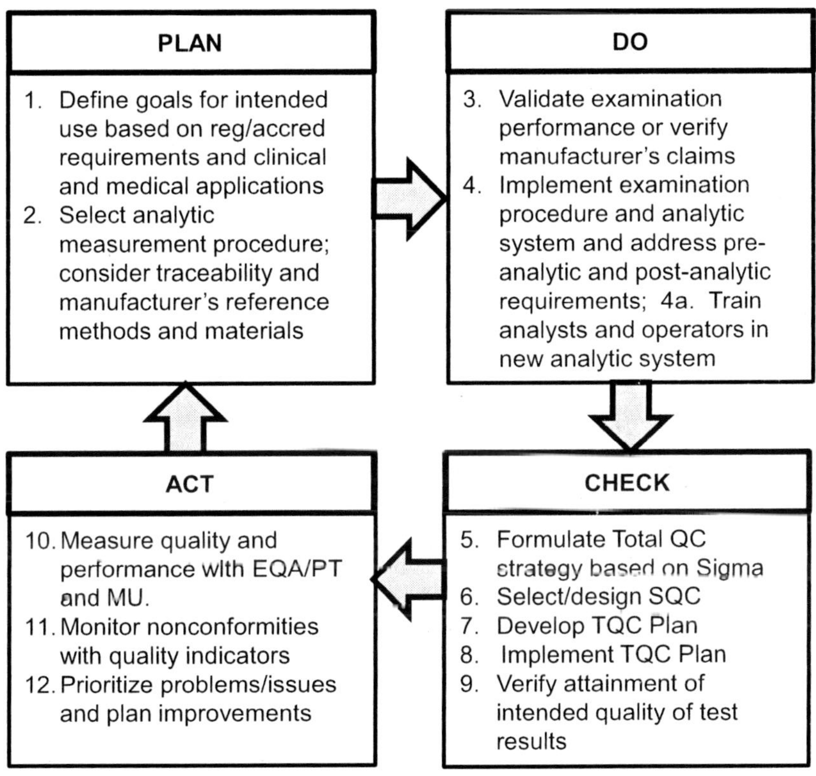

Figure 8-1. Plan-Do-Check-Act model for implementing a Six Sigma Quality System

- The PLAN stage begins with defining goals for intended use, then selecting examination procedures, paying particular attention to traceability and process capability.
- The DO stage involves the validation of measurement performance, assessment of pre-examination and post-examination processes that are critical for implementation of the total examination process, and training of personnel on the new total examination process. The sigma performance of each examination should be determined based on the quality requirements defined earlier and the precision and bias that is experimentally determined for each examination procedure.
- The CHECK stage involves formulating a Total QC strategy based on the sigma quality of the examination procedure, then selecting a Statistical QC procedure, assessing the need for additional controls in the Total QC Plan based on sigma priorities for control mechanisms, then implementation of QC procedures that will verify attainment of the intended quality of examination results.
- The ACT stage requires ongoing monitoring of measurement performance through EQA and PT programs, along with determination of Measurement Uncertainty from QC data obtained under intermediate precision conditions. Other Quality Indicators should also be employed to monitor failures and nonconformities. Finally, the monitoring results should be expressed in DPM and Sigma-metrics, problems identified and prioritized, and improvements planned.

Figure 8-2 provides a more detailed flowchart for managing the quality of examinations on the basis of Six Sigma concepts and metrics. The top half of this model focuses on making quality *measureable* by defining intended use for a test (Step 1), selecting a measurement or examination procedure that is capable of achieving the quality required for intended use (Step 2), assessing the critical performance characteristics of the examination to demonstrate the capability of the measurement procedure on the sigma Scale (Step 3), then implementing the examination procedure (Step 4). Steps 1 and 2 correspond to the PLAN phase of the PDCA cycle and steps 3 and 4 to the DO phase.

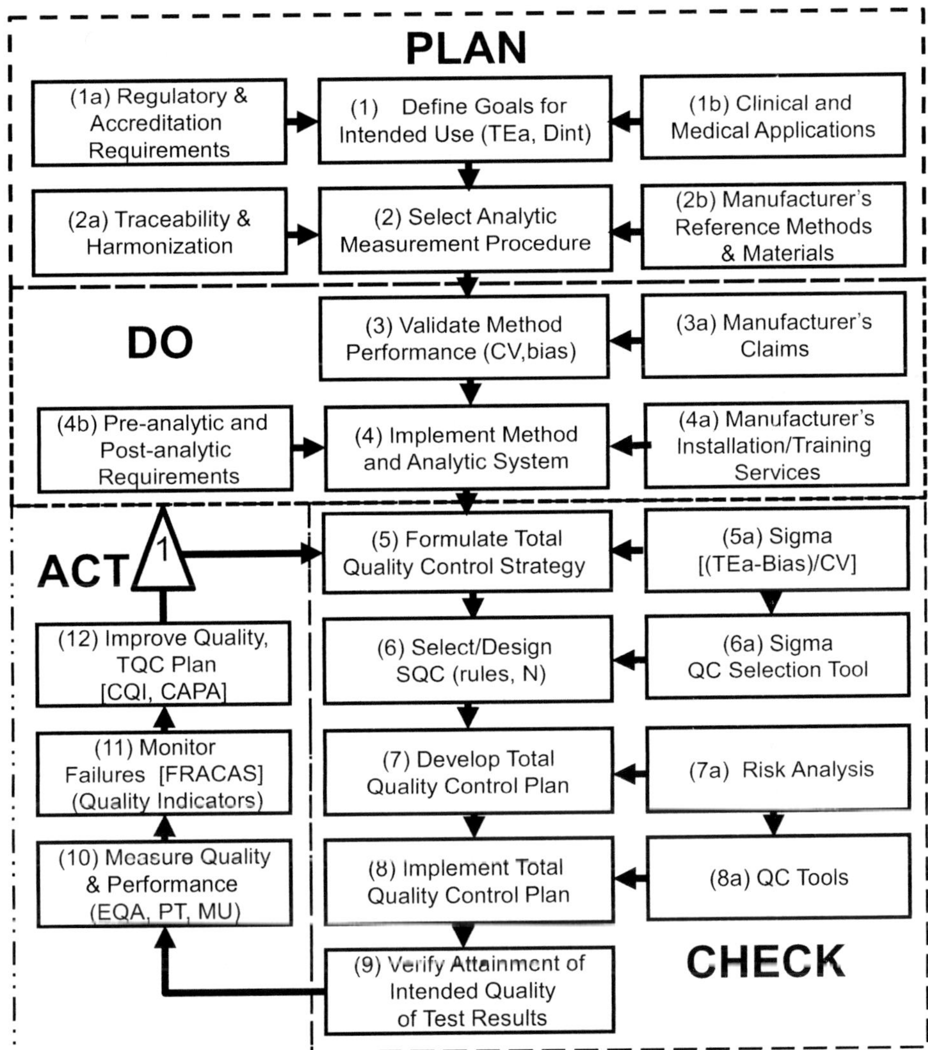

Figure 8-2. Detailed flowchart of PDCA model for implementing a Six Sigma Quality System

The bottom half of the model is about making quality *manageable.* The Sigma-metric that was determined earlier becomes the driving force for formulating a Total QC strategy (Step 5), selecting a Statistical QC procedure that can detect medically important errors (Step 6), developing a comprehensive or Total QC Plan (Step 7) and implementing that plan (Step 8) to verify the attainment of the intended quality of examination results (Step 9). Steps 5 through 9 correspond to the CHECK phase in the PDCA cycle. Steps 10, 11, and 12 are about monitoring and measuring quality and performance with the goal of identifying failures and taking corrective and preventive actions to improve quality. Those steps correspond to the ACT phase in the PDCA cycle.

Making quality measureable (PLAN and DO Phases)

Step 1 is to define quality goals for intended use. ISO 15189 [3] employs the term "intended use" to describe the intended application of a laboratory test. Intended use is a broad term that includes such things as type of specimen, type of sample, amount of sample, etc. Here we are particularly concerned with defining the analytical quality that is required.

Regulatory and accreditation considerations vary from country to country, but always include a requirement for Proficiency Testing or External Quality Assessment. That is an important consideration because the format for stating goals in such programs is the Allowable Total Error (TE_a) that must be achieved. Clinical and medical applications may also utilize goals in the form of TE_a, but it is also possible to format goals in terms of a Clinical Decision Interval (D_{int}) which represents the gray zone or difference between test values that lead to different medical decisions. Other types of goals, such as those based on biologic variation, are also commonly used. Such goals may be expressed in terms of the maximum allowable standard deviation (SD) or coefficient of variation (CV), maximum allowable bias, and biologic allowable total error (TE_b) which can be calculated from precision and bias goals [4].

Step 2 is to select an analytic measurement procedure, or "method" in layman's terms, or "examination procedure" in ISO terminology. ISO 15189 states that *the laboratory shall select examination* *procedures which meet the needs and requirements of users and are appropriate for the examination being undertaken.* There are many factors to be considered. Some have to do with practical factors that are essential for the use in the laboratory. For example, specimen type, sample size, test menu, cost, etc. Others are concerned with performance characteristics, such as precision, bias, reportable range, detection limit, etc. Another critical characteristic is traceability to reference methods and materials [5].

Traceability is defined as a *property of the results of a measurement or the value of a standard whereby it can be related to stated references, usually national or international standards, through an unbroken chain of comparisons all having stated uncertainties.* Traceability is the key to achieving comparability of test results from method to method and laboratory to laboratory. Traceability depends on the manufacturer's reference methods and materials that are used to assign values to the calibrators and laboratories need to ensure that traceability is documented for their examination procedures.

Harmonization is a term for what happens when no standardization is possible. When standards for certain tests cannot be established, either because there is no agreed-upon standard, or all current assays are fundamentally measuring different things, the results cannot be traditionally compared. At best, the differences between methods can be acknowledged and minimized. There are many methods on the market where harmonization is the only possible goal.

Step 3 is **method validation**, which is critical for establishing the capability of the analytic method or examination procedure. ISO 15189 requires that a laboratory *shall only use examination procedures that have been validated as suitable for their intended use.* That's why it is critical to carefully define "intended use" in step 1. US CLIA regulations require that a laboratory must verify a manufacturer's claims for reportable range, precision, bias and reference range, and in some cases, also analytical sensitivity or detection limit and analytical specificity or interference and recovery.

To get started with a method validation study, it is necessary to become familiar with the operation of the method. This will take training and practice to establish a working method. During this familiarization period, it is useful to determine reportable range, i.e., the low to high values for which the method is useful. Following this familiarization period, preliminary validation experiments should be performed. These are the short experiments for within-run replication, recovery, interference, and possibly detection limit. If the results of all these preliminary experiments show acceptable performance, then the final validation experiments are performed. These experiments take a longer time, typically 20 days for the long-term replication experiment and at least 5 days for the comparison of methods experiment.

Finally, if all these experiments show acceptable performance, the method can be implemented for routine operation. That requires establishing QC procedures, training personnel, and monitoring routine performance, i.e., managing the quality of the testing process.

Decisions on the acceptability of method performance should be judgments on errors. Remember that method evaluation is all about errors, what types and how large. A method provides acceptable performance when the observed errors are smaller than the defined allowable error. A method is NOT acceptable when the observed errors are larger than the defined allowable error. The key to the decision is "how good does the test need to be" for its intended clinical use. And remember that step 1 in this Six Sigma Quality System is the definition of quality goals and requirements.

A **Method Decision Chart** can be used to judge the acceptability of method performance [6]. An example is shown in Figure 8-3, where the chart has been prepared for an Allowable Total Error of 7.0%, which is applicable to HbA1c. The observed inaccuracy, or percent bias, is described on the y-axis and the observed imprecision, or percent CV, is described on the x-axis. The different diagonal lines from top to bottom represent performance at the levels of 2-sigma, 3-sigma, 4-sigma, 5-sigma, and 6-sigma. To judge acceptability, an **operating point** is plotted that represents the observed inaccuracy (as the y-coordinate) and the observed imprecision (as the x-coordinate).

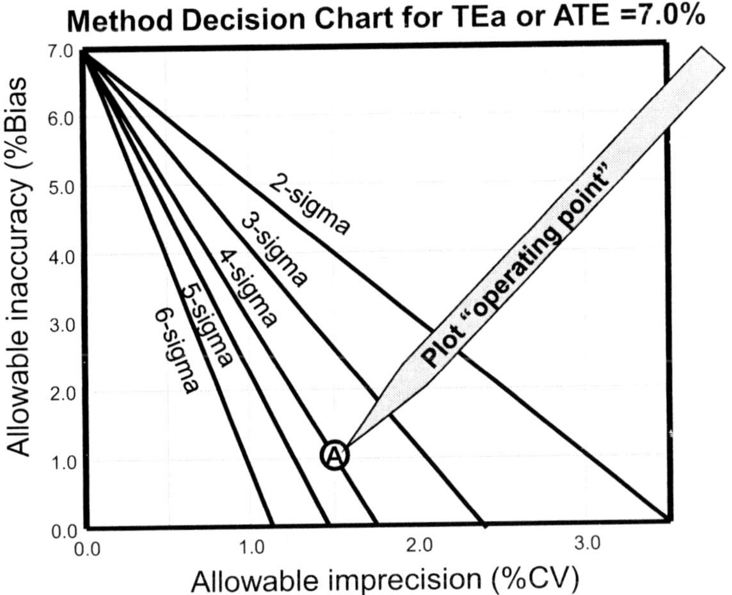

Figure 8-3. Method Decision Chart. Prepared for HbA1c where CAP PT criterion is 7.0%. Allowable inaccuracy (%Bias) is plotted on the y-axis vs allowable imprecision (%CV) on the x-axis. Diagonal lines represent, from left to right, 6-sigma, 5-sigma, 4-sigma, 3-sigma, and 2-sigma quality. Operating point (A) shows a method having a bias of 1.0% and a CV of 1.5%, which demonstrates 4-sigma quality [(7-10/1.5]

In the example shown here, point A shows a HbA1c method with a bias of 1.0% and a CV of 1.5%, which falls on the 4-sigma line. You can confirm the sigma value by calculation using the simple formula Sigma = (TE_a-bias)/CV, which gives (7-1.0)/1.5, or 6/1.5, or 4 sigma.

Step 4 is to implement the examination procedure and the analytic system. Laboratories must establish Standard Operating Procedures (SOPs) to minimize the operating variability from analyst to analyst and from day to day in routine service.

SOPs should follow the manufacturer's directions for use, including recommendations for maintenance and Quality Control. In addition, SOPs need to consider regulatory and accreditation requirements for ongoing validation and quality control. Pre-analytic and post-analytic requirements and processes must be defined to assure proper acquisition of specimens, processing of samples, and interpretation and reporting of test results. The manufacturer often provides support for the installation of new equipment and the initial training of key analysts, but the laboratory must plan for ongoing training of new analysts and periodic assessment of their competency.

Making quality manageable (CHECK and ACT Phases)

Step 5 begins the CHECK phase of Deming's PDCA cycle, which focuses on Quality Control (QC). The Sigma-metric that was determined earlier guides the formulation of a Total QC strategy. In this model, the sigma performance of the examination procedure is the key to selecting an appropriate TQC strategy. Remember that the Sigma-metric shows the relationship between the quality goal or requirement that is defined in Step 1 and the precision and bias that are determined from method validation studies in Step 3.

General guidance on how the Sigma-metric should influence Quality Control is shown in the simple prioritization matrix shown in Figure 8-4. Based on the observed sigma, we can prioritize the importance of SQC, the need for Other QC mechanisms, and the need for Quality Improvement (QI).

- Hi-sigma methods (≥5.5) can rely on SQC, follow manufacturer's directions for use and preventive maintenance and other regulatory and accreditation requirements.
- Moderate-sigma methods (3.6 to 5.4) need to balance SQC, other QC, and Quality Improvement. Quality Improvement here should focus on reducing any method bias and systematizing or automating operations to reduce variability.
- Low-sigma methods (≤ 3.5) require maximum SQC, but will need additional control mechanisms. One strategy may be to focus on Quality Improvement to move the method into a higher sigma category. Sometimes this may even mean changing examination procedures and acquiring new analytic systems. Another strategy is to focus on "Other QC" and add control mechanisms that are specific for the expected failure modes of the testing process.

HI-Sigma Strategy	MOD-Sigma Strategy	LOW-Sigma Strategy
SQC	SQC	SQC
Other QC	Other QC	Other QC
QI	QI	QI

Figure 8-4. Sigma Total Quality Control Strategy for prioritizing the need for Statistical QC, Other QC, and Quality Improvement.

Other QC mechanisms are described in CLSI EP23A [7]. SQC should be a high priority for daily use in most applications. EQA or PT is often required 3 or 4 times a year by regulations and accreditation. Trueness controls refer to reference materials that have assigned values and can therefore be used to assess method bias. Integrated liquid controls may be found in analytic systems where Statistical QC has been built into the analyzer. Other common controls that may be built-in by the manufacturer include function tests and procedural controls that check specific factors or operations, electronic checks for instrument components, and calibration checks. Patient data controls include repeat patient testing, delta checks, implausible values, patient population algorithms (such as Average of Normals, AoN), as well as correlation algorithms (e.g., anion gap). It should be obvious that implementation of all these controls will take considerable time and effort, therefore it is important to prioritize applications.

Step 6 is to select an optimal Statistical QC (SQC) procedure on the basis of the Sigma-metric that has been determined. The objective is to select the right control rules and right number of control measurements to detect medically important errors while at the same time minimizing false alarms or false rejections. This objective must consider the quality required for the test, as well as the performance observed for the method. That's why the Sigma -metric provides the best guidance. The selection can be supported using available quality-planning tools, such as the Sigma SQC Selection Tool recommended in the CLSI C24A3 guidance for Statistical QC. Another tool – the Chart of Operating Specifications, or OPSpecs Chart – is available and is structured similarly to the Method Decision Chart that is used to judge acceptability during Method Validation.

Figure 8-5 shows a Sigma SQC Selection Tool [8]. Probability for rejection is plotted on the y-axis versus the size of the medically important Systematic Error on the lower x-axis. The upper x-axis provides the related Sigma Scale. The different power curves correspond to the list of QC procedures in the key at the right. Given a calculated sigma of 4.0, a vertical line is drawn at 4 sigma on the x-scale. Then it is of interest to identify the particular power curves that would provide the a desired probability of 0.9 or 90% chance of detecting the medically important error. For this example, the two best choices are a $1_{2.5s}$ single rule procedure or a $1_{3s}/2_{2s}/R_{4s}/4_{1s}$ multirule procedure, each requiring a total of 4 control measurements to achieve the desired error detection. The y-intercepts of these power curves at the lower left corner of the graph identify the probabilities for false rejections, which are suitably low. The final choice between these SQC procedures will depend on practical matters of ease of implementation in the laboratory.

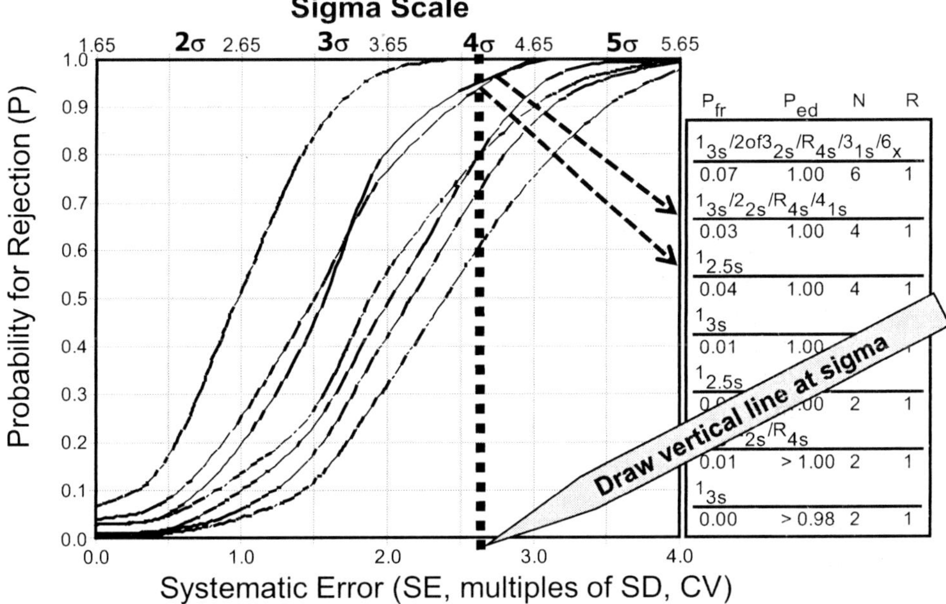

Figure 8-5. Sigma SQC Selection Graph. Probability for rejection is shown on y-axis versus the size of systematic error on the lower x-axis (given in multiples of the SD or CV) and the Sigma-metric of the method on the upper x-axis. The curves represent different SQC procedures, top to bottom, as shown in the key at the right, top to bottom. Vertical line represents a method having 4-sigma quality and illustrates selection of SQC procedures that have a total of 4 control measurements per run.

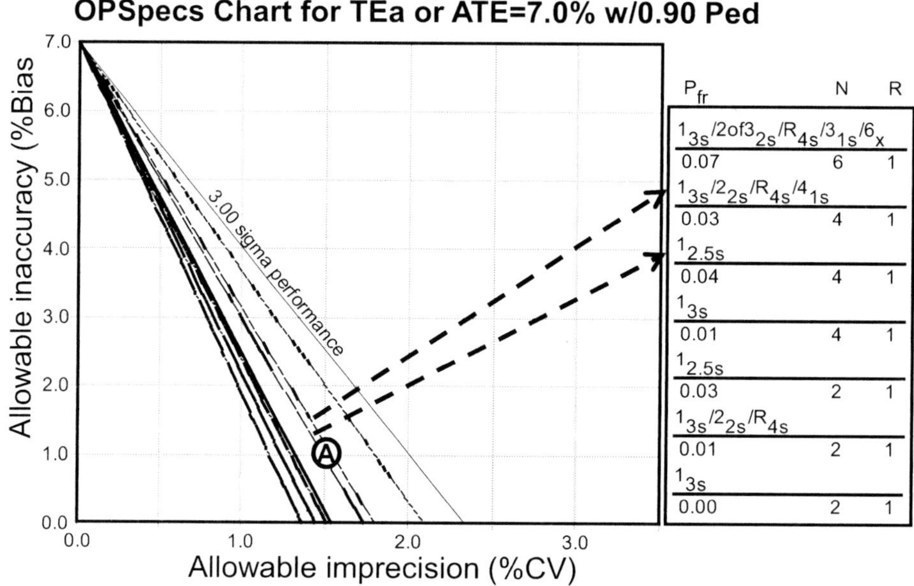

Figure 8-6. Chart of Operating Specifications. Prepared for HbA1c where CAP PT criterion is 7.0%. Allowable inaccuracy (%Bias) is shown on the y-axis vs allowable imprecision (%CV) on the x-axis. The different lines below 3-sigma line represent different SQC procedures, as identified in the key at the right. Point A shows a method having a 1.0% bias and 1.5% CV and illustrates the selection of SQC procedures that have a total of 4 control measurements per run.

Figure 8-6 shows a Chart of Operating Specifications [9], which is similar in format to the Method Decision Chart. This chart has been prepared for a quality requirement of 7.0%. The Y-axis shows the observed inaccuracy or %Bias and is scaled the same as the Method Decision Chart. The X-axis shows the observed imprecision or %CV and is scaled the same as the Method Decision Chart. Only the lines on the graph are different! They now represent different QC procedures, as identified from top to bottom by the list in the key at the right side of the chart. To use the OPSpecs tool, just like with the Method Decision Chart, you start by plotting your operating point, i.e., your observed %Bias as the y-coordinate and your observed %CV as the x-coordinate. Every line above the operating point identifies a QC procedure that has at least the necessary 90% error detection.

The lines above but closest to the operating point will identify the most cost-effective QC procedures, i.e., they will have the fewest controls and fewest rules and therefore be least costly to implement. In this example, a 2.5s rule or multirule with 4 control measurements will be cost-effective.

Step 7 provides for a broader or Total Quality Control Plan (TQC Plan) based on principles of risk management. This approach follows the ISO 14971 guidance for use of risk analysis by manufacturers of medical devices [10]. Manufacturers have performed risk analysis in the design and evaluation of new analytic systems for many years, however risk analysis is a new approach in medical laboratories and applications are just beginning. CLSI provides guidance for applications in medical laboratories through its trademarked guideline, EP23A[7].

Risk is defined as a "combination of the probability of occurrence of harm and the severity of that harm." This is a "2-factor" model that considers "probability of occurrence" and "severity of harm." Most industrial applications make use of a 3-factor model that includes "Detection."[7] CLSI EP23A defines a Quality Control Plan as "*a document that describes the practices, resources, and sequences of specified activities to control the quality of a particular measuring system or test process to ensure requirements for its intended use are met.*" [7]

It's important to note: a laboratory's strategy to mitigate risks is different than that of the manufacturer.

For occurrence, laboratories need to validate method performance characteristics, or safety characteristics, to ensure they are acceptable for their intended use. Method validation is important to ensure that precision, bias, detection limit, interference, etc., are acceptable for the intended use. A laboratory then monitors "events," for example, changes in reagents, calibrators, maintenance, replacement of parts during service, etc. Finally, a laboratory can prioritize applications of risk-based TQC plans on the basis of the expected occurrence of errors, which is predictable based on sigma.

For example, control systems for analytic methods that have a high sigma of 5.5 or greater can depend mainly on Statistical QC plus the manufacturer's recommended controls. Moderate sigma methods between 5.4 and 3.6 may be controllable with optimized SQC procedures, but may also require maximization of the controls recommended by the manufacturer. The need for more and better control increases and as the Sigma-metric gets lower. Low sigma methods of 3.5 or less require maximum SQC plus maximum manufacturer's controls plus patient data QC plus risk analysis controls. Poor performing methods require maximum care and attention if they are to produce clinically useful test results.

A TQC Plan is the laboratory strategy for detection of problems and recovery via corrective actions. Table 8-7 illustrates the idea [11].

TQC Plan	Frequency	Recovery	Disclosure
Analyst/operator controls			
Standard Operating Procedure	Yearly SOP review	Director review	No
Operator training	Every operator	Supervisor review	No
Operator checklists	Daily	Supervisor review	No
System maintenance	Manuf. Schedule	Manuf. Repair	No
Operator competency	Yearly	Re-train	No
Pre-analytic controls			
Inspect samples (ILH)	Every sample	Request new sample	Yes
Analytic controls			
Electronic checks	Manuf.	Manuf. Instructions	No
Function tests	Manuf.	Manuf. Instructions	Sample condition
Process tests	Manuf.	Manuf. Instructions	No
Calibration checks	Manuf./Reg.	Supervisor review	No
Statistical QC	Startup + Monitor	TS guidelines	No
Trueness control	Calibration	TS guidelines	No
Periodic EQA, PT	3/year	CA plan	No
Implausible values	Each test result	Repeat test	Yes
Post-analytic controls			
Confirm/call critical values	Each critical test	Repeat test	Yes
Monitor Turn-Around Time	Each STAT test	Call test result	Yes

Figure 8-7. Illustration of the information that may be included in a laboratory Total Quality Control Plan.

Detection should first focus on the careful design of Statistical QC procedures to assure detection of medically important errors. SQC design requires identifying the right control rules and the right number of control measurements on the basis of the quality required for the test and the precision and bias observed for the method. Then, the controls must be analyzed in each run plus whenever there is a change or "event" that needs to be checked. SQC should provide a "safety net" for catching errors in the laboratory.

The laboratory strategies for mitigating the effects of severity are to identify problems *prior* to reporting results in order to perform corrective actions. This should include specimen problems that may cause erroneous results, thus pre-analytic factors should be considered when developing the TQC Plan. Finally, the laboratory should disclose "information for safety." Some of this information is common today, such as reference ranges for tests. Other information for safety that may be helpful would be potential interferences and interpretative guidance.

Step 8 is to implement the TQC Plan. While many different control mechanisms may be considered, some are more important than others. Statistical QC should always be part of the plan. Other controls may be added to detect specific failure modes that are problematic for a particular test or analytic system. The plan should also include pre analytic and post-analytic controls to monitor the total examination process.

Implementation of a TQC Plan will depend on the computer support that is available. The analyzer's own software may support built-in controls and possibly SQC. Middleware can provide broader support for pre-analytic controls, such as specimen indices, as well as analytic controls based on patient test results, such as plausibility checks, patient data consistency algorithms, and possibly patient population algorithms such as Average of Normals. A laboratory information system is often necessary to implement delta checks, interpretive controls, and provide information for safety (reference ranges, interpretive comments, limitations due to specimen or sample stability, etc.).

Step 9 is the overall objective of the CHECK stage of Deming's PDCA cycle. In the language of ISO 15189, *the laboratory shall design internal quality control systems to verify the attainment of the intended quality of results.* That objective requires that Statistical QC procedures must be properly designed based on the quality requirement for a test and the imprecision and bias observed for a method. Quality-planning tools are available to accomplish this objective. Such QC design is also possible for some patient data controls, such as Average of Normals algorithms. For other controls, it is much more difficult to document their performance characteristics and assure they will detect medically important errors. But the absence of that data does not mean these cntrols are to be avoided, only that they must be bolstered by more data-driven controls.

Step 10 starts the ACT phase of the PDCA cycle. This includes measuring quality and performance to document the actual quality that is achieved and ensure that quality requirements are fulfilled. For analytical performance, bias can be monitored by periodic Proficiency Testing or External Quality Assessment programs. Or, more continuous monitoring can be provided by Peer Comparison programs where a group of laboratories make use of the same QC materials. Imprecision can be monitored with internal QC data. Measurement Uncertainty can be estimated from QC data obtained under "intermediate precision conditions," which involves a single method operating under routine conditions that include changes in reagent lots, calibration, maintenance, personnel, etc. Such QC data would typically be collected over a period of a few months in order to obtain the 100 or more control measurements that are needed to provide a reliable estimate of the method SD or CV.

PT and EQA results could be presented in the format of a Method Decision Chart, as shown in Figure 8-8, to demonstrate the quality being achieved on a regional, national, or global scale. This figure shows results from a CAP survey of HbA1c methods in 2013 where the criterion for acceptable performance was a TE_a of 7.0%. This particular survey sample had a reference value of 7.11 %Hb, which is in the critical concentration range for diagnosis and monitoring of diabetes. Each point on the chart represents a method subgroup and shows the quality achieved relative to the regions defined by the lines for 2 and 3 sigma.

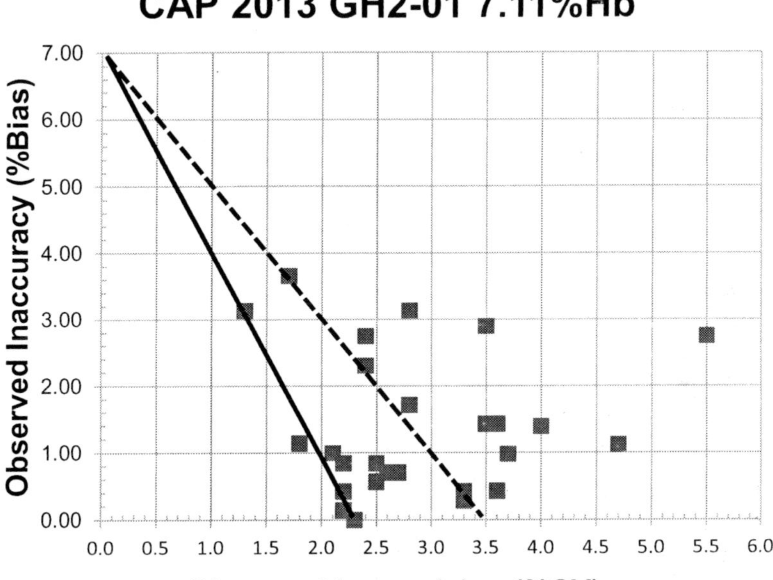

Figure 8-8. Assessment of Sigma Quality from Proficiency Testing Data. Region above the dashed line represents less than 2-sigma quality. Region below the solid line represents 3-sigma quality or better. Region between the lines represents 2 to 3 sigma quality.

The low quality on the Sigma Scale indicates that test results from method to method and laboratory to laboratory do not show the consistency that is needed to broadly apply clinical treatment guidelines.

Step 11 includes monitoring of nonconformities to document actual failure rates or defect rates. This is often discussed as occurrence management. Various Quality Indicators can be used to monitor pre-examination, examination, and post-examination processes.

Quality on the sigma Scale can be assessed by counting the nonconformities or defects, calculating the defects per million (DPM), then using standard conversion tables to translate DPM to values on the sigma Scale [9]. Quantitative estimates of defect rate can also be used as part of a Failure Reporting and Corrective Action System [FRACAS] to identify failure modes, prioritize the need for corrective actions, preventive actions, and additional controls. FRACAS is an extension of Failure Mode and Effects Analysis [FMEA], which is a tool commonly employed in risk assessment.

Step 12 focuses on improving quality, which may include improving the TQC Plan as well as improving all phases of the examination processes. Corrective and preventive actions should naturally lead to continual quality improvement. Nonconformities, failures, and defects should lead to improvement efforts. Risk management should be an integral part of quality improvement because of its focus on identifying potential failure modes and mitigating their effects. Fundamental improvements in laboratory testing often depend on new technology, which would then cycle back to the beginning of the Six Sigma Quality System (Step 1) to review the quality required for intended use, select new analytic systems, etc.

Requirements for implementing a Six Sigma Quality Management System

To implement a scientifically-based quality process, a Six Sigma Quality Management System provides an objective and quantitative approach that will guarantee that the analytical quality of test results is acceptable for their intended clinical use.

6σQMS Policy: The laboratory shall document Quality Policies, Processes, and Procedures in a Quality Manual.

This is the starting point! As you proceed with development and implementation of a 6σQMS, you must document the policies, procedures and procedures that are necessary to measure and manage qualty in a quantitative way.

In the effort to establish a 6σQMS, the following activities will be essential:

1. Appoint an Analytical Quality Manager who has competencies to plan, implement, monitor, and improve the Six Sigma Quality System.

2. Train key supervisors, analytic system specialists, and analysts to understand Six Sigma concepts, metrics, and application tools.

3. Define quality goals, objectives, and requirements for intended use for each laboratory examination.

4. Select examination procedures on basis of traceability and expected analytic performance. Estimate the sigma capability from manufacturer's data for performance claims or, when available, from independent method validation studies.

5. Validate analytical performance of new examination procedures against the defined quality requirements. Utilize Method Decision Charts to determine the Sigma-metric from the performance data collected in your laboratory and judge acceptability.

6. Formulate a Total Quality Control strategy on the basis of your observed Sigma-metric to balance SQC, manufacturer's recommended controls, and regulatory/accreditation requirements.

7. Select SQC procedures on the basis of the quality required for a test and the imprecision and bias observed for the examination procedure. Utilize Sigma SQC Selection Tools or Charts of Operating Specifications to select appropriate control rules and the total number of control measurements needed to detect medically important errors.

8. Optimize risk-based Total Quality Control Plans for individual tests and analytic systems to provide control mechanisms that are effective for expected failure-modes. Add controls to monitor pre-examination and post-examination processes.

9. Estimate measurement uncertainty from intermediate-term SQC data and evaluate against defined quality goals.

10. Estimate ongoing bias from PT or EQA programs. Use this estimate of bias, along with the intermediate estimate of imprecision, to calculate and monitor the Sigma-metrics of your processes.

11. Identify issues and prioritize improvements that to fulfill requirements for intended use. Employ Quality Indicators that monitor the total examination process. Determine nonconformities

in terms of defect rates (or frequency of errors) and evaluate on the sigma scale. When possible, utilize risk management tools to identify potential failure modes that are unique to the particular examination process.

12. Review annually the quality goals for intended use, the quality achieved, the TQC Plan, and the plan for improvement.

References

1. Plebani M. The CCLM contribution to improvements in quality and patient safety. Clin Chem Lab Med 2013;51:39-46.

2. Jassam N, Yundt-Pacheco J, Jansen R, Thomas A, Barth JH. Can current analytical quality performance of UK laboratories support evidence-based guidelines for diabetes and ischaemic heart disease? A pilot study and a proposal. Clin Chem Lab Med 2013;51(8):1579-84.

3. ISO 15189. Medical laboratories – Requirements for quality and competence. ISO, Geneva, 2012.

4. Westgard JO. The need for a system of quality standards for modern quality planning. Scand J Clin Lab Invest 1999;59:483-486.

5. Miller WG, Myers GL, Gantzer ML, et al. Roadmap for harmonization of clinical laboratory measurement procedures. Clin Chem 2011;57:1108-1117.

6. Westgard JO. Basic Method Validation, 3rd ed. Madison WI:Westgard QC, Inc., 2008.

7. CLSI EP23A. Laboratory Quality Control Based on Risk Management. Clinical Laboratory and Standards Institute, Wayne, PA, 2011.

8. CLSI C24A3. Statistical Quality Control for Quantitative Measurement Procedures: Principles and Definitions. Clinical and Laboratory Standards Institute, Wayne, PA, 2006.

9. Westgard JO. Six Sigma Quality Design & Control, 2nd ed. Madison WI:Westgard QC, Inc., 2006.

10. ISO 14971. Medical devices – Application of risk management to medical devices. ISO, Geneva, 2007.

11. Westgard JO. Six Sigma Risk Analysis: Designing analytic QC Plans for the medical laboratory. Madison WI:Westgard QC, Inc., 2011.

9. Defining Quality for Intended Use

In many laboratories, the practice of defining quality goals or requirements is relatively new.

What is the situation in your laboratory? Have you defined quality goals for all your tests, for some of your tests, or for none of your tests? An extension of this question would be to review your laboratory policies and practices for your Quality Management System. Is it an established practice in your laboratory to define quality goals and requirements? If not, you should start by defining a quality policy that requires careful consideration of the needs of patients, physicians, and other users of laboratory testing services.

6σQMS Policy: Quality requirements shall be defined for each test to identify critical performance characteristics that must be achieved to satisfy the intended clinical use of each laboratory test.

There are many characteristics that are important, such as type of specimen, turnaround time, report format, etc. Our focus is on analytical quality, where the standard of practice for defining quality specifications is a set of recommendations from the 1999 Stockholm Conference on "Strategies to Set Global Analytical Quality Specifications in Laboratory Medicine" [1]. First, note that this document uses the term "quality specifications," which in Europe is understood to mean quality *requirements*. There is a long history of discussions of this topic in the *Clinical Chemistry* literature, going back to the 1960s. Many papers debated the types and sources of different kinds of quality requirements. The outcome of the Stockholm conference was a consensus statement on the "Hierarchy of quality specifications," i.e., a recommendation for which some forms of quality specifications/requirements are preferred over others. Here is the complete recommendation:

"CONSENSUS STATEMENT. The main outcome of the conference was agreement that the following hierarchy of models should be applied to set analytical quality specifications.

1. *Evaluation of the effect of analytical performance on the clinical outcomes in specific clinical settings*

2. *Evaluation of the effect of analytical performance on clinical decisions in general:*
    a. *Data based on components of biological variation*
    b. *Data based on analysis of clinicians' opinions*
3. *Published professional recommendations*
    a. *From national and international expert bodies*
    b. *From expert local groups or individuals*
4. *Performance goals set by*
    a. *Regulatory bodies*
    b. *Organizers of External Quality Assessment (EQA) schemes*
5. *Goals based on the current state of the art*
    a. *As demonstrated by data from EQA or Proficiency Testing schemes*
    b. *As found in current publications on methodology*

When available, and when appropriate for the intended purpose, models higher in the hierarchy are to be preferred to those at lower levels."

All these different sources and recommendations can be considered, with priority given to the highest level in the Stockholm hierarchy of quality specifications. Goals for a specific clinical applications are preferred, goals based on biologic variability come next, followed by recommendations from professional and expert groups, followed by quality requirements established in EQA or PT programs. At the bottom of the hierarchy are "state of the art" recommendations, which describe the performance available from current laboratory methods.

6σQMS Process: Analytic goals shall be established for each test based on an assessment of specific clinical diagnostic and treatment requirements for the test, goals based on biologic variability, recommendations from expert groups, criteria for performance in proficiency testing and External Quality Assessment programs, and "state of the art" performance.

Let's consider HbA1c, where there are existing clinical diagnosis and treatment guidelines, expert group recommendations, data on biologic variation, and established Proficiency Testing criteria for acceptable performance. A good starting point is to find a review article in the recent scientific literature. The February 2011 issue of *Clinical Chemistry* was devoted to diabetes and included a review of the "Status of hemoglobin A1c measurement and goals for improvement" by authors from the National Glycohemoglobin Standardization Program (NGSP) steering committee [2] (which can be considered an expert professional group). This review described the efforts to improve HbA1c testing since 1996 when NGSP was established. It described the NGSP network, its relationship to the International Federation of Clinical Chemistry (IFCC) network, and the traceability of the US NGSP reference method to the IFCC higher order method. It reviewed the clinical use of HbA1c for diagnosis of diabetes and provided new guidelines on the clinical use for monitoring treatment.

ADA intended clinical use guidelines. The American Diabetes Association (ADA) recommends the following classification of patients on the basis of their HbA1c values [3]:

- ≤5.6 %Hb is considered normal;
- 5.7 to 6.4 %Hb represents pre-diabetes;
- 6.5 %Hb is the cutoff for diagnosis of diabetes;
- 7.0 %Hb is the target for treatment;

The diagnostic guideline identifies a "gray zone" between 6.5 and 5.6 %Hb that represents a "clinical decision interval," where a patient with a test result of 6.5 %Hb is classified as non-diabetic and a patient with a test result of 6.5% %Hb is classified as diabetic. Ideally, the total error or uncertainty of a test result of 6.5 %Hb should be less than 0.9 %Hb, or 14%, to avoid misclassification.

Biologic variability. A database on biologic variation has been developed by a group of Spanish clinical chemists, initially published in the Stockholm conference report [4], but now periodically updated online. Over 350 quantities are included in this database. The database provides the following information for HbA1c:

- 1.9% for CV_I for individual or within-subject coefficient of variation
- 5.7% CV_G for group coefficient of variation
- 1.4% CV_A for minimum analytical precision specification, $\%CV_A$
- 2.3% Bias for minimum analytical bias specification
- 4.6% TE_a for calculated biologic allowable total error

These analytic performance goals are calculated from CV_I and CV_G, following the recommendations by Fraser [5]:

- Allowable CV = $0.5\ CV_I$
- Allowable Bias = $0.25\ (CV_I^2 + CV_G^2)^{1/2}$
- $TE_a = 1.65(0.5CV_I) + 0.25(CV_I^2 + CV_G^2)^{1/2}$

Physician treatment practice. It has been recommended that treatment be re-evaluated if HbA1c is 7.5 %Hb or higher [2]:

"...many physicians have suggested that 0.5% HbA1c is a 'clinically significant change.' Importantly, treatment guidelines and algorithms from the ADA/EASD and National Institute for Clinical Excellence in the UK recommend evaluating new treatment regimens in terms of whether HbA1c is lowered by 0.5 percentage points or more. Therefore it is important to be sure that a change of this magnitude is statistically significant and not due to analytical variation.

Given that a change of 0.5 %Hb is considered clinically significant and needs to be monitored for effective treatment, there are two situations to be considered. (a) The first involves consecutive measures to evaluate a change in a patient's test values and (b) the second considers the significance of a patient value versus a target value of 7.0 %Hb. For the first situation, here is the analysis, as discussed in the NGSP review paper [2]:

Taking a statistically significant difference of 0.5 %HbA1c and an HbA1c concentration of 7% as the goal for HbA1c, one can use the reference change value (RCV), also called critical difference to calculate an appropriate goal in terms of a method's CV. For sequential results to be significantly different, the numbers must differ by more than the combined variation inherent in the 2 results:

$RCV(\%) = 2^{(1/2)} \times 1.96 \times [(CV_A)^2 + (CV_I)^2]^{(1/2)}$

Where CV_A is the analytical CV of the method (within-laboratory CV) and CV_I is the within-subject biological variation.

For HbA1c the CV_I is low, <1% when estimated in individuals without diabetes. If the analytical CV of the HbA1c method is 2% (feasible for many commercially available HPLC systems), then the RCV (95% probability) is <0.5 %HbA1c...

Therefore, the CV that is required within a single laboratory and within a single method should be less than 2.0% in order to measure clinically important changes. Note that in this clinical application, method bias is not a consideration because the focus is only on the difference between two consecutive measurements on the same method.

However, in the second situation, comparison to a target value of 7.0, method bias does need to be considered. Here's the recommendation from the NGSP review:

In the situation in which a physician wants to look at the difference between a patient result and a goal of 7% HbA1c, both the bias and variability (%CV), in other words the total error, of the method must be taken into account.

For example, if a method has 0.0 bias, a CV of 3.5% is required to have 95% confidence that the HbA1c result for a patient with a 'true' result of 7% will read between 6.5 and 7.5% (±7%). If there is a bias of 0.2 %HbA1c, the CV requirement would tighten to 2.3%...

In this second clinical treatment situation, the CV of the method can be larger if the bias is zero. If bias is as large as 0.2 %Hb, then essentially the same CV is needed as in the first scenario, approximately 2%.

NGSP certification criteria. The National Glycohemoglobin Standardization Program (NGSP) provides professional guidance to manufacturers in the form of certification of HbA1c methods as providing "equivalent performance." The NGSP certification process for manufacturers (or laboratories) involves 40 patient samples tested by the manufacturer (or laboratory) and compared to results from an NGSP reference method. Performance is considered acceptable if 37 of 40 test results agree within 7.0% [6].

CAP PT criteria. The College of American Pathologists provides a whole blood survey for HbA1c that is widely recognized for the quality of its survey samples. The criterion for acceptable performance was 15% in 2007, tightened to 12% in 2008, 10% in 2009, 8% in 2010, 7% in 2011, and 6.0% in 2014 [6]. The CAP allowable error of 7.0% at a concentration of 7.0 %Hb would be 0.49 %Hb.

Given the many different forms of quality goals and recommendations that are available, the laboratory will need to compare the requirements. Most laboratories find goals for the Allowable Total Error to be most practical because they are readily available from their PT and EQA surveys. In addition, a Biologic Allowable Total Error is included in the in the Ricos database. Use of Allowable Total Error goals prepares the laboratory for clinical goals in the form of a clinical decision interval, which expands the total error to include pre-analytic components of errors, as well as within-subject biologic variation. Goals defined through clinical decision intervals rank at the top of the Stockholm "hierarchy" and therefore are the most desirable form for quality goals. Note, however, they require more complex quality-planning models; the only practical way to apply these goals is with computer software programs developed expressly for this purpose.

6σQMS Procedure. Prepare an error grid to compare different quality requirements, assess which are most critical, and define the quality requirement for the test in your laboratory.

It is difficult to compare the various recommendations for intended clinical use, performance specifications for precision and bias, and Total Error criteria for proficiency testing. In part this is because they are specifications for different types of errors, e.g., imprecision of 1.4%, bias of 2.3%, total error of 4.6%, but also because they may be in different units, e.g., 0.5 %Hb critical change for treatment. The actual specifications disagree as well: 4.6% TE_b calculated from biologic variation terms, 7.0% TE_a by NGSP, 6.0% TE_a for CAP 2014 PT criterion.

An error grid can compare these quality requirements. Historically, error grids have been used for demonstrating the performance of glucose meters [7,8], but recently have been recommended by the US FDA for use in the approval of *all* waived medical devices, such as Point-of-Care tests. Figure 9-1 shows the FDA's example of an error grid [9].

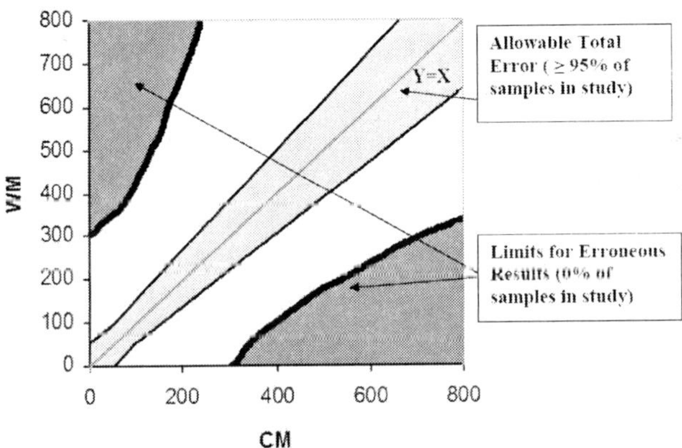

Figure 9-1. Concept of error grid. From Guidance for Industry and FDA Staff: Recommendations for Clinical Laboratory Improvement Amendments of 1988 (CLIA) Waiver Applications for Manufacturers' of Invitro Diagnostic Devices. Jan 30, 2008, Food and Drug Adminstration

The generic form of an error grid is a comparison graph where the result by a "test method" is plotted on the y-axis vs the result by a "comparative method" on the x-axis. A zone of acceptable performance is indicated by lines drawn above and below the line of identity, and 95% of the results should fall within this zone. More important, zones of *unacceptable* performance are also indicated to identify where results would lead to inappropriate patient treatment. There should be NO results in the unacceptable zones. FDA expects a manufacturer to specify an Allowable Total Error to define the zone for acceptable performance in any data submission for a waived test. To provide guidance on preparation of error grids, CLSI has published document EP27 [10]. While the intent of EP27 is to use an error grid for evaluation of method comparison data, it can also be used to compare different requirements for quality and identify those that are most demanding.

Figure 9-2 shows the comparison of quality goals and requirements for HbA1c.

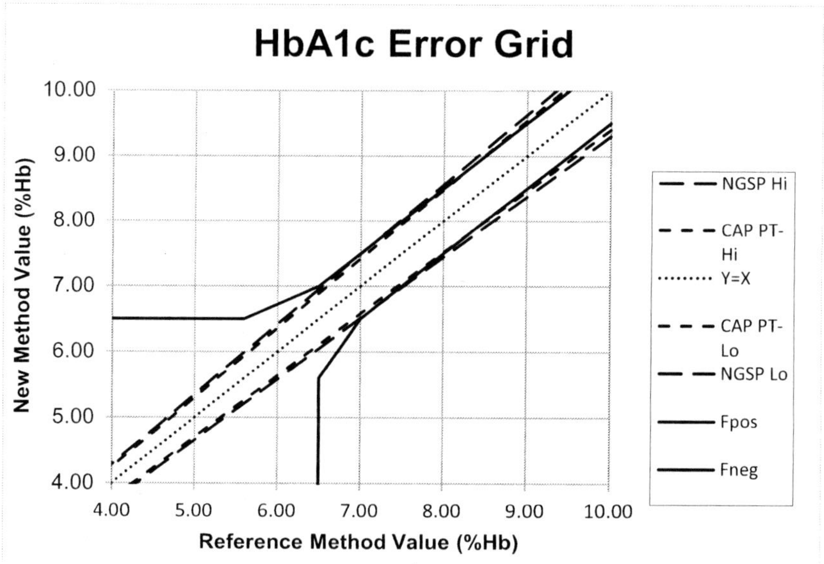

Figure 9-2. 2013/14 comparison of HbA1c quality requirements for intended clinical diagnosis and treatment, NGSP certification requirements, and CAP proficiency testing criterion for acceptability.

Note that the x-axis and y-axis are both scaled from 4 to 10 %Hb, the dotted line from corner to corner represents the line of ideal agreement. The solid lines represent the clinical diagnostic and treatment goals. The lower part represents the diagnostic criterion (clinical decision interval from 5.6 to 6.5 %Hb) and the upper part (above 7) represents the treatment criterion (0.5 %Hb change). The longer dashed lines represent the NGSP certification requirement of 7% and the shorter dashed lines represents the CAP 2014 requirement of 6%. From this comparison, the laboratory should define its quality requirement as 6% or 7% TE_a. Both are sufficiently rigorous to support the diagnostic and treatment decisions in the critical range from 5.5 to 8.0 %Hb.

HbA1c goals are in good alignment, as of 2014, but they have not always been so. Figure 9-3 shows the comparison as of early 2011.

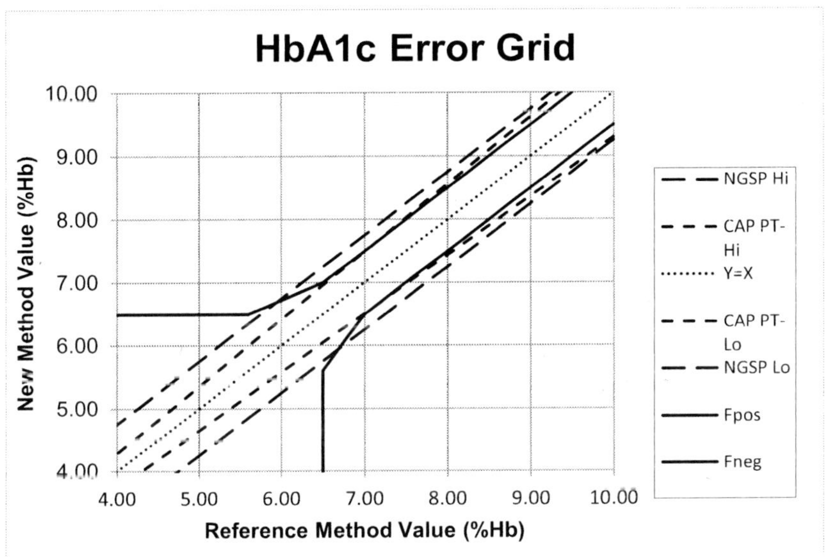

Figure 9-3. 2011 comparison of HbA1c quality requirements for intended clinical diagnosis and treatment, NGSP certification requirements, and CAP proficiency testing criterion for acceptability.

At that time, the NGSP criterion was ± 0.75 %Hb, rather than the current ± 7%. The CAP criterion was 7%, which was more demanding than the certification requirement. That meant that laboratories were required to meet a tighter standard of performance than the manufacturers' certification requirement. NGSP recognized this shortcoming and tightened its certification requirement.

What's the point?

Many laboratory scientists get confused by the types of quality goals and requirements. Just "how good" does a lab test need to be? Figure 9-4 reviews the different types of quality goals and requirements that are found in the literature [11].

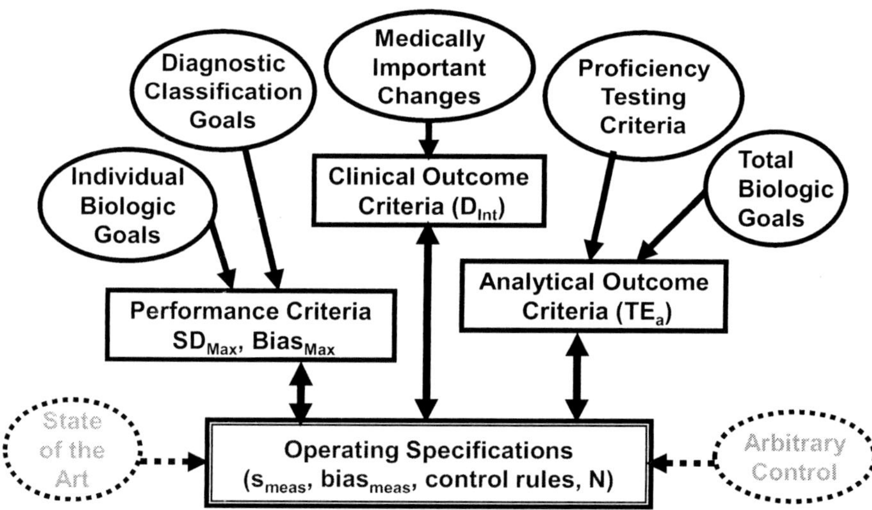

Figure 9-4. Systems perspective on various types of analytical goals and quality requirements.

- The right side in this diagram shows analytical outcome criteria in the format of an Allowable Total Error (TE_a). These can be found in Proficiency Testing and External Quality Assessment guidelines, and can also be calculated from biologic goals.

- The middle of the diagram shows clinical outcome criteria that represent medically important changes in test results. They may be described as "Decision Interval Criteria" that represent the "gray zone" between different test results that lead to different clinical decisions.
- The left side shows performance criteria in the form of the maximum allowable inaccuracy, or bias, and the maximum allowable imprecision, or Standard Deviation or Coefficient of Variation. Recommendations from expert groups are often presented in these terms. In addition, these criteria can be determined from studies on within-subject biologic variation, which is why they are often called "biologic goals."
- Finally, at the bottom, the diagram shows "operating specifications", which represent the precision, bias, and QC that are necessary for daily operation in the laboratory. Such operating specifications can be derived from the defined quality goals and represent the method performance and QC needed at the bench level.

To reiterate our earlier advice, most laboratories find goals for the Allowable Total Error to be most practical. These goals are already available from PT and EQA surveys. In addition, it is possible to calculate the Biologic Allowable Total Error from the extensive studies found in the "Ricos database". Ideally, labs used to TE_a goals will eventually transition to clinical goals in the form of clinical decision intervals, which expand the total error model to include pre-analytic components of error, as well as within-subject biologic variation. Clinical goals rank at the top of the Stockholm "hierarchy" and therefore are the most desirable quality requirements.

TE_a goals are also synonymous with the Six Sigma concept of "tolerance limits" which facilitates the adoption and adaptation of Six Sigma tools. For example, the relationship between TE_a and precision and bias can be described as a Sigma-metric:

$$\textbf{Sigma} = [(\%TE_a - \%bias)]/\%CV$$

Here's a quick example: if TE_a were 7.0%, bias 2.3%, and CV 1.4%, sigma would be 3.36 [(7.0-2.3)/1.4], which is actually a "borderline" method in the laboratory, i.e., the sigma is so low that the method will require extensive QC to monitor routine performance. If bias could be reduced to 0.0, then sigma would be 5.0 [(7-0)/1.4], which would be much more reliable and controllable method in the laboratory.

The point is that quality requirements/specifications/goals are distinct from the strategies needed to achieve the goals. With examination procedures, goals for intended use must be translated into "operating specifications" for the imprecision, bias and QC that is needed at the bench level. That's where Six Sigma concepts, principles, and tools become useful for evaluating the quality of examination procedures, selecting Statistical QC procedures, prioritizing applications of Risk-based QC Plans and the need for different control mechanisms, and assessing the existing proficiency of laboratory tests on the sigma scale.

References

1. Hyltoft Petersen P, Fraser CG, Kallner A, Kenny D. Strategies to Set Global Analytical Quality Specifications in Laboratory Medicine. Scand J Clin Lab Invest 1999;59(7):475-585.

2. Little RR, Rohlfing CL, Sacks DB. Status of hemoglobin A1c measurement and goals for improvement: From chaos to order for improving diabetes care. Clin Chem 2011;57:205-214.

3. American Diabetes Association. Standards of Medical Care in Diabetes – 2013. Diabetes Care 2013;36:S11-S66.

4. Ricos C et al. Current databases on biologic variation. Scand J Clin Lab Invest 1999;59:491-500.

5. Fraser CG. Biological Variation: From principles to practice. Washington DC:AACC Press, 2001.

6. NGSP website: www.ngsp.org, accessed 9/14/2013.

7. Clark WL, Cox D, Gonder-Fredrick LA, et al. Evaluating the clinical accuracy of systems for self-monitoring of blood glucose. Diabetes Care. L987;10:622-628.

8. Parkes JL, Slatin SL, Pardo S. Ginsberg BH. A new consensus error grid to evaluate the clinical significance of inaccuracies in the measurement of blood glucose. Diabetes Care 2000;23:1142-1148.

9. Guidance for Industry and FDA Staff: Recommendations for Clinical Laboratory Improvement Amendments of 1988 (CLIA) Waiver Applications for Manufacturers' of *In Vitro* Diagnostic Devices. Jan 30, 2008, Food and Drug Administration.

10. CLSI EP27. How to Construct and Interpret an Error Grid for Diagnostic Assays. Clinical and Laboratory Standards Institute, Wayne, PA, 2009.

11. Westgard JO. The need for a system of quality standards for modern quality management. Scand J Clin Lab Invest 1999;59:483-486.

10. Selecting an Examination Procedure

ISO 15189 [1] states that the laboratory shall select examination procedures which meet the needs and requirements of users and are appropriate for the examination being undertaken.

There are many factors to be considered. Some are practical factors that are essential for the application in the laboratory, e.g., type of specimen, sample size, instrument throughput, test menu, cost, etc. Others are concerned with performance characteristics, such as precision, trueness or bias, detection limit, reportable range, etc.

There are many different examination procedures available for most laboratory tests today. Virtually all examination procedures that are used in US laboratories have been approved by the US Food and Drug Authority and their routine operation is governed by the CLIA regulations. Approval by the FDA requires that manufacturers document their claims for performance by submitting experimental evidence from field studies. The underlying principle here is "truth in labeling," which means that the manufacturer's data must be consistent with their performance claims for precision, trueness or bias, reportable range, reference range, detection limit, and interferences.

This regulatory approach does not require that different examination procedures give the same results, only that any difference in results be properly described in the manufacturer's claims. Thus systematic differences between examination procedures that have been documented by the manufacturer may be accepted as long as the laboratory verifies the manufacturer's claims and the appropriateness of the reference range or ranges for the intended patient population. This verification of claims is a serious weakness in many accreditation programs, including ISO 15189 accreditation. A better approach is for laboratories to validate that performance meets the quality required for intended use.

Comparability of the results from different examination procedures is a critical issue today! With utilization of national and global evidence-based guidelines for diagnosis and treatment of diseases, it is generally assumed that different examination procedures provide equivalent results. HbA1c provides a good example where there are global guidelines for diagnosis (HbA1c ≥ 6.5 %Hb) and treatment (HbA1c ≤ 7.0 %Hb) of diabetes. Figure 10-1 shows the results for a proficiency testing sample having an assigned reference value was 7.11 %Hb [2]. There is good consistency among the 27 examination subgroups, but they do not all provide the same results. For example, it would be possible for a patient to get a result as high as 7.9 %Hb or as low as 6.1 %Hb (disregarding the examination subgroup third from left that is known to have interference from the anticoagulant used in the survey sample).

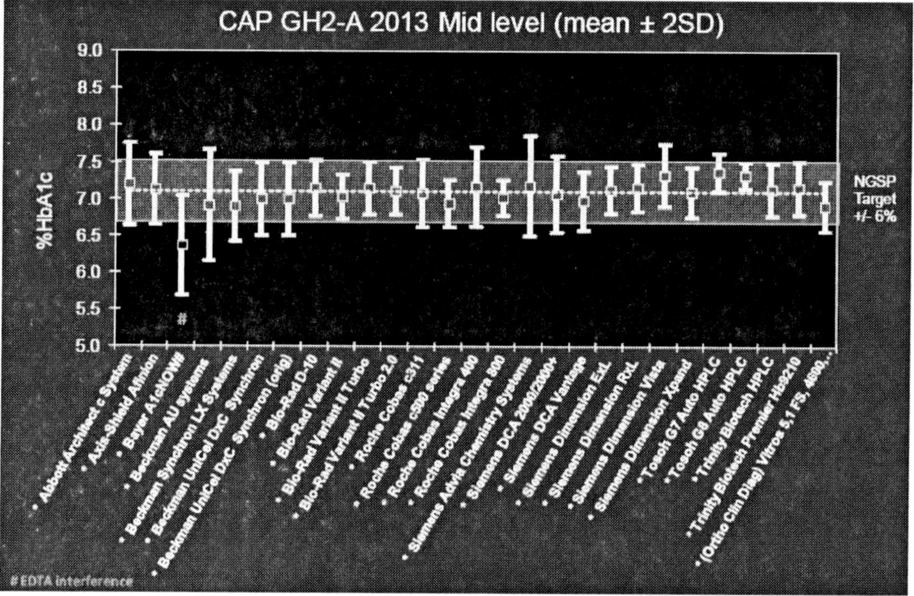

Figure 10-1. Observed mean and range of survey results for 27 HbA1c examination subgroups for a CAP sample with assigned reference value of 7.11 %Hb. Note that one examination subgroup (third from left) is affected by anti-coagulant in sample. Source: www.ngsp.org

EQA and PT programs provide measures of comparability when the survey samples satisfy conditions for commutability. The process for achieving comparability is often referred to as "harmonization" [3] and requires that trueness be demonstrated by traceability to reference measurement procedures and reference materials.

Traceability is defined as a property of the results of a measurement or the value of a standard whereby it can be related to stated references, usually national or international standards, through an unbroken chain of comparisons all having stated uncertainties [4]. Traceability is the key to achieving comparability of test results from method to method and laboratory to laboratory. Traceability depends on the manufacturer's reference measurement procedures and reference materials that are used to assign values to the calibrators used in the laboratory. ISO 15189 requires that laboratories "record the metrological traceability of the calibration standard" as part of the technical documentation for an examination procedure. The CLIA program does not have any comparable requirement, but US laboratories should pay attention to ISO's guidance in this area.

6σQMS Policy. The laboratory shall select examination procedures that are traceable to reference measurement procedures, certified reference materials, or accepted harmonization procedures that achieve the quality required for intended use.

The International Committee of Weights and Measures (CIPM) and the International Bureau of Weights and Measures (BIPM) have created the Joint Committee for Traceability in Laboratory Medicine (JCTLM) to identify, review, and publish lists of higher order certified reference materials and reference measurement procedures. The "preamble" states that the "goal of obtaining comparability of laboratory diagnostic test results will be reached only when common reference systems can be established for worldwide use." [5]

"The Joint Committee on Traceability in Laboratory Medicine (JDTLM) was created to meet the need for a worldwide platform to promote and give guidance to internationally recognized and accepted equivalence of measurements in laboratory medicine and traceability to appropriate measurement standards. These are embodied in ISO 17511, 17025, and 18153."

JCTLM maintains databases for reference materials and reference methods that can be accessed at their website www.bipm.org/jctlm.

6σQMS Process. In selecting examination procedure, the laboratory shall ensure that the manufacturers of analytic systems provide evidence that the calibration of examination procedures is traceable to reference measurement procedures, certified reference materials, or accepted harmonization procedure.

The important issue here is the "truth" of the values that are assigned to calibrator materials.

It is expected that the correctness of the assigned values is known and should be expressed as a statement of measurement uncertainty. This is a requirement of ISO 15189, but not of the US CLIA regulations.

According to Thienpont *et al* [6], *"metrological traceability is considered the basis for achieving comparability of measurement results in laboratory medicine."* Figure 10-2 provides an example of a traceability chain that shows the relationships between reference materials (shown on the left side) and reference methods (shown on the right side).

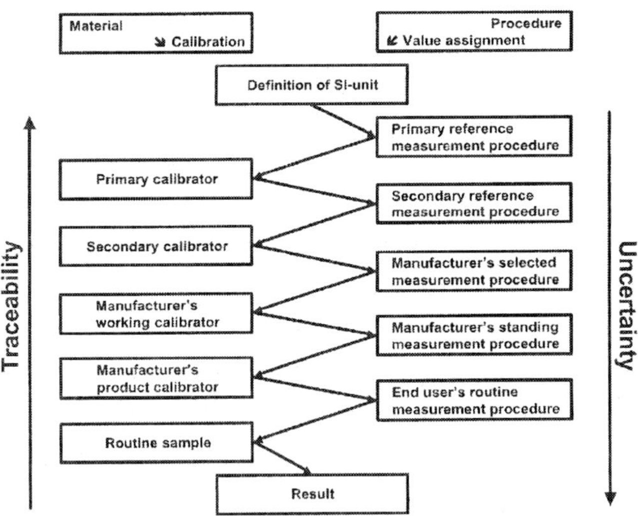

Figure 10-2. Traceability chain showing relationships between reference materials (left side) and reference measurement procedures (right side). From Thienpont [6] with permission.

The idea is to use higher order reference methods and materials to assign values to lower order methods and materials, ending with calibrators with traceable values being used in routine service laboratories. The end test result should be traceable, or related to the "truth" as represented by the assigned value.

The traceability chain flows from the top down, beginning with the definition of SI-unit, primary reference measurement procedure, primary calibrator, secondary reference measurement procedure, secondary calibrator, manufacturer's selected measurement procedure, manufacturer's working calibrator, manufacturer's standing measurement procedure, manufacturer's product calibrator, terminating at the end user's routine measurement procedure, which provides the analysis of a routine sample and produces a test result. The arrow on the right side indicates that uncertainty in the assigned values increases for lower order methods and materials. Uncertainty is the measure of the quality of the traceability chain!

This traceability model is the ideal and is applicable for sodium, potassium, calcium, glucose, and similar "simple" clinical chemistry measurands. However, it is difficult to apply more broadly in laboratory medicine due to what Thienpont calls "physico-chemical complexity" [6] where biologic matrices are complex and can influence the analytical results, measurands are often a class of substances rather than a single species, and different measurement procedures sometimes demonstrate specificity to one or a few of the substances in that class. Therefore, other traceability models are needed that begin with international conventional reference measurement procedures, international conventional calibrators, international protocols for value assignment, and even manufacturer's selected measurement procedures. Thus, for diagnostic tests in laboratory medicine, the issues are complex and involve five possible models for establishing traceability and comparability:

- Model I: Definition of SI unit and complete set of reference measurement procedures and materials;
- Model II: International conventional reference measurement procedure and International conventional calibrator;
- Model III: International conventional reference measurement procedure and Manufacturer's working calibrator;

- Model IV: International protocol for value assignment along with Manufacturer's selected measurement procedure;
- Model V: Manufacturer's selected measurement procedure along with Manufacturer's working calibrator.

Models II to V allow establishment of "medical traceability," whereby comparability of analytical processes is assured and test results can be interpreted against common decision-making criteria. Given the increased complexity and difficulty of medical traceability, there is a need for ongoing assessment to assure traceability [6]:

"To assure metrological traceability at any time, the Directive requires that the IVD manufacturer install a systematic procedure to review post-production experiences and implement any necessary corrective actions. In addition, this legislation may also be needed for post-market vigilance from a third party, i.e., for external quality assessment (EQA). To fulfill this objective, EQA has to meet the requirements detailed in the CEN 14316 standard. In essence, they require the use of survey samples that simulate as closely as possible the relative properties of the samples on which the IVD MDs are intended to be used. In addition, the EQA design should enable device-specific and procedure-specific evaluation of results."

HbA1c provides a good example of the efforts required to establish medical traceability, as shown in Figure 10-3. To provide comparative results and to assign values to standards, an IFCC network of laboratories provides the global mechanism for harmonization in which an IFCC reference measurement procedure has been developed. EQA and PT surveys are an integral part for measuring the comparability of field methods, such as the CAP program in the US. While HbA1c provides a model system for physico-chemically complex examinations, enormous efforts will be needed to accomplish harmonization for many of the examinations performed in medical laboratories today.

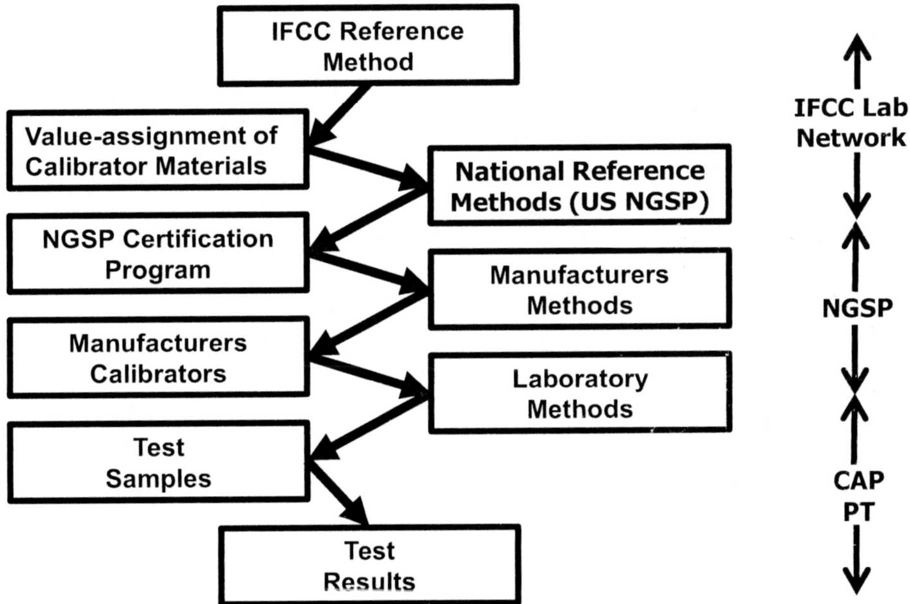

Figure 10-3. Traceability chain for "physio-chemically complex" examination for HbA1c. Test results are traceable to an IFCC reference method via national standardization programs, such as the US NGSP certification program. Comparability is monitored through EQA orPT surveys, e.g., the College of American Pathologists (CAP) program.

6σQMS Process. In selecting new examination procedures, the laboratory shall assess the performance capability by calculation of Sigma-metrics based on manufacturer's claims for precision and bias or from published method performance studies.

Meanwhile, laboratories need to select examination procedures that have the capability of providing the performance necessary to satisfy the quality required for intended use, while also taking into account traceability. Method performance data obtained from independent field studies is the preferred source, but will not always be available, in which case it will be necessary to make a careful assessment of the data used by the manufacturer in establishing performance claims.

6σQMS Procedure. Calculation of a Sigma-metric from published performance data.

While there are a common set of experiments that are expected in a method evaluation study, there is no standard way of presenting the experimental results, particularly the choice of statistics for summarizing the data. It requires considerable skill to read through the study and extract the important information. Published studies seldom declare any quality requirements, therefore they typically describe only performance, with little objective discussion of whether or not performance is acceptable. Therefore, the laboratory scientist must impose the "Sigma-metric framework" on a typical published study, find the needed experimental data, judge whether the experimental conditions provide reliable results, extract and interpret the critical statistics, and define the quality requirement that is appropriate for determining acceptability for that examination in the analysts own laboratory.

Directions for calculation of a Sigma-metric

1. For the examination of interest, define quality in terms of an Allowable Total Error (TE_a) at a critical medical decision level (X_c);
2. Assess imprecision from data collected in a replication experiment (SD, %CV), preferably a study performed over at least a one month period;
3. Determine Bias from data collected in a comparison of methods experiment (bias, %Bias);
    a. Utilize regression statistics when available and calculate $Y_c = a + b^*X_c$, where a is the y-intercept, b is the slope, and Y_c is the concentration by the new method that corresponds to X_c by the comparative method;
    b. Calculate bias as the difference Y_c minus X_c.
4. Calculate sigma as (TE_a – Bias)/SD where all terms are in concentration units or (%TE_a – %Bias)/%CV where all terms are in percent.

Example Application. Calculation of Sigma-metrics for HbA1c POC device.

Information on the performance of new analytic systems and examination procedures is provided by manufacturers in their labeling claims, often found in poster presentations at professional meetings and sometimes in published evaluation studies. For HbA1c, a published evaluation study is available [7] that focuses on Point-of-Care devices and evaluates their precision and bias following CLSI protocols (EP5 and EP9). Given that this is a peer-reviewed paper, consensus protocols have been followed for the experimental design and data analysis, and the authors are from one of the IFCC HbA1c reference laboratories, this study provides a reliable source of performance data.

Precision results were presented for 6 different examination procedures, but one is selected here to illustrate the validation of performance. An imprecision table showed the CVs observed at two concentrations, one a normal level (~5 %Hb) and the other a high abnormal (~11 %Hb). The experiment followed the CLSI EP5 protocol – 2 levels measured twice per day for 20 days. Unfortunately, the levels might have been better chosen. If analyzing only 2 levels, then the design would be better if the chosen concentrations were 6.5 and 9.0 %Hb. With 3 levels, the design might have focused on 5.5, 7.0, and 9.0 %Hb. However, it is not always possible to find controls at the right concentrations and it is necessary to work with those that are available.

The observed performance for our example examination procedures is given as a CV of 1.8% at a concentration of 5.1 %Hb and 3.7% at a concentration of 11.2 %Hg. Units can be confusing when dealing with HbA1c, where %Hb represents concentration units and %CV represents the size of the standard deviation relative to the mean value of the control material. If a patient sample had a true value of 6.5%Hb, the imprecision of the method can be used to describe the range of values that might be expected for that patient, e.g., 6.5 %Hb ± 1.96 SD would describe the range which should include 95% of the expected values. That range can be calculated from the CV, assuming the CV observed applies at a value of 6.5 %Hb.

- For a CV of 1.8%, the SD would be 0.12 %Hb (1.8*6.5/100), the 1.96 SD range would be ± 0.23, which shows that a patient with a true value of 6.5 %Hb would have a test result between 6.27 to 6.73 %Hb.
- If the CV were 3.7%, on the other hand, the SD would be 0.24 %Hb (3.7*6.5/100), the 95% range ± 0.47, meaning the patient would have a value between 6.03 to 6.97 %Hb.

That's quite a difference and it is reasonable to consider that the CV at a level of 6.5% would likely be between these two estimates, perhaps the average, which would be a CV of 2.8%.

Comparison results are shown Figure 10-4 for the examination procedure chosen for this discussion. The reference examination results are the average of three secondary reference methods.

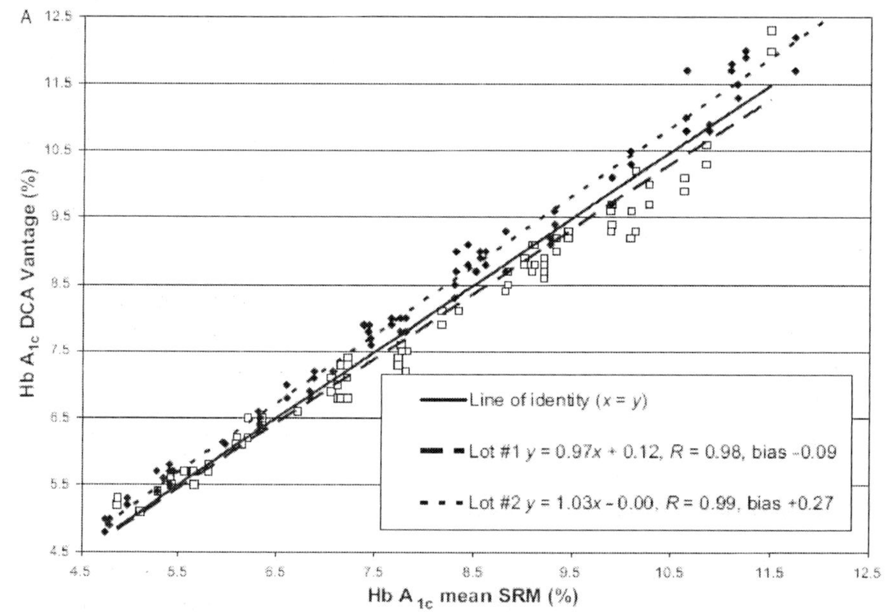

Figure 10-4. An example of results from a comparison of examination procedures for a HbA1c candidate procedure on the y-axis versus reference procedure results on the x-axis. Statistical results in the form of regression equations are shown for two different reagent lots. From Lenters & Slingerland [7] with permission.

Two different lots of reagents have been studied, thus there are two sets of regression statistics. For example, the regression equation for lot #1 is $y = 0.97x + 0.12$. Remember the form of this equation is $y = a + b*x$, where a is the y-intercept and b the slope of the regression line. Ideally, the slope should be 1.00 and the y-intercept should be 0.00, so the observed slope is too low by 3% (0.97-1.00 or 0.03, which multiplied by 100 describes a proportional error in units of %) and the observed intercept is high by 0.12 %Hb (which describes a constant error).

The regression equation can be used to calculate the expected value for the test method (Y_c) that corresponds to a chosen value (X_c) by the reference method, e.g., if the true value were 6.5 %Hb by the reference method, what value is expected by the test method?

$$Y_c = 0.97*X_c + 0.12$$

$$= 0.97*6.5 + 0.12$$

$$= 6.30 + 0.12$$

$$= 6.42 \text{ \%Hb}$$

The systematic error is simply $Y_c - X_c$, or -0.08 %Hb, which is an absolute bias of 1.2% at the critical diagnostic cutoff of 6.5 %Hb [(100*0.08)/6.5=1.2%]. Thus, even though the slope and the y-intercept are not ideal, they offset or compensate at this critical medical cutoff and the inaccuracy, or systematic error, or bias, is estimated as 1.2 %. [Note that the bias of 0.09 shown in the statistical results in Figure 10-3 was obtained from data analysis using paired t-test statistics.]

These calculations can be repeated for the second reagent lot, as follows:

$$Y_c = 1.03*X_c - 0.00$$

$$= 1.03*6.5 - 0.0$$

$$= 6.70 \text{ \%Hb}$$

$$Y_c - X_c = 6.7 - 6.5 = 0.2 \text{ \%Hb}$$

$$\text{\%Bias} = (100*0.2/6.5) = 3.1\%$$

Thus the bias varies with different reagent lots and from this study is estimated as being between 1.2% and 3.1%.

The Sigma-metric is calculated from the quality required for intended use, defined as an Allowable Total Error, and the observed bias and imprecision [8]. All terms must be in the same units, either concentration units or units of percent. PT criteria for acceptable performance are often defined in terms of percent, so the equation is as follows:

$$\textbf{Sigma} = (\%TE_a - \%Bias)/\%CV$$

At the time of this evaluation study was published in 2010, the CAP criterion for acceptable performance was a TE_a of 8.0%. Given the lowest observed bias of 1.2% and an average CV of 2.8%, sigma is calculated to be 2.4 [(8.0-1.2)/2.8], which is quite low. Keep in mind the goal for World Class Performance is a sigma of 6 and the lowest sigma recommended for production processes is 3 sigma. If the more optimistic estimate of precision were used, i.e., a CV of 1.8%, then sigma would be estimated as 3.8 [(8.0-1.2)/1.8], which is considerably better, but still far from the goal for World Class Quality. If the larger estimate of bias were used, the Sigma-metrics would be lower; likewise, if the 2013 TE_a criterion of 7.0% were used, the Sigma-metrics would be even lower.

What's the point?

Traceability and process capability (performance on the sigma scale) are both important considerations in selecting examination procedures. Traceability is a prerequisite to achieving comparability of results, yet many laboratories do not adequately consider this critical characteristic, probably because of its metrological complexity. A careful assessment of the performance of different examination procedures in EQA and PT surveys provides a more practical approach and more realistic evidence of comparability of results.

As stated by Armbruster [9], "*... few health care laboratories have the time and resources to establish traceability and ensure accuracy. In the clinical laboratory, the only practical approach is for those assays for which certified reference materials are available to* *be properly traceable using the concepts of metrology to ensure appropriate calibration of methods and trueness of patient test results. The practical measure is bias, which is inherent in the systematic concept of accuracy, through the concept of TE_a."*

Laboratories can also assess process capability, which is the ability of the examination procedure to achieve the quality required for intended use and is readily evaluated by calculation of Sigma-metrics. The use of Sigma-metrics will be discussed in later chapters and graphical tools will be described to support applications in the validation of examination procedures and the design and selection of Statistical QC procedures. One of these tools, the Normalized Method Decision Chart, is very effective for summarizing the sigma performance of multiple tests to aid in the assessment of the capability of new analyzers. Many examples are provided on the Westgard Website, as well as a detailed series of lessons related to the Lenters and Slingerland paper on HbA1c POC devices.

References

1. ISO 15189. Medical laboratories – Requirements for quality and competence. ISO, Geneva, 2012.
2. NGSP website, www.ngsp.org, accessed June 2nd, 2014.
3. WG Miller, GL Myers, ML Gantzer, SE Kahn, ER Schonbrunner, LM Thienpont, DM Bunk, RH Christenson, JH Eckfeldt, SF Lo, CM Nubling, CM Sturgeon. Special Report: Roadmap for Harmonization of Clinical Laboratory Measurement Procedures. Clin Chem 2011;57:1108-1117.
4. BIPM website www.bipm.org/utils/en/pdf/Preamble.pdf Accessed June 2nd, 2014.
5. In Vitro Diagnostic Medical Devices. Measurement of quantities in biological samples; Metrological traceability of value assigned to calibrator and control materials. EN/ISO 17511. 2002
6. Thienpont LM, Van Utfanghe K, Cabaleiro DR. Metrological traceablity of calibration in the estimation and use of common medical decision-making criteria. Clin Chem Lab Med 2004;42:842-850.
7. Lenters-Westra E, Slingerland RJ. Six of eight Hemoglobin A1c Point-of-Care instruments do not meet the general accepted analytical performance criteria. Clin Chem 2010;56:44-52.
8. Westgard JO. Six Sigma Quality Design & Control: Desirable precision and requisite QC for laboratory measurement processes, 2nd ed. Madison WI:Westgard QC, Inc., 2006.
9. Armbruster D. Accuracy controls: Assessing trueness (bias). In Quality Control in the Age of Risk Management, Westgard JO and Westgard SA, eds. Clin Lab Med 2013;33:125-137.

11. Validating Performance of an Examination Procedure

Section 5.5 of ISO 15189 instructs laboratories to evaluate the performance of examination procedures [1]: *The laboratory shall select examination procedures which have been validated for their intended use. The identity of persons performing activities in examination processes shall be recorded. The specified requirements (performance specifications) for each examination procedure shall relate to the intended use of that examination.... The independent verification by the laboratory shall confirm through obtaining objective evidence that the performance characteristics for the examination procedure are met."*

Verification refers to the confirmation of a manufacturer's claims for performance, whereas **Validation** refers to the assessment that performance is adequate for the intended use of test results. Verification assumes that manufacturers have performed extensive validation studies, thus allowing the laboratory to simply confirm the manufacturer's performance claims. Validation is required anytime the laboratory wants to evaluate performance relative to requirements for intended use. Validation represents a higher level of experimental documentation that is needed to establish performance claims and to make sure performance is acceptable for the intended use of a test. The two terms – verification and validation — are often used interchangeably, but they have different meanings in accreditation guidelines and government regulations.

Validation is also required is whenever a laboratory modifies a manufacturer's recommended procedure. Laboratories are not allowed to modify a manufacturer's method in any way unless they perform the experimental studies to prove that the modified method provides acceptable performance for the intended use. Factors such as using a different specimen type, dilution, sample size, different reaction conditions – all require validation by the laboratory.

Another challenge is **Laboratory Developed Tests (LDTs)** where there generally are no commercial methods available. LDTs are commonly seen in infectious disease testing and molecular diagnostics, where the laboratory develops its own reagent and reaction conditions. Again, the laboratory takes on a higher level of responsibility because no outside studies document method performance.

6σQMS Policy. Thne laboratory shall validate the performance of all examination procedures to ensure the quality required for intended use is achieved.

For purposes of our Six Sigma Quality System, **validation** is required for critical performance characteristics such as imprecision and inaccuracy. Merely confirming that an examination procedure meets a manufacturer's claims does not ensure that the requirements for intended use are satisfied. Manufacturers generally do not make any claim for the quality of an examination procedure, often they only make claims for performance characteristics, such as imprecision, accuracy, reportable range and reference range, and sometimes also for analytical specificity (interference, recovery) and analytical sensitivity (detection limit). Performance contributes to quality, but quality depends on the net effect of all the individual performance characteristics, particularly precision and accuracy.

6σQMS Process. The laboratory shall perform an evaluation study that includes experiments for analytic range, replication, comparison of methods, confirmation of reference range, and when appropriate, detection limit, interference, and recovery. Experimental results should be analyzed graphically and statistically and the Sigma-metric determined to judge the acceptability of the examination procedure for its intended use.

The organization of a method validation study is illustrated in Figure 11-1, which identifies 3 phases, the types of errors that are to be determined, and the types of experiments that are performed to estimate these errors.

- The first phase is to become familiar with the operation of the measurement procedure. This takes training and practice to establish a working method. During this familiarization period, it is useful to determine reportable range, i.e., the low to high values for which the method is useful.

Familiarization Setup Method	Reportable Range	Linearity Series
Preliminary Experiments	Random Error	Replication Within Run
	Constant Systematic Error	Interference
	Proportional Systematic Error	Recovery
Final Experiments	Random Error	Replication Between Runs
	Systematic Errors	Comparison of Methods
	Reference Limits	Test Normal Subjects

Figure 11-1. Organization of a method validation study.

- Following this familiarization period, the second phase is to perform the preliminary validation experiments. These are the short experiments for within-run replication, recovery, interference, and possibly detection limit.
- Once the results of all these preliminary experiments show acceptable performance, then the third phase experiments are performed. These experiments take a longer time, typically 20 days for the long-term replication experiment and at least 5 days for the comparison of methods experiment.

Finally, when all these experiments show acceptable performance, the method can be implemented for routine operation. That requires establishing QC procedures, training personnel, and monitoring routine performance, i.e., managing the quality of the testing process.

The method validation process involves different studies or statistical experiments Each of these studies involve protocols and statistical data analysis, as described in our book *Basic Method*

Validation [2]. Specific protocols are available from the Clinical and Laboratory Standards Institute (CLSI) for evaluation of precision performance (EP5), linearity (EP6), interference testing (EP7), bias estimation from comparison of methods (EP9), evaluation of detection limits (EP17), and verifying reference intervals (EP28). These protocols are available from the CLSI website in electronic or printed form [3, cost is typically $170 per document].

Ultimately, the laboratory obtains an estimate of imprecision in terms of an SD or %CV and an estimate of accuracy in terms of bias or %Bias. The laboratory then needs to determine whether the observed imprecision and bias provide acceptable performance relative to the quality required for intended use. (Unfortunately, the CLSI protocols do not include this final step of determining the acceptability of examination procedures for their intended use.)

A decision of the acceptability of an examination procedure for its intended use should be based on the size of the errors that have been observed in comparison to the amount of error that is allowable, i.e. TE_a as defined earlier. The total error that is observed is the combined effect of the observed bias and SD or CV. Total Error combines bias with a multiple of the SD or CV to describe a worst-case error condition, i.e., how large the error could be if the systematic error (bias) and the random error (SD or CV) are in the same direction, as described in Figure 11-2. In this figure, TV represents the True Value and Bias represents the average difference or systematic error observed from a comparison of methods experiment. The distribution of random errors, or imprecision, is determined from the replication experiment. Because random error can be either positive or negative, the worst case error condition always considers the error in the same direction of the bias. Common practice is to estimate Total Error as bias + 2 SD. However, other multiples have been recommended and the practical meaning of "Six Sigma" is that the multiple should be 6 to achieve World Class Quality.

A practical way for a laboratory to perform this step is to use a Sigma-metrics tool called the Method Decision Chart [2].

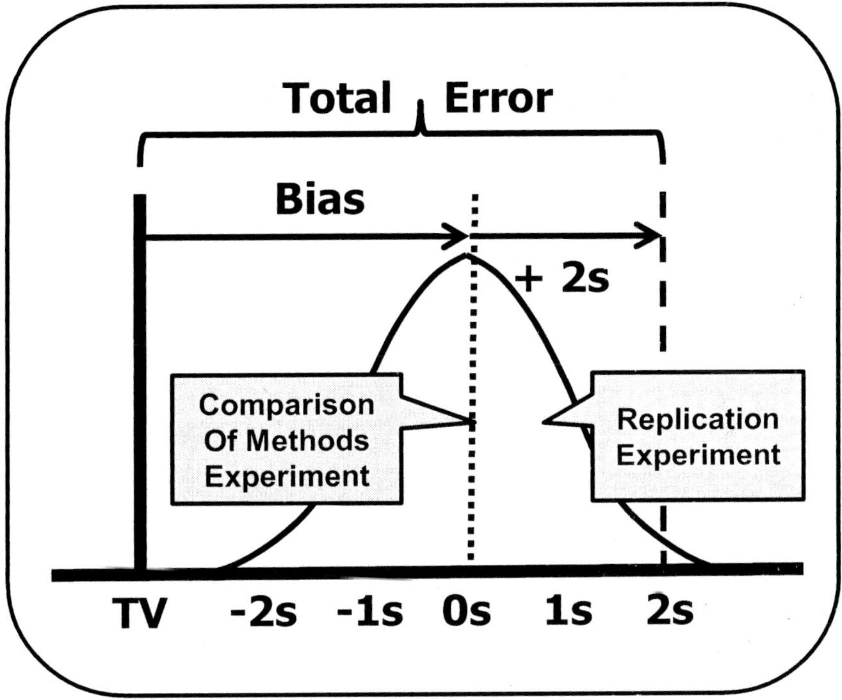

Figure 11-2. Concept of Total Error as total effect of observed bias and observed imprecision.

6σQMS Procedure. Prepare a Method Decision Chart to determine quality on the sigma scale and assess the acceptability of precision and bias for intended use.

A Method Decision Chart is a graphic tool that shows the observed inaccuracy (bias) on the y-axis and the observed imprecision (SD or CV) on the x-axis. It is prepared for a defined quality requirement in the form of an Allowable Total Error (TE_a). Lines are drawn for various Total Error criteria of the form Bias + m*SD, where m corresponds to a multiple of the CV or a multiple of sigma.

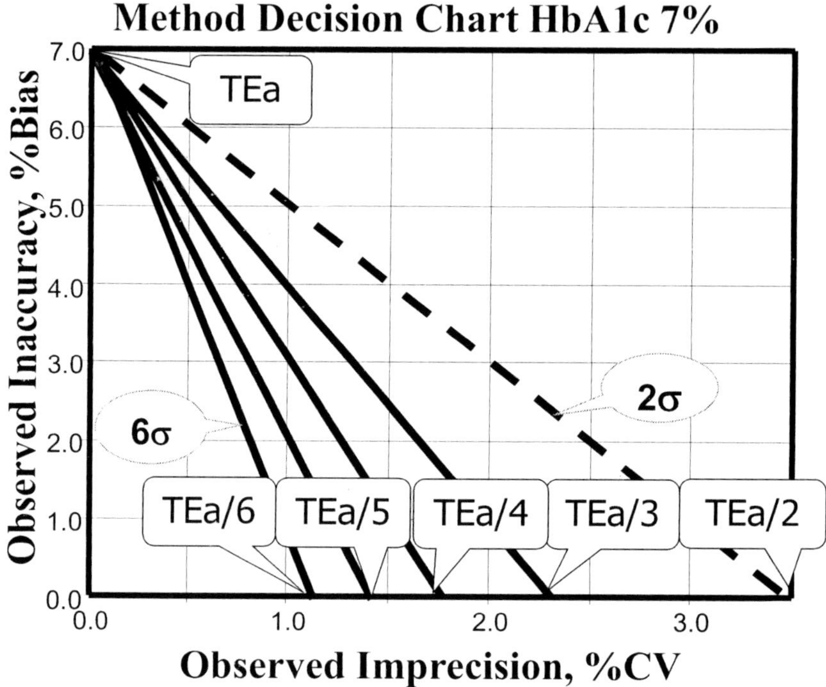

Figure 11-3. Preparation of a Method Decision Chart for HbA1c where TE_a is 7.0%.

Figure 11-3 illustrates the preparation of a Method Decision Chart to judge the acceptability of an examination procedure. This example is for HbA1c where the quality required for intended use has been defined as an allowable Total Error (TE_a) of 7.0%. Each of the lines represents a different level of sigma, from 6-sigma on the furthest line to the left, through 5-sigma, 4-sigma, 3-sigma, and 2-sigma for the furthest line on the right.

Directions: Preparing a Method Decision Chart for HbA1c

1. Scale the y-axis from 0% to TE_a of 7.0%. Label this axis as "observed inaccuracy" in units of %Bias.

2. Scale the x-axis from 0% to half of TE_a, which is 3.5%. Label this axis "observed imprecision" in units of %CV.

3. Draw lines for the various Total Error Criteria. This can be done by determining the y-intercept and x-intercept for each line, as described below:

   - For the Bias plus 2s TE criterion, if the x-value or s were zero, then the y-intercept would be equal to TE_a or 7.0%. If the y-value were zero, then the x-intercept would be TE_a divided by 2, or 3.5.
   - For the Bias plus 3s TE criterion, the y-intercept is again 7.0 and the x-intercept is 7.0 divided by 3, or 2.33.
   - For the Bias plus 4s TE criterion, the y-intercept is 7.0 and the x-intercept is 7.0 divided by 4, or 1.75.
   - For the Bias plus 5s TE criterion, the y-intercept is 7.0 and the x-intercept is 7.0 divided by 5 or 1.40.
   - For the Bias plus 6s TE criterion, the y-intercept is 7.0 and the x-intercept is 7.0 divided by 6, or 1.17.

One disadvantage of the OPSpecs chart is the need to prepare a new chart for each test having a different quality requirement. An alternative is to prepare a "normalized" Method Decision Chart, then calculate the coordinates of the operating point as a percentage of the quality requirement. In that way, the same chart can be used for many different examination procedures, e.g., to summarize performance of a new multitest system.

Directions: Preparing a Normalized Method Decision Chart

1. Scale the y-axis from 0% to TE_a of 100%. Label this axis as "observed inaccuracy" in units of %Bias.
2. Scale the x-axis from 0% to half of TE_a, or 50%%. Label this axis "observed imprecision" in units of %CV.
3. Draw lines for the various Total Error Criteria. This can be done by determining the y-intercept and x-intercept for each line, as described here.

- For the Bias plus 2s TE criterion, if the x-value or s were zero, then the y-intercept would be equal to TE_a or 100%. If the y-value were zero, then the x-intercept would be TE_a divided by 2, or 50%.
- For the Bias plus 3s TE criterion, the y-intercept is again 100% and the x-intercept is 100/3 or 33%.
- For the Bias plus 4s TE criterion, the y-intercept is 100% and the x-intercept is 100%/4, or 25%.
- For the Bias plus 5s TE criterion, the y-intercept is 100% and the x-intercept is 100%/5 or 20%.
- For the Bias plus 6s TE criterion, the y-intercept is 100% and the x-intercept is 100%/6, or 16.7%.

Example Application 1. Use of a Method Decision Chart for HbA1c

Figure 11-4 shows the application for 3 different HbA1c examination procedures using a Method Decision Chart prepared for TE_a of 7.0%. The Observed %Bias is plotted as the y-coordinate and the Observed %CV as the x-coordinate to locate the "operating point" for each examination procedure.

- Point A represents an examination procedure with a 2.0% bias and 1.0% CV, whose operating point falls on the 5-sigma line [(7-2)/1].
- Point B represents a 1.0% bias and 1.5% CV, which falls on the 4-sigma line [(7-1)/1.5].
- Point C represents a 2.0% bias and 2.0% CV, which falls between the 3-sigma and 2-sigma lines. In this case, the actual sigma value is 2.5 [(7-2)/2].

The first two examination procedures (A, B) provide acceptable performance, but the second one (B) requires more QC effort to monitor and maintain performance. The third example (C) does not satisfy the needs for intended use and should not be implemented in the laboratory.

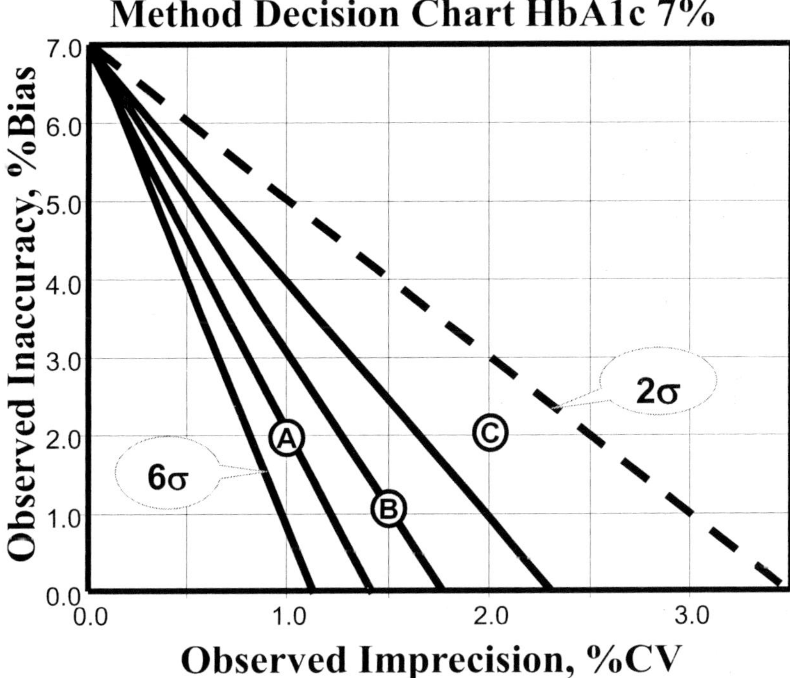

Figure 11-4. Method Decision Chart for HbA1c with TE_a of 7.0%. Point A represents an examination procedure having a bias of 2.0% and CV of 1.0%; Point B shows a bias of 1.0% and CV of 1.5%; Point C shows a bias of 2.0% and a CV of 2.0%.

Example Application 2. Use of Normalized Method Decision Chart.

Figure 11-5 shows a normalized Method Decision Chart. To use this normalized chart, a normalized operating point must be calculated, as follows:

- Y-coordinate = 100*(%Bias/%TE_a)
- X-coordinate = 100*(%CV/%TE_a)

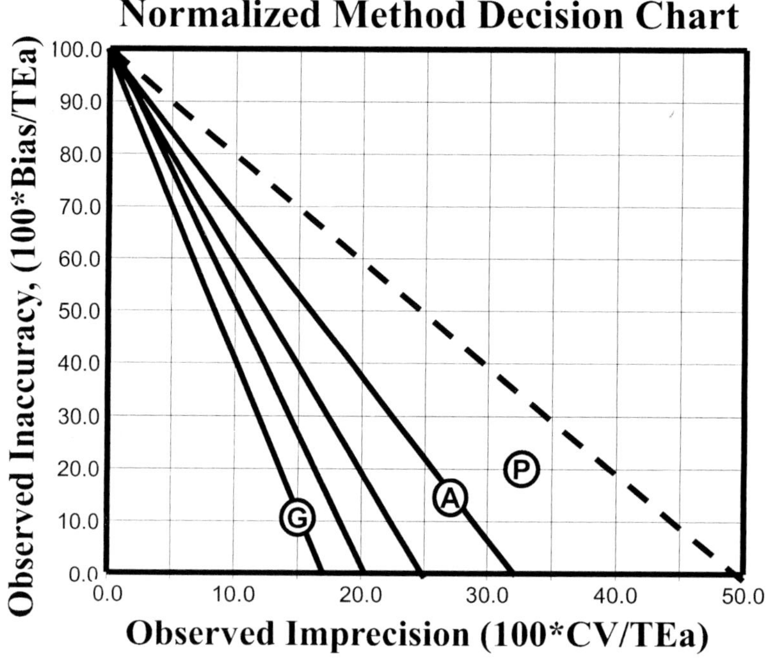

Figure 11-5. Normalized Method Decision Chart where observed inaccuracy is calculated as 100(Bias/TE$_a$) and observed imprecision is calculated as 100*(CV/TE$_a$), when original parameters are all in units of %. Example G is a laboratory glucose examination procedure, P a point of care glucose meter, and A is a HbA1c examination procedure.*

To illustrate the use of this normalized chart, this single chart can be used to show the performance of a laboratory glucose method, a Point-of-Care glucose meter, and an HbA1c method.

- Point G represents a a laboratory glucose examination procedure where TE$_a$ is 10.0%, bias is 1.0%, and CV is 1.5%, the y-coordinate is 10.0% (100*1.0/10.0) and the x-coordinate 15.0% (100*1.5/100);
- Point P represents a Point-of-Care glucose meter where TE$_a$ is 15%, bias is 3.0%, and the CV is 5.0%, the y-coordinate is 20% (100*3.0/15.0) and the x-coordinate is 33.3% (100*5.0/15.0);

- Point A represents a HbA1c examination procedure where TE_a is 7.0%, bias is 1.0%, and CV is 2.0%, the y-coordinate is 14.3% (100*1.0/7.0) and the x-coordinate is 28.6% (100*2.0/7.0) .

What's the point?

Validating the performance of examination procedures to ensure they satisfy the needs for intended use is necessary if quality is to be effectively managed in the medical laboratory. Existing evaluation protocols are often focused on estimation of performance characteristics, such as imprecision and bias and verification of manufacturers' claims, rather than judging the acceptability for intended use. Because manufacturers seldom make a claim for quality, the laboratory has responsibility for defining the quality required for intended use and judging acceptability on basis of the performance observed in the laboratory.

The approach recommended here – use of a Method Decision Chart – provides a graphical display of the observed bias and precision relative to lines that describe different total error criteria or different levels of quality on the sigma scale. Examination procedures with sigma performance of 5 or better are desirable to minimize the time and effort needed to monitor and maintain performance. Examination procedures with sigma performance of 4 need more QC, but are still acceptable for routine operation. Examination procedures with sigma performance of 3 or less should not be implemented because they cannot be adequately controlled under routine operations.

References

1. ISO 15189. Medical laboratories – Requirements for quality and competence. ISO, Geneva, 2012.
2. Westgard JO. Basic Method Validation, 3rd ed. Madison WI:Westgard QC, Inc., 2008.
3. Clinical and Laboratory Standards Institute, Wayne PA, www.clsi.org
    a. EP05A2. Evaluation of Precision Performance of Quantitative Measurement Methods. 2004.
    b. EP06A. Evaluation of the Linearity of Quantitative Measurement Procedures. 2003.
    c. EP07A2. Interference Testing in Clinical Chemistry. 2005
    d. EP09A3. Measurement Procedure Comparison and Bias Estimation Using Patient Samples. 2013.
    e. EP28A3C. Defining, Establishing, and Verifying Reference Intervals in the Clinical Laboratory. 2010.
    f. EP17A2 Evaluation of Detection Capability for Clinical Laboratory Measurement Procedures. 2012.
    g. EP14A2. Evaluation of Matrix Effects. 2005.

12. Designing SQC Procedures

All laboratories perform quality control, but merely analyzing controls does not ensure that the necessary quality is achieved. The necessary quality must be defined, as discussed in chapter 10. The performance of the examination procedure must be validated to achieve the quality for intended use, as discussed in chapter 12. In addition, Statistical QC procedures (SQC) must be properly designed and properly implemented to detect medically important errors that occur during routine service operation.

ISO 15189 [1] imposes a demanding requirement in Section 5.6.2.1 with the statement *"the laboratory shall design quality control procedures that verify the attainment of the intended quality of results"*. It is recommended that quality control materials be examined at a frequency that reflects the stability of the examination procedure and the patients' consequence of harm if erroneous results are produced. The laboratory should apply statistical control rules to make decisions on the acceptability of analytical results and the need to reject runs and repeat patient testing.

6σQMS Policy. The laboratory shall design Statistical Quality Control procedures to ensure the quality of routine testing meets the needs of the intended use of examination procedures.

Guidance on the design of SQC procedures can be found in ISO 15198 (which should not be confused with 15189). The 15198 document [2] provides guidance to manufacturers on how to design SQC procedures and validate their performance:

"For existing IVD medical devices, conventional statistical quality control procedures (e.g. as described in CLSI C24) are considered adequate unless evidence from risk-monitoring activities indicates [other] quality control procedures are essential for maintaining risk at an acceptable level. In such cases, the quality control procedures shall be validated .... NOTE: Demonstration that a statistical quality control procedure will detect results that exceed predetermined limits does not require induction of actual failure modes. Validation may be based on statistical evaluation of the simulated effects of imprecision and/or bias on actual performance data obtained in routine operating mode."

There are two important considerations here: (a) SQC procedures can be readily validated based on existing information on their rejection characteristics, as determined from simulation studies documented in the clinical chemistry literature. (b) Validation of other non-SQC control procedures will require induction of actual failure modes to determine whether the QC procedures can detect medically important errors. Manufacturers can do this when they are validating new systems, but laboratories will find it very difficult to induce specific failures to validate detection of individual controls. SQC is important in the laboratory because it is an independent control mechanism that can be designed to detect medically important errors.

Quality-Planning Tools make it practical for laboratories to select the right SQC procedures. Power curves [3, 4] and critical-error graphs [5] have been used for planning SQC procedures for many decades. Today's version of the critical-error graph is known as the Sigma-metrics SQC Selection Tool and its application is illustrated in the CLSI C24A3 guidance for Statistical QC procedures [6]. Charts of Operating Specifications [7, 8] are a related tool and there are "normalized" charts that are available for manual applications [9]. There also are computer programs available, both an standalone automatic QC design program [10] and an online production tool.

6σQMS Process. The laboratory shall select SQC procedures on the basis of the quality required for intended use, the imprecision and bias observed for the examination procedure, and the known rejection characteristics of different control rules and different numbers of control measurements.

ISO 15198 makes reference to CLSI C24 [6], which discusses the principles of SQC and describes a process for selecting appropriate control rules and the number of control measurements to detect medically important errors. While C24A3 provides a Sigma SQC Selection Tool, it is also possible to employ Charts of Operating Specifications, thus there are two planning tools that are practical for use in the laboratory.

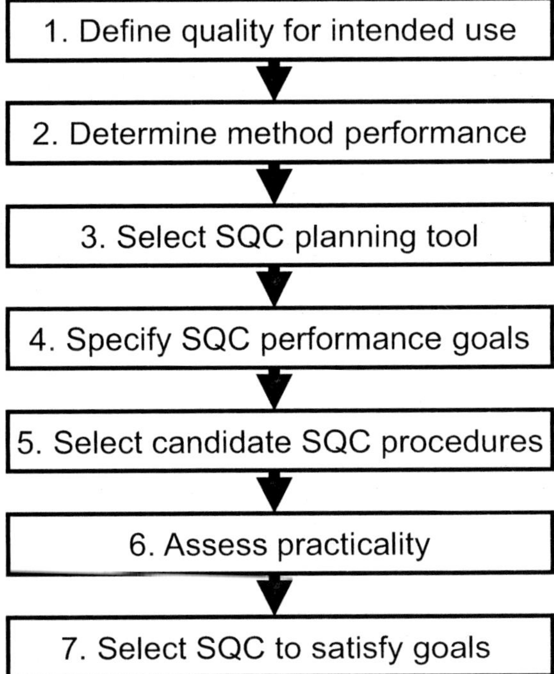

Figure 12-1. Process for selecting SQC procedures to ensure quality required for intended use.

Figure 12-1 describes the SQC selection process. Quality for intended use should be defined in terms of an Allowable Total Error (TE_a). Method performance should be determined to estimate imprecision (CV) and accuracy (bias). With that information, it is possible to calculate the Sigma-metric and use the Sigma SQC Selection Tool from C24A3 or to plot the operating point on a Chart of Operating Specifications (OPSpecs chart). The general goals for SQC performance are to achieve a 0.90 probability of error detection (P_{ed}) and a low probability of false rejection (P_{fr}). Candidate SQC procedures that achieve these goals are identified and their practicality assessed for implementation in the laboratory. Then the final SQC procedure is selected to identify the control rules and number of control measurements that will be implemented in the laboratory.

6σQMS Procedure 1. Selection of appropriate control rules and the total number of control measurements using a Sigma SQC Selection tool.

Figure 12-2 shows the Sigma SQC Selection Tool that can be used when running 2 levels of controls. This graph shows probability for rejection on the y-axis and the size of systematic error on the bottom x-axis. The medically important systematic error can be calculated as $[(TE_a - bias)/CV] - 1.65$, which is equivalent to the value of Sigma-metric minus 1.65. That relationship allows the x-axis to be scaled in terms of sigma, as shown at the top of the graph.

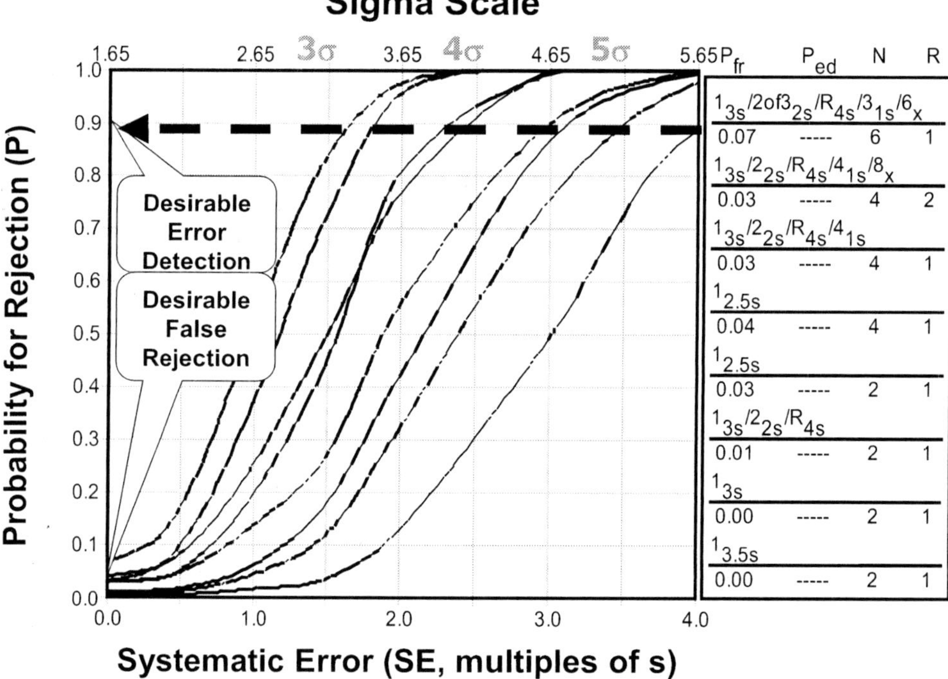

Figure 12-2. Sigma SQC Selection Tool for 2 levels of controls. The probability for rejection is plotted on y-axis versus the size of systematic error on bottom x-axis and the Sigma-metric on the top x-axis. The different power curves correspond, top to bottom, to the list of control rules and N in the key at the right side.

The graph shows the power curves for 8 different QC procedures. The curves from top to bottom on the graph correspond to the list of QC procedures from top to bottom in the key at the right side. For example, the second curve from the bottom represents a QC procedure with 2 control measurements and 3s control limits. The top curve represents a multirule QC procedure with 6 control measurements per run.

The idea is to select the QC procedure that provides a low probability of false rejection, as shown by the y-intercept of the power curves, preferably less than 0.05 or a 5% chance of false rejection, and a high probability of error detection, preferably 0.9 or 90% detection of medically important systematic errors, as shown by the dashed line at the top.

To select an appropriate SQC procedure, the Sigma-metric for an examination procedure is located on the top x-scale and a vertical line is drawn to intersect the power curves. The probability for error detection is estimated at the intersection of the vertical and power curve, reading the value from the scale on the y-axis. The probability of false rejection is estimated from the y-intercept of the selected power curve.

Figure 12-3 on the following page provides a similar Sigma SQC Selection Tool for 3 levels of controls, which will be applicable for examination procedures, such as immunoassays, hematology, etc.

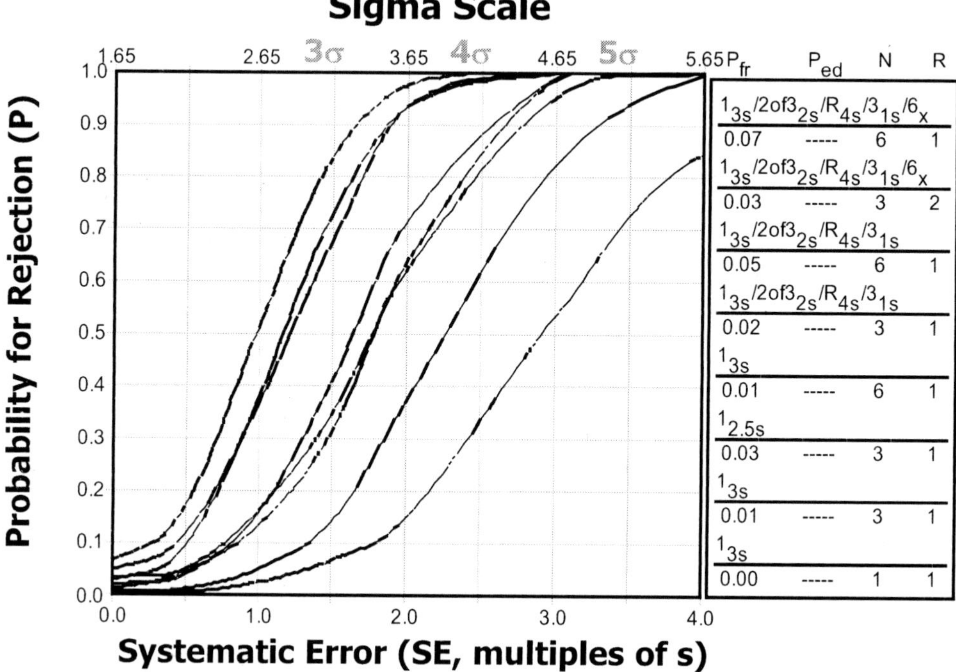

Figure 12-3. Sigma SQC Selection Tool for 3 levels of controls. The probability for rejection is plotted on y-axis versus the size of systematic error on bottom x-axis and the Sigma-metric on the top x-axis. The different power curves correspond, top to bottom, to the list of control rules and N in the key at the right side.

To select an appropriate SQC procedure, identify the Sigma-metric on the scale at the top, drop a vertical line, observed where that line intersects the power curves, then read the probabilities for error detection on the y-axis.

Directions for Using a Sigma SQC Selection Tool

1. Identify the test and method for the intended application.

2. Define a quality requirement in form of Allowable Total Error (TE_a).
3. Identify a critical decision concentration (X_c) that is of interest for the test and its application with your patient population.
4. Decide whether to use 2 or 3 levels of controls.
5. Determine the imprecision of your method (SD, CV%) at or near the critical decision concentration or level (X_c).
6. Determine the inaccuracy of your method (Bias, Bias%) at or near X_c.
7. Calculate the Sigma-metric from the defined TE_a and the observed imprecision and the observed inaccuracy.
    a. Sigma = (TE_a% - Bias%)/CV% where all terms are in %, or
    b. Sigma = (TE_a – Bias)/SD where all terms are in concentrations units.
8. Calculate the critical Systematic Error (ΔSE) that needs to be detected, which is simply Sigma – 1.65.
9. Utilize the Sigma-metrics Tool for either 2 or 3 levels of control, whichever is chosen for your application. Locate either the Sigma value on the x-scale at the top of the graph, or ΔSE value on the x-scale at the bottom of the graph. Draw a vertical line that intersects the power curves.
    a. Try to achieve a P_{ed} of 0.90 or 90% chance of detection, with the lowest N and the simplest control rules.
    b. If a P_{ed} of 0.90 cannot be achieved, then select the control procedure that gives you maximum error detection.
10. Recommend a QC procedure for use with your method.
11. Document your recommendation.

Example: Selection of SQC Procedures for HbA1c

Sigma Scale

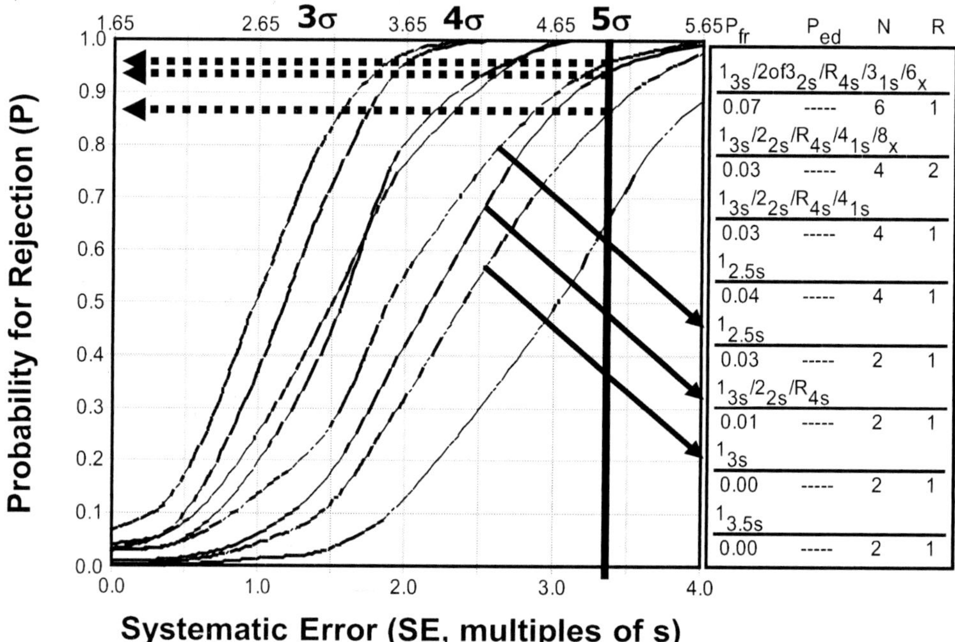

Figure 12-4. Example application for 5-sigma method and 2 levels of controls.

Sigma 5.0. Figure 12-4 shows an examination procedure that corresponds to our earlier HbA1c example A. Note that the 4 power curves on the left all achieve 100% error detection, but require 4 to 6 control measurements per run. The curves of most interest are the next 3 which require fewer control measurements and the probabilities for error detection are about 0.96, 0.94, and 0.87. These 3 control procedures can be identified in the key at the right as $1_{2.5s}$ with N=2, $1_{3s}/2_{2s}/R_{4s}$ with N=2, and 1_{3s} with N=2. Considering the goals for SQC performance, all three satisfy the goal for $P_{fr} \leq 0.05$ and two of those also satisfy the goal for $P_{ed} \geq 0.90$. Therefore, the best choices would be to implement $1_{2.5s}$ with N=2 or $1_{3s}/2_{2s}/R_{4s}$ with N=2. However, in some situations, it may be appropriate to implement 1_{3s} with N=2 because that is a simpler SQC procedure.

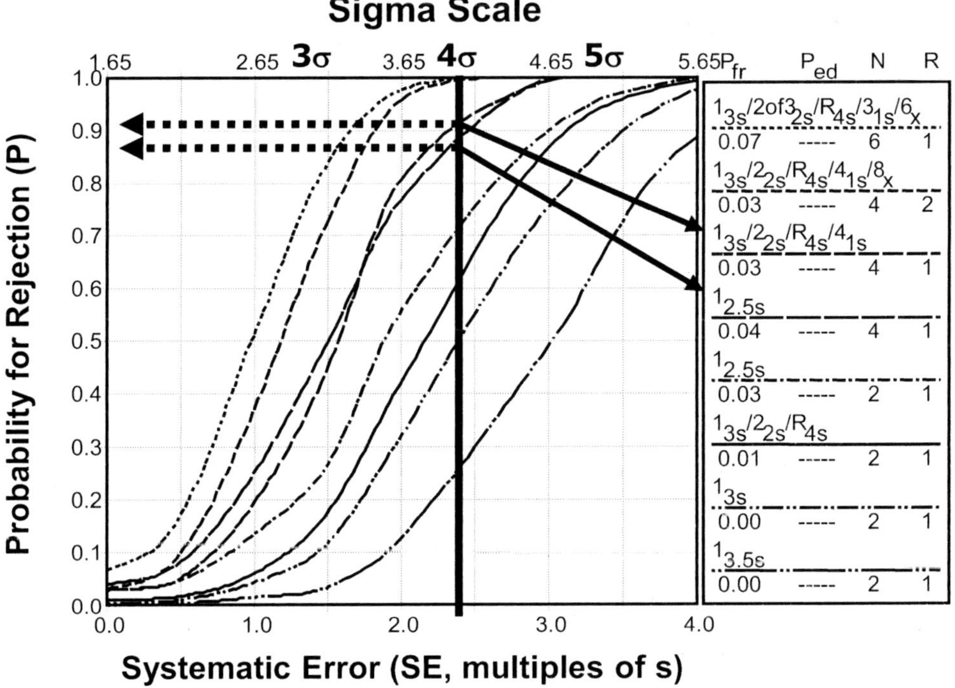

Figure 12-5. Example application for 4-sigma testing process and 2 levels of controls.

Sigma 4.0. Figure 12-5 provides an examination procedure that corresponds to our earlier HbA1c example B. The two SQC procedures of most interest here are the $1_{3s}/2_{2s}/R_{4s}/4_{1s}$ multirule with N=4 or the $1_{2.5s}$ single rule with N=4. The two are very close in performance with P_{fr} of 0.03 and 0.04, respectively, and P_{ed} of 0.91 and 0.88, respectively. In principle, the multirule procedure is a better choice, but the performance is so close that either would be appropriate. The decision between the two may be based on practical issues in implementing the rules. Some SQC software may not support multirules, other software may not support use of 2.5s control limits. Manual applications may be simpler if a single rule is used. On the other hand, if implementation of 2.5s control limits seems too difficult, it may be easier to implement the multirule QC procedure, even for manual applications.

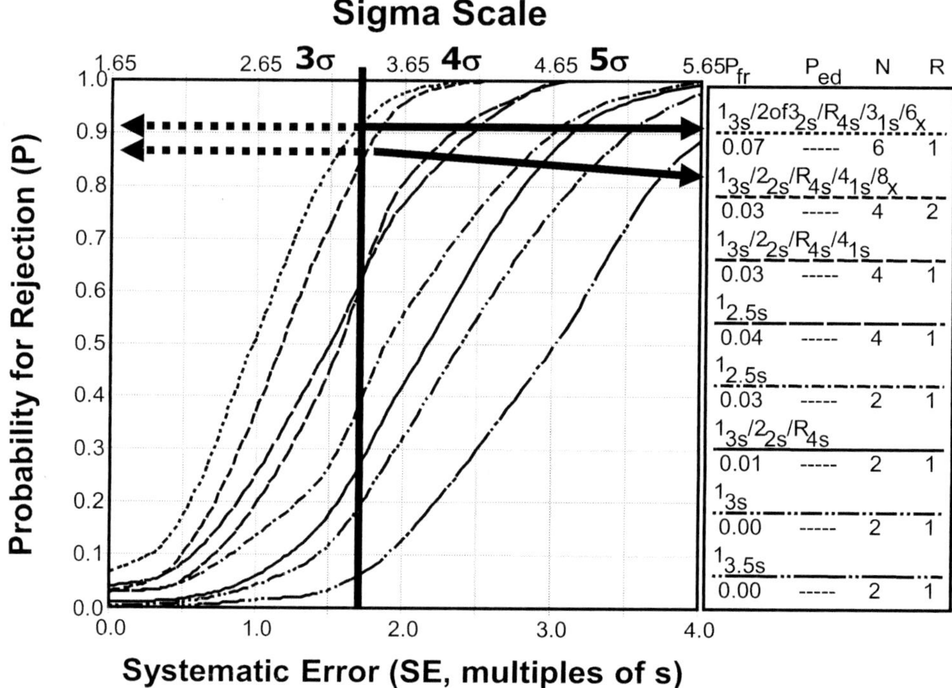

Figure 12-6. Example application for 3.3-sigma method and 2 levels of controls.

Sigma 3.3. Figure 12-6 shows illustrates the minimum Sigma-metric performance of a method that still allows the laboratory to implement an "affordable" SQC procedure. The appropriate SQC procedures are both multirule procedures, one with 6 control measurements per run and the other with 4 control measurements per run, but with inspection of controls over 2 runs (that's the meaning of R=2 in the key). The best choice would be the N=6 procedure because it provides the necessary error detection in a single run. The difficulty, of course, is that it is expensive to analyze that many controls. The alternative is to analyze 4 controls and then employ an 8_x rule to look back at control data from the previous run to obtain the necessary 8 measurements. Neither is ideal, but the real problem is that the method is so poor that it is difficult and costly for a laboratory to implement the appropriate SQC.

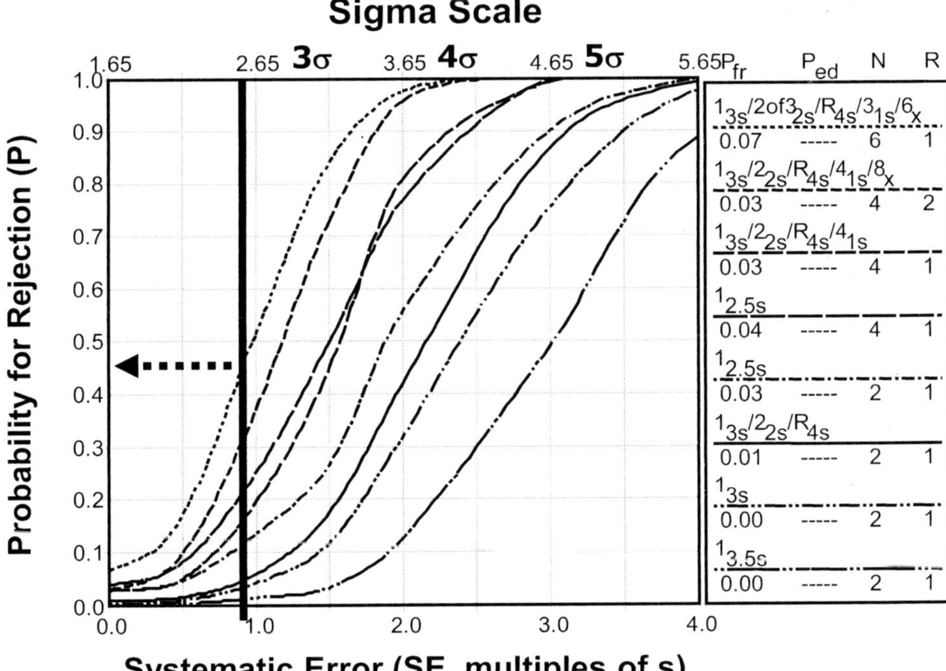

Figure 12-7. Example application for 2.5-sigma method and 2 levels of controls.

Sigma 2.5. Figure 12-7 shows an examination procedure that corresponds to our earlier HbA1c example C. A multirule procedure with N=6 can provide a P_{ed} of about 0.45, or a 45% chance of detecting a medically important error.

6σQMS Procedure 2. Selection of appropriate control rules and the total number of control measurements using Charts of Operating Specifications.

A second tool that is practical for manual applications is the Chart of Operating Specifications, or OPSpecs chart. This tool also allows you to set specifications for allowable precision and allowable bias. The format and layout of the OPSpecs chart is the same as the Method Decision Chart, which is also an advantage, particularly if you already use the Method Decision Chart in your method validation studies.

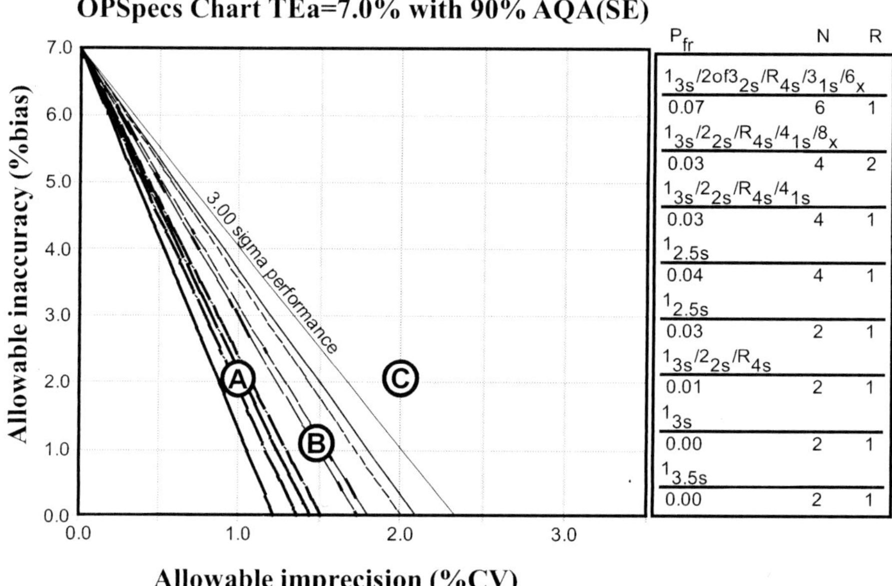

Figure 12-8. OPSpecs Chart prepared for TE_a of 7.0%, 2 levels of controls, and 90% detection for systematic errors. Allowable inaccuracy, or bias, is shown on the y-axis versus allowable imprecision or SD or CV on the x-axis. Points A, B, and C correspond to HbA1c examples.

Figure 12-8 shows an OPSpecs chart prepared for an Allowable Total Error of 7% and a 90% chance of detecting a medically important systematic error (see label at top). The y-axis shows the allowable inaccuracy, or %Bias, and the x-axis shows the allowable imprecision, or %CV, similar to the layout of the Method Decision Chart. The diagonal lines correspond top to bottom to the different QC procedures listed in the key at right, top to bottom. Note also that there is a line that represents 3-sigma performance, exactly like the Method Decision Chart. That makes it clear that examination procedures performing below 3-sigma cannot be adequately controlled by SQC procedures with Ns of 6 or less. Our earlier HbA1c example for 2.5-sigma examination procedure (Point C) falls into that category. The 4-sigma example (Point B) shows the need for a total N of 4. The 5-sigma example (Point A) indicates that an N of 2 would be appropriate for that examination procedure.

There also are "normalized" forms of the OPSpecs Chart, as shown in Figures 12-9 and 12-10. These charts are convenient for use with any TE_a requirement, though it requires some additional calculations to be performed, as described in the directions that follow.

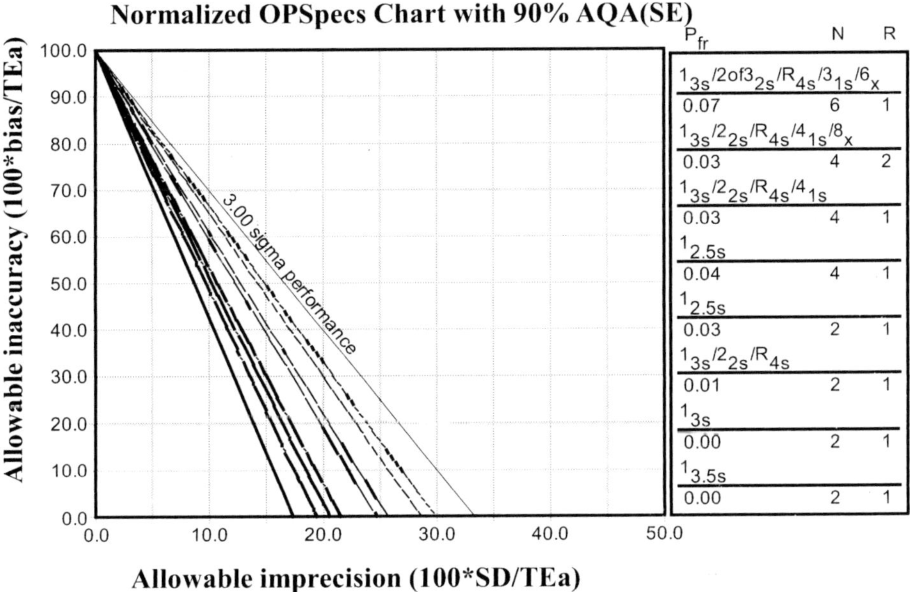

Figure 12-9. Normalized OPSpecs Chart prepared for 2 levels of controls and 90% detection for systematic errors. Allowable inaccuracy, or bias, is shown on the y-axis versus allowable imprecision or SD or CV on the x-axis. Observed inaccuracy is calculated as 100(Bias/TE_a) and observed imprecision is calculated as 100*(CV/TE_a) when the parameters are all expressed in units of %.*

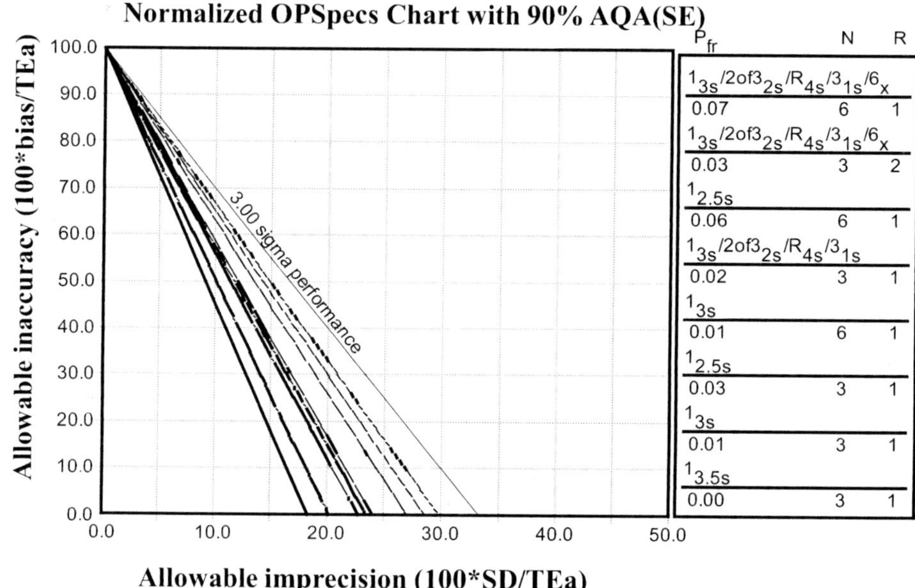

Figure 12-10. Normalized OPSpecs Chart prepared for 3 levels of controls and 90% detection for systematic errors. Allowable inaccuracy, or bias, is shown on the y-axis versus allowable imprecision or SD or CV on the x-axis. Observed inaccuracy is calculated as 100(Bias/TE_a) and observed imprecision is calculated as 100*(CV/TE_a) when original parameters are all expressed in units of %.*

Directions for Using Normalized OPSpecs Charts

1. Identify the test and method for the intended application.
2. Define a quality requirement in form of Allowable Total Error (TE_a).
3. Identify a critical decision concentration (X_c) that is of interest for the test and its application with your patient population.
4. Decide whether to use 2 or 3 levels of controls.
5. Determine method imprecision (SD, CV%) at or near X_c.
6. Determine method inaccuracy (Bias, Bias%) at or near X_c.

7. Express the imprecision and inaccuracy in percent by reference to the critical decision level (X_c) of interest.

   a. $(SD/X_c)*100 = CV\%$

   b. $(Bias/X_c)*100 = Bias\%$

8. Calculate a "normalized operating point" by expressing the observed imprecision and inaccuracy as a percent of the allowable Total Error.

   a. X-coordinate = $(CV\%/TE_a\%)*100$

   b. Y-coordinate = $(Bias\%/TE_a\%)*100$

9. Plot the normalized operating point on the Normalized OPSpecs Charts using the chart for either 2 control levels or 3 control levels.

10. Inspect the Normalized OPSpecs charts and select control rule(s) whose allowable limits for imprecision and inaccuracy are above the operating point. Identify the control rule(s) from the key at the right.

    a. Try to achieve a P_{ed} of 0.90 or 90% chance of detection, with the lowest N and the simplest control rules.

    b. If a P_{ed} of 0.90 cannot be achieved, then select the control procedure that gives you maximum error detection.

11. Recommend a QC procedure for use with your method.

12. Document your recommendation.

Westgard Sigma Rules™

Figures 12-11 and 12-12 summarize our guidance for adapting QC rules to account for the sigma quality observed for an examination procedure. We describe this guidance as "Westgard Sigma Rules™" to differentiate this recommendation from the "original" multirule procedure commonly known as "Westgard Rules". Observe that there is a Sigma-scale at the bottom of these figures. That scale provides guidance for which rules should be included for an examination procedure that achieves the designated quality on the Sigma-scale.

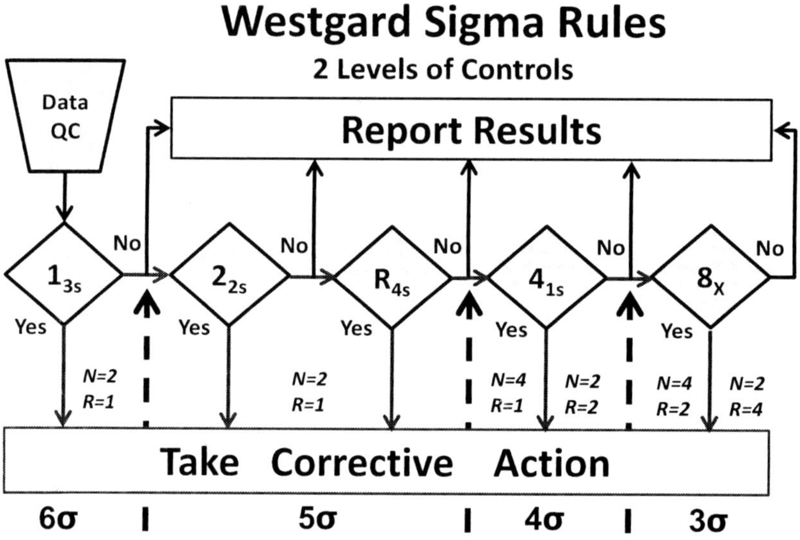

Westgard Sigma Rules

2 Levels of Controls

Data QC

Report Results

1_{3s} No / Yes — N=2 R=1

2_{2s} No / Yes — N=2 R=1

R_{4s} No / Yes

4_{1s} No / Yes — N=4 R=1; N=2 R=2

8_{X} No / Yes — N=4 R=2; N=2 R=4

Take Corrective Action

6σ | 5σ | 4σ | 3σ

Figure 12-11. Westgard Sigma Rules™ for 2 levels of control

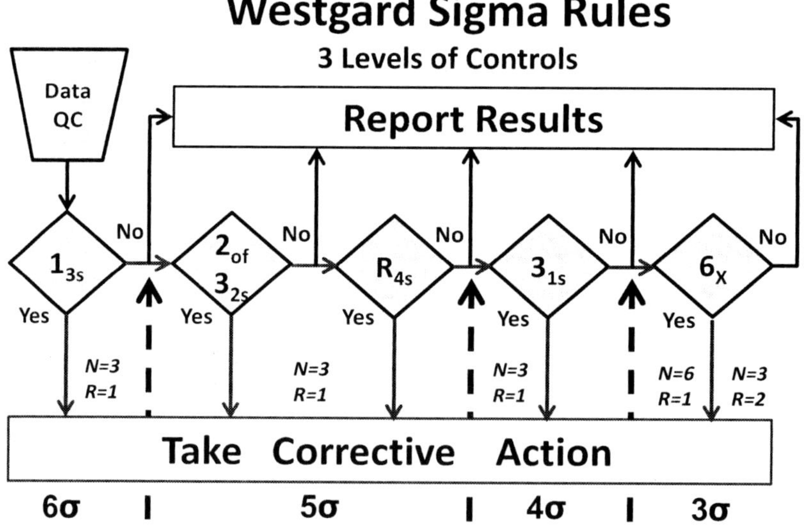

Figure 12-12. Westgard Sigma Rules™ for 3 levels of control

How do "Westgard Sigma Rules™" work?

Figure 12-11 shows how the control rules should be selected relative to sigma performance at the bottom of the figure. The dashed vertical lines that originate at the Sigma Scale show the extent of the rules that should be applied for an examination procedure. For example, a 6-sigma examination procedure would utilize only a single control rule, 1_{3s}, with 2 control measurements in each run (one on each level of control). A 5-sigma examination procedure should use three rules, $1_{3s}/2_{2s}/R_{4s}$, with 2 control measurements in each run (N=2, R=1). A 4-sigma examination procedure should add a fourth rule, implementing a $1_{3s}/2_{2s}/R_{4s}/4_{1s}$ multirule, preferably with 4 control measurements in each run (N=4, R=1), or alternatively, 2 control measurements in each of 2 runs (N=2, R=2), using the 4_{1s} rule to inspect the control rules across both runs. This second option suggests dividing a day's work into 2 runs and monitoring each with 2 controls. An examination procedure with a Sigma-metric less than 4 must use a multirule that includes the 8_x rule, which can be implemented with 4 control measurements in each of 2 runs (N=4, R=2) or alternatively with 2 control measurements in each of 4 runs (N=2, N=4). The first option suggests dividing a day's work into 2 runs with 4 control measurements per run, whereas the second option suggests dividing a day's work into 4 runs and monitoring each with 2 controls.

Figure 12-12 provides similar information for 3 levels of controls. A 6-sigma examination procedure may be controlled with a 1_{3s} rule and 1 measurement on each of 3 levels of controls. A 5-sigma process should add the $2of3_{2s}$ and R_{4s} rules for use with 1 measurement on each of 3 levels of controls. A 4-sigma process should add a 3_{1s} rule for use with 1 measurement on each of 3 controls. If sigma is less than 4, the 6_x rule should be added and N increased to 6, which suggests that the 3 levels of controls be analyzed in duplicate in one run (N=6, R=1) or the day's work divided into 2 runs with 3 control measurements per run (N=3, R=2). If a 9_x rule were substituted for the 6_x rule, then a day's work could be divided into 3 runs with 3 controls per run (N=3,R=3).

What's the point?

ISO's guidance to design internal quality control procedure to verify the attainment of the intended quality of results can be easily accomplished by using QC-planning tools, such as the Sigma SQC Selection Graph or OPSpecs Charts. An even simpler tool, the Westgard Sigma Rules™ diagram, is introduced here to aid laboratories in adapting existing multirule QC procedures to provide more efficient practices for well-performing (high sigma) examination procedures.

References

1. ISO 15189. Medical laboratories – Requirements for quality and competence. ISO, Geneva, 2012.
2. ISO 15198. Clinical laboratory medicine – in vitro diagnostic medical devices – Validation of user quality control procedures by the manufacturer. Geneva, 2004.
3. Westgard JO, Groth T. Power functions for statistical control rules. Clin Chem 1979;25:863-869.
4. Westgard JO, Barry PL. Cost-Effective Quality Control: Managing the quality and productivity of analytical processes. Washington DC:AACC Press, 1986.
5. Koch DD, Oryall JJ, Quam EF et al. Selection of medically useful quality-control procedures for individual tests done in a multitest analytical system. Clin Chem 1990;36:230-233.
6. CLSI C24A3. Statistical quality control for quantitative measurement procedures. Clinical and Laboratory Standards Institute, Wayne PA, 2006.
7. Westgard JO. Charts of Operational Process Specifications (OPSpecs Charts) for assessing the precision, accuracy, and quality control needed to satisfy proficiency testing criteria. Clin Chem 1992;38:1226-1233.
8. Westgard JO. Assuring analytical quality through process planning and quality control. Arch Path Lab Med 1992;116:765-769.
9. Westgard JO. Assuring the Right Quality Right: Good Laboratory Practices for verifying the attainment of the intended quality of test results. Madison WI:Westgard QC, Inc., 2007.
10. Westgard JO, Stein B. An automatic process for selecting statistical QC procedures to assure clinical or analytical quality requirements. Clin Chem 1997;43:400-403.

13. Formulating a Total Quality Control Plan

The emphasis in the Six Sigma Quality Management System is on the analytical quality of the examination procedure because it is critically important to achieve comparability of test results for today's evidence-based medicine. However, it is also important to consider what might go wrong in the pre-examination and post-examination phases and add other control mechanisms to detect specific failure modes. The control plan should then cover the total examination process, hence the name Total Quality Control Plan (TQC Plan).

A TQC Plan can be formulated by application of risk management principles, concepts, and tools. ISO 14971 provides guidance to manufacturers to employ risk management techniques in the planning and development of new analytic systems [1]. Manufacturers, in turn, are passing the risk management approach along to medical laboratories through development of new laboratory guidelines such as CLSI EP23A [2]. According to EP23A, a Quality Control Plan (abbreviated QCP) is *"a document that describes the practices, resources, and sequences of specified activities to control the quality of a particular measuring system or test process to ensure requirements for its intended use are met."*

The EP23A process for developing a QCP is shown in Figure 13-1 (following page). *Note that this is not a figure from the EP23 trademarked guideline.* Rather, this is *our perspective* of its recommendations. The actual EP23A presents multiple figures to describe the methodology and that information is combined into a single figure here. The EP23A approach depends on formation of a project team to ensure knowledge of the total examination process. In step 1, input information is collected and reviewed to assess requirements. In step 2, the process is mapped to identify possible failure modes, then the risk of each failure mode is estimated in step 3, prioritized for importance, and evaluated for acceptability in step 4. For high priority failure modes, step 5 initiates a risk control strategy to mitigate the effects. Recommended control mechanisms are identified in step 6 from the "QC Tool Box." The selected controls are then assembled together into a QCP in step 7.

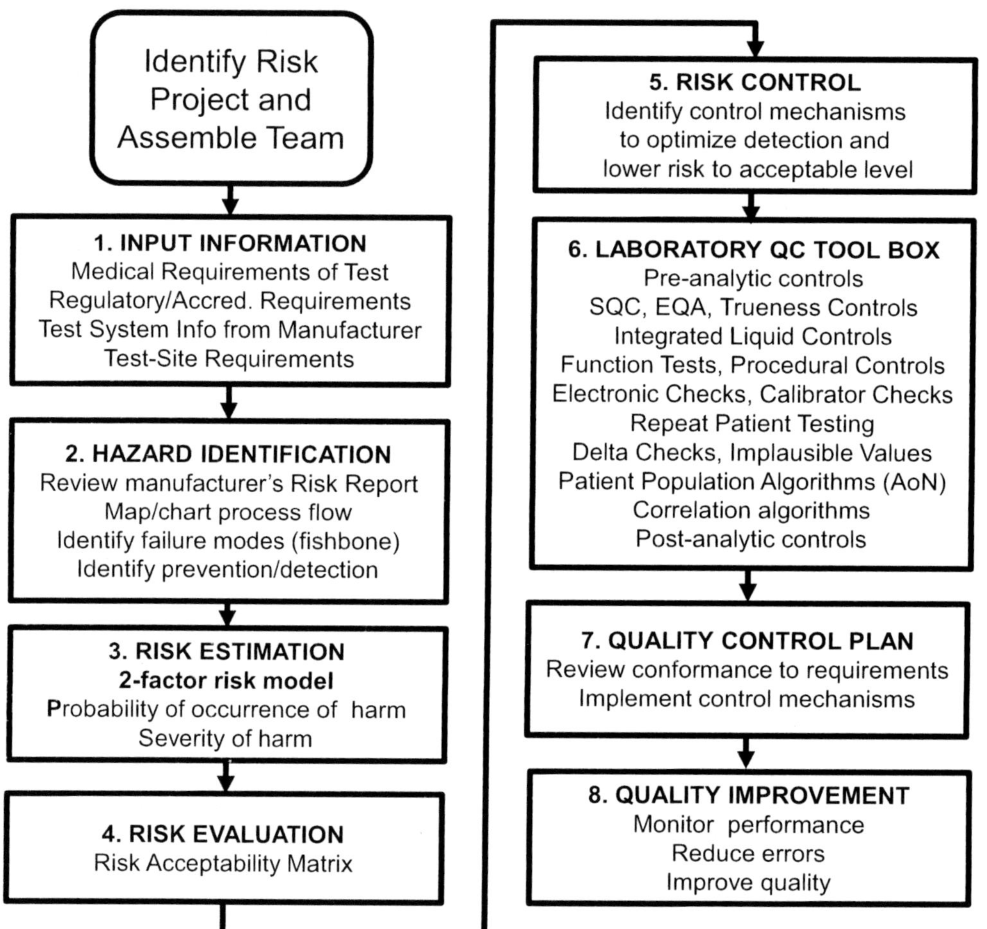

Figure 13-1. Description of the CLSI EP23A Process for Developing a Quality Control Plan (QCP) based on Risk Management ***(Note: this is our interpretation)****.*

Once implemented, performance of the total examination process is monitored (Step 8) to identify sources of errors and opportunities for improvement. Clearly, developing a QCP is a complicated task. The CLSI process is over-simplified and may lead to qualitative, even arbitrary, assessments of the need for different controls and the appropriate frequency for those controls.

In the US, CLIA regulations permit laboratories to implement "Individualized Quality Control Plans" (called IQCP) as one option for complying with regulatory requirements for quality control. US accreditation organizations, such as TJC, CAP, A2LA and COLA may adopt similar requirements as part of being "deemed" to inspect laboratories for regulatory compliance. The IQCP option became available to laboratories in 2014, but there will be an "education and transition period" of 2 years during which laboratories will *not* be cited as being out of compliance if they use EQC instead of IQCP. Remember, *no* IQCP is required if laboratories comply with the CLIA minimum "default" regulation to analyze 2 levels of controls per day for an examination procedure. Given the steep learning curve for risk management practices and procedures, laboratories will be well advised to meet the default requirement even when implementing a TQC, QCP, or IQCP, whichever term you choose to use.

6σQMS Policy. The laboratory shall formulate a Total Quality Control Plan (TQC Plan) to ensure the quality of the total examination process and shall include the analysis of a minimum of two levels of controls per day.

The inclusion of "a minimum of two levels of controls per day" is an important management strategy during the time when risk management concepts are being introduced to the medical laboratory. SQC provides a general control for the examination procedure and identifies many different failures that cause errors in test results. However, SQC by itself doesn't detect all error conditions. The advantage of a TQC Plan is to add other control mechanisms for specific purposes, e.g., inspection of samples for lipemia, icterus, and hemolysis. This is an important step for detecting sample conditions that may lead to invalid test results. The inspection can be a visual control by the analyst or a spectrophotometric control by the analyzer. Likewise, a review of test results to identify critical values is an important control for the post-examination process and should lead to both confirmation of the test result and immediate delivery of the test report.

It is desirable for medical laboratories to begin applying risk management techniques, but it is essential that they also adhere to the basics of analytical quality management. Risk management is NOT a substitute for selecting examination procedures on the basis of traceability and performance, validating the performance of examination procedures for their intended clinical use, and the design of SQC procedures to verify the attainment of the intended quality of test results. Risk management should add to these basic practices to solve specific problems or address specific failure modes.

6σQMS Process. The laboratory shall prioritize the use of control mechanisms in a TQC Plan on the basis of the documented sigma performance of the examination procedure and the potential failure modes of the total examination process.

Based on the observed sigma of the examination procedure, a general strategy is to prioritize the needs for SQC, other QC mechanisms, and the need for Quality Improvement (QI). Hi-sigma methods can rely on SQC, follow manufacturer's directions for use and preventive maintenance and other regulatory and accreditation requirements. Moderate-sigma methods need to balance SQC, other QC, and Quality Improvement. Quality Improvement here should focus on reducing any method bias and systematizing or automating operations to reduce variability. Low-sigma methods should employ SQC, but will need to depend more on other specific control mechanisms. One strategy may be to focus on Quality Improvement in order to move the method into a higher sigma category. Sometimes this may even mean changing methods and acquiring new analytic systems. Another strategy is to focus on other QC mechanisms, which is where the guidance from CLSI's EP23A on the use of risk management becomes useful.

The essence of risk management is to identify potential failure modes, assess the frequency or probability of occurrence, the severity of harm that could result, and the detection capability of controls. These 3 factors – occurrence, severity, and detection – should be evaluated and their overall impact assessed. In industrial applications, each factor is typically assessed on a scale from 1 to 10, then the scores multiplied together to give a Risk Priority Number (RPN = OCC*SEV*DET). This is done for each possible failure mode using a tool called Failure Mode and Effects Analysis (FMEA). The failure modes are then prioritized for mitigation, i.e., actions to lower or eliminate the risk of future failures and future errors.

In industry, the first priority for mitigation is Occurrence, then Detection, and finally Severity. Ideally Occurrence is mitigated by "design for safety" to eliminate failure-modes. Industry then discloses the "safety characteristics" that are achieved. For analytic systems, example safety characteristics are the imprecision and bias, i.e., the manufacturer's performance claims. Next industry focuses on Detection by building control mechanisms into the product or process, with the objective of identifying problems when they occur. Finally, industry deals with Severity by providing instructions for "safe use" and precautions for "use errors." For analytic systems, these may include types of specimens, reference ranges, cutoffs, etc., as well as recommendations for Quality Control.

For mitigating risks in a medical laboratory, the best guidance comes from Krouwer [3]. For Occurrence, a laboratory should attempt to prevent or reduce problems. For Detection, a laboratory should add or improve control mechanisms. For Severity, a laboratory should plan for recovery and disclosure when failures occur.

In dealing with Occurrence, however, laboratories are at a disadvantage; they are limited in their ability to make modifications to the examination procedures and analytical systems. Modification of a manufacturer's procedure and directions for use are not advised, particularly in US laboratories, since CLIA regulations do not allow laboratories to make changes to the manufacturer's directions for operation. If an examination procedure is modified, it is reclassified as "highly complex, " and the laboratory takes on additional responsibilities for managing quality. The main mitigation strategy for dealing with Occurrence is for the laboratory to assure that "safety characteristics" are satisfactory via method validation studies.

The second mitigation strategy in a laboratory is to add or improve control mechanisms to optimize detection. Detection is the main emphasis of the EP23A guidance and the purpose of developing a TQC Plan. The EP23A document suggests many possible control mechanisms available in the laboratory's "QC Tool Box". These include analyst and operator controls, manufacturer's built-in controls, use of controls, and use of patient samples for control purposes.

In assessing the usefulness of various controls, it is important to understand that controls are *not* created equal! For the various control mechanisms, there are differences in the control objectives, coverage, and detection. For example, one control might focus on proper operation, another on a particular analyzer component, another on analytical stability or systematic errors, and others on random errors. The coverage may different, from a single patient sample to an analytical run to multiple runs to a reagent or calibration lot. Finally, the detection capability of many controls is unknown, except for statistical quality control procedures and sometimes for patient data controls. This is a critical issue when developing a TQC Plan whose purpose is detection of medically important errors. It should not be assumed that running a control actually controls quality unless the detection characteristics are known and documented.

To mitigate severity, the laboratory's options include planning for recovery and disclosure of information for safety. Recovery means taking action following detection of a problem. This requires troubleshooting the problem, identifying the cause, making the necessary correction, and then verifying that performance is now acceptable. Disclosure relates to the information that the laboratory provides to aid the understanding of the test result. This is called "information for safety" in industrial terminology. In a laboratory, this may mean disclosing certain problems with specimens that limit the accuracy of test results, possible interferences in the test, guidance for interpretation of the test result, etc.

Given that whole books have been written about the application of risk management in medical laboratories [4,5], our approach here is to recommend the use of Six Sigma concepts and metrics to prioritize applications and control mechanisms. Six Sigma is inherently risk-driven with its focus on tolerance limits to define defects, its relationship to the process capability of the examination procedure, and its usefulness for identifying appropriate SQC procedures.

Figure 13-2 describes a process for formulating a TQC Plan on the basis of the sigma performance that has been documented for the examination procedure in a particular medical laboratory. First, to deal with occurrence, the laboratory should validate "safety characteristics" through method validation studies. Second, to deal with detection, the laboratory should prioritize the need for SQC versus other controls. For high-sigma methods, the laboratory can depend primarily on SQC. For low-sigma methods, risk analysis can identify specific controls appropriate for the analytic method. The laboratory should then assess the practicality and reliability of the various controls, assemble the list, and specify their frequency of use. Third, to deal with severity, the laboratory should specify how to recover from each failure and whether to disclose safety information. Finally, the TQC Plan should be evaluated. This means evaluation of the residual risks when all the controls are included. Then the laboratory must document the plan and implement the controls.

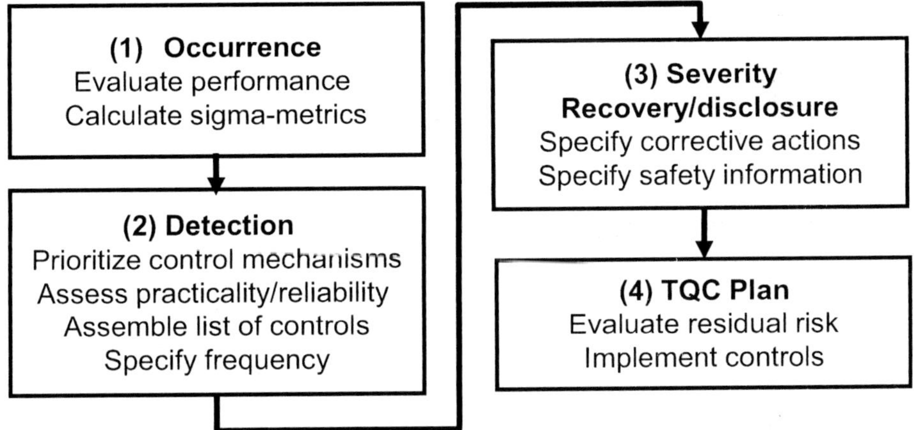

Figure 13-2. Sigma strategy for a Total Quality Control Plan (TQC Plan).

6σQMS Process. A TQC Plan should specify control mechanisms, frequency of controls, guidance for recovery, and disclosure of information for safety to ensure the quality of the total examination process.

The essentials of formulating a TQC Plan are to identify control mechanisms, specify their frequency or how often they are to be used, and provide directions for recovery and disclosure. Recovery is concerned with what to do when problems are detected. This means providing trouble-shooting guidelines and plans for corrective actions. Disclosure is concerned with providing any information that to assist in the safe use of the test results.

Control mechanisms. Figure 13-3 illustrates the mechanisms that might be included in a QC Plan. There could be analyst or operator controls, such as Standard Operating Procedures and operator training. There may also be operator checklists, maintenance schedules, and periodic assessment of operator competency. There could be built-in analyzer controls, such as electronic checks, function tests, process tests, and calibration checks. There should also be two levels of stable control materials for traditional statistical QC. There may also be certified reference materials used for "trueness controls" and periodic External Quality Assessment or Proficiency Testing will be required. Finally, there may be patient data controls such as "implausible values" and "delta checks."

TQC Plan	Frequency	Recovery	Disclosure
Analyst/operator controls			
Stand. Op. Procedure	Yearly SOP review	Director review	No
Operator training	Every operator	Supervisor review	No
Operator checklists	Daily	Supervisor review	No
System maintenance	Manuf. Schedule	Manuf. Repair	No
Operator competency	Yearly	Re-train	No
Pre-examination controls			
Inspect samples (ILH)	Every sample	Request new sample	Yes
Examination controls			
Electronic checks	Manuf.	Manuf. Instructions	No
Function tests	Manuf.	Manuf. Instructions	Sample Cond
Process tests	Manuf.	Manuf. Instructions	No
Calibration checks	Manuf./Reg.	Supervisor review	No
Statistical QC	Startup + Monitor	TS guidelines	No
Trueness control	Calibration	TS guidelines	No
Periodic EQA, PT	3/year	CA plan	No
Implausible values	Each test result	Repeat test	Call
Delta checks	Each test result	Repeat test	No
Post-examination controls			
Confirm/call crit values	Each critical test	Repeat test	Yes
Monitor TAT	Each STAT test	Call test result	Yes

Figure 13-3. Example of information that may be included in a laboratory Total Quality Control Plan.

Figure 13-4 shows a prioritization matrix that ranks the importance of various controls for methods with high sigma (≥5.5), moderate sigma (3.6 to 5.4), and low sigma (≤3.5). The different QC Tools are grouped as Analyst/Operator Controls, Built-in Analyzer Controls, Stable Control Materials, and Patient Data Analysis.

Recommended QC Tool	Sigma >5.5	Sigma 3.5-5.5	Sigma <3.5
Analyst/operator controls			
Stand. Op. Procedure	Essential	Essential	Essential
Operator training	High	High	High
Operator checklists	High	High	High
System maintenance	High	High	High
Operator competency	High	High	High
Built-in analyzer controls			
Electronic checks	Low	Moderate	High
Function tests	Low	Moderate	High
Process tests	Low	Moderate	High
Calibration checks	Low	Moderate	High
Integrated controls	Low	Moderate	High
Stable control materials			
Statistical QC	Essential	Essential+	Essential++
Frequency of QC	Low	Moderate	High
SQC with peer comparison	Low	Low	Low
Periodic EQA, PT	Regulatory	Regulatory	Regulatory
Trueness controls	Low	Low	Low
Patient data analysis			
Implausible values	High	High	High
Delta checks	Low	Moderate	High
Correlation algorithms	Low	Moderate	High
Repeat patient testing	Low	Moderate	High
Population statistics	Low	Moderate	High

Figure 13-4. Sigma priorities for inclusion of controls in Total Quality Control Plan.

- Analyst/operator controls consist of Standard Operating Procedures (SOPs), operator training, operator checklists, system maintenance, and operator competency. These controls have a high priority in all analytic quality systems.

- Built-in analyzer controls represent manufacturers' controls such as electronic checks, function tests, process tests, calibration checks, and integrated controls. Their priority is low when sigma is high, moderate for moderate sigma, and high priority when sigma is low.

- Stable control materials are used for SQC which is essential for all methods, though the frequency of controls should increase as sigma decreases. SQC with peer comparison is an "accuracy control" that has low utility because it does not generally provide immediate information about problems. Likewise, most PT and EQA programs (particularly in the US) provide only periodic information, but they are often regulatory requirements that are essential. "Trueness controls" represent reference materials with assigned values that are also analyzed infrequently.

- Patient data QC includes implausible values, delta checks, correlation algorithms, repeat patient testing, and population statistics. Implausible values have a high priority for all methods, whereas the need for other patient controls increases as sigma decreases.

The priority and balance of SQC and other controls should be based on your "Sigma TQC Strategy." SQC should always be included, then specific controls can be added on basis of risk analysis. Finally, pre-analytic and post-analytic controls can be added to monitor the total examination process. Detection is an important consideration. Is detection known or unknown? One of the major advantages of SQC is that detection *is known* and the control rules and number of control measurements can be selected to assure detection of medically important errors. Practicality is also important. The controls must be implementable in your laboratory.

Frequency of controls. There has been a lot of discussion of the probability of occurrence of various failure modes and how each might be addressed by various control mechanisms. The frequency of those controls must be defined in the TQC Plan, as discussed earlier. For built-in controls, frequency is usually established by the manufacturer. Some controls, such as patient sample indices, evaluate each sample. Others continuously monitor instrument functions and generate conditional flags when appropriate.

For laboratory controls, frequency should be guided by the schedule of known events, as well as the expected occurrence of unscheduled events, even unknown unscheduled events. An "event" refers to a change in operating conditions or procedures. For example, the daily startup of an analytic system often involves preparing and loading new reagents, calibrating the measurement procedure, then loading patient samples for analysis. System startup involves many changes from earlier operation, thus it is an event that should be checked by controls. Likewise, system maintenance, any interruption in service that requires changes to reagents or components, new lots of reagents and calibrators, and even new operators are events that should influence the frequency of controls. Known and scheduled events can be readily addressed in the plan.

Unknown events require careful consideration of the possible consequences if failures occur in the middle of ongoing operations. One major consideration is the number of patient samples that might be compromised and require repeat analyses. For example, is it safe to test controls only at the beginning of an analytic run, two levels once a day, as required by the US CLIA regulations, even though the analyzer continuously reports results for the rest of the day? Or should controls be distributed throughout the analytic run and results reported only at the end of the run, as in batch operation? Clearly, the mode of operation – continuous versus batch – should influence the frequency of controls and the intervals for reporting or releasing test results. Safe operation for the continuous release of test results dictates a startup SQC design at the beginning of the analytic run and a monitor SQC design periodically throughout the analytic run. Guidance in this area is evolving, as shown by the work of Parvin [8].

Recovery. There has been little emphasis on recovery, except by Krouwer [3] (see also www.krouwerconsulting.com). Given that the focus of the TQC Plan is on detection, it is critical to define what can be done for corrective action, or recovery, i.e., what should the analyst do when a particular failure is detected. Ideally, the problem should be corrected and the patient samples re-analyzed under in-control conditions before reporting the test results. Some delay will be incurred, but the corrective action will prevent the more serious consequences from erroneous test results.

In many laboratories, the practice is simply to repeat the controls (without any corrective action) until their results fall back within the control limits. This repeat-repeat practice is harmful to both the patient and the laboratory. It usually arises because SQC procedures have not been properly designed to employ the right control rules (limits) and right number of control measurements. Often 2s control limits are being used with a minimum of 2 controls, giving a false rejection rate of nearly 10% even when the method is operating normally and without error. Under these conditions, it's no wonder that analysts and operators lose confidence in the control system and pay less attention to correcting problems. Thus, for recovery to be successful, the first requirement is to employ the proper SQC design. The second requirement is to provide directions for corrective actions as part of the Analytic QC Plan so analysts and operators know what to do in response to out-of-control signals.

Disclosure. Remember, the idea here is to convey information that is critical for the safe use of a laboratory test result. Sometimes the safest information is to *not* report a test result, even though that may trigger unfavorable responses and behaviors from physicians and patients, e.g., not reporting a potassium result on a hemolyzed sample because it is known the result will be too high, or not reporting a glucose result on a sample that was not promptly removed from the cells because it is known that the result will be too low. In some cases, the test result may be qualified by identifying potential hazardous conditions that may affect the result. For example, there may be known interferences for patients with certain treatments and certain drugs. A large database of such interfering materials has been developed by Young [9] and can be implemented in a laboratory information system to automatically provide information for safe use. Otherwise, specific directions must be provided for specific disclosures that should accompany the reporting of a test result.

In addition to specific information that relates to an individual patient sample and test result, there should be general disclosures of reference intervals, cutoffs, and expected ranges for patient conditions. There are recommendations for flagging reported test results to indicate their change from previous results and whether such changes represent a real change in patient status, taking into account both the measurement and biologic variability [10]. For example, Fraser has devised a reporting system that "flags" results as follows: > higher than reference limit; < lower than reference limit; >>higher than reference limit and clinically important; << lower than reference limit and clinically important; * significant change (95% confidence level); ** highly significant change (99% confidence level). These latter two flags relate to the calculation of a "reference change value" that takes into account both analytical variation and within-subject biological variation.

6σQMS Process. The laboratory should implement multi-stage SQC designs to ensure quality throughout the analytic run.

Defining the frequency of SQC is still a difficult issue that requires considerable judgment. Guidance can be found in CLSI C24A3 – Statistical QC for quantitative measurement procedures [7]. This guidance defines a quality control strategy as *"the number of control materials, the number of measurements to be made on those materials, the location of those materials in an analytical run, and the statistical quality control rules applied."* In addition, the document describes "run length" which relates to how often controls should be analyzed.

Some of the important characteristics that are to be considered in defining run length are identified in this statement from C24A3.

> *"For purposes of quality control, the laboratory must consider the stability of the analytical testing process, its susceptibility to problems that may occur, and the risk associated with undetected error."*

There are 3 important characteristics – stability, susceptibility, and risk. Stability relates to how long the process is expected to operate without problems. Susceptibility relates to the problems that may arise and lead to erroneous test results being produced. Risk is concerned with the impact of erroneous test results on patient care. Run length is related to the frequency of analyzing controls. According to C24A3:

- *"the length of the analytical run must be defined appropriately for the specific analytical system and specific measurement procedure... In laboratory operations, control samples should be analyzed during each analytical run to monitor method performance... The laboratory should consider many factors, such as the number of patient samples, the cost of re-analysis, workflow patterns, operator competency, criticality of tests, and impact of errors."*

- An analytical run is defined as *"interval or period of time or series of measurements during which the accuracy and precision of the measurement procedure is expected to be stable; between which events may occur causing the measurement process to be more susceptible (i.e., greater risk) to error that are important to detect."*

Again, the important characteristics are stability, susceptibility, and risk. Plus, an important concept is the "events" that may occur and cause changes in the performance of the measurement process. Events turn out to be the key to a practical understanding of run length and the frequency of SQC. There are "expected events" that are known, scheduled, and expected changes in the operation of the measurement procedure. There are also unexpected events, or unexpected changes in the operation of the measurement process, as already noted earlier, by Parvin[8].

Here's a strategy for determining how often to analyze controls. For expected events, the SQC design should be based on the right rules and right number of control measurements to detect medically important errors. Controls should be analyzed whenever an "event" occurs that requires validation of the testing process. For unexpected events, controls should be analyzed periodically to monitor the process during routine operation.

For additional guidance, the principles of risk management are useful. Risk management provides a methodology for identifying possible "unexpected events" and ranking their importance. It begins by asking what changes or failures might occur, then considers the probability of failure, and the severity of harm from such a failure. Next it considers what control mechanisms could be implemented to detect failures, assesses the frequency for application of those control mechanisms, and identifies the corrective actions that should follow.

A practical strategy for setting SQC frequency is suggested here:

- Regulatory compliance provides the minimum requirement – for example, US CLIA rules require 2 levels of control materials be analyzed every day.
- To this minimum, the laboratory should add "Event QC", i.e., analyze controls to assess the significance of known or expected changes in the testing process.
- Then, the laboratory should consider "Unexpected Events" and add QC periodically to monitor the process during routine operation.

These different phases of operation may require implementation of different SQC designs, or multi-stage SQC that includes a "startup design" and a "monitor design". The "startup design" should fulfill the need to verify the attainment of the quality required for the intended use of the test results. The "monitor" design may employ single controls and simple control rules, such as 1_{3s}, to detect unexpected events.

What's the point?

The laboratory community is at a very early stage of risk-based quality control. It is difficult to provide specific guidance and practical procedures, particularly when guidelines are vague and regulations have not been directly issued. Attempts to simplify risk management will probably result in qualitative and subjective assessments. Quantitative and objective assessments are possible with the application of Six Sigma principles and the characterization of risk in terms of defect rates, as outlined in our book, *Six Sigma Risk Analysis* [4]. (The fact that it takes an entire book to describe a proper approach for risk-based quality control plans is evidence of the complexity.) There's a great need for education and training for laboratory analysts. We advise labs to proceed cautiously.

In a medical laboratory, implementation of a TQC Plan will depend on the particular analytic and information systems available. The implementation of built-in controls depends on the manufacturer and the implementation of SQC and patient data QC procedures depends on the computer support and resources of the laboratory. Those considerations should be part of the earlier assessment of feasibility of different control mechanisms. At the point where a TQC Plan has been defined, the capabilities for implementation should have already been established, or acquisition of those capabilities should already be underway. Implementation will be a unique process in each laboratory because of the particular characteristics of the analytic system and the information processing system.

In the dawn of this new age of risk management, the laboratory should not abandon its most proven practices for managing the analytical quality of examination procedures. The laboratory must plan QC with care, beginning with the definition of the quality needed for the intended medical use or clinical application of the test. Examination procedures must be validated for their intended use to ensure patient safety. Next, the SQC design should account for the imprecision and bias observed for the measurement procedure. It should also account for the known performance characteristics of the SQC procedure, i.e., error detection and false rejection. Finally, the frequency of SQC should account for expected and unexpected events. Expected events are those known changes that occur and require validation that the testing process still operates properly. Unexpected events are unknown changes that must be detected by periodic monitoring or by specific controls implemented as part of a TQC Plan.

References

1. ISO 14971. Medical devices – Applications of risk management to medical devices. ISO, Geneva, 2007.
2. CLSI EP23A. Laboratory Quality Control Based on Risk Management. Wayne PA:Clinical and Laboratory Standards Institute, 2011.
3. Krouwer JS. Managing risk in hospitals: Using integrated fault trees and failure modes and criticality analysis. Washington DC: AACC Press, 2004.
4. Westgard JO. Six Sigma Risk Analysis: Designing analytic QC Plans for the medical laboratory. Madison WI:Westgard QC, Inc., 2011.
5. Westgard JO, Westgard SA eds. Quality Control in the Age of Risk Management. Clinics in Laboratory Medicine. Philidelphia:Elsevier 2013:33(1).
6. ISO 15189. Medical laboratories – Requirements for quality and competence. ISO, Geneva, 2012.
7. CLSI C24A3. Statistical quality control for quantitative measurement procedures. Clinical and Laboratory Standards Institute, Wayne PA, 2006.
8. Parvin C. Assessing the impact of the frequency of quality control testing on the quality of reported patient results. Clin Chem 2008;54:2049-2054.
9. Young DS. Effects of drugs on clinical laboratory tests. Washington DC:AACC Press, 2000.
10. Fraser CG. Biological Variation: From Principles to Practice. Washington DC:AACC Press, 2001.

14. Monitoring Nonconformities

The implementation of a Six Sigma Quality System and Total Quality Control Plans (TQC Plan) requires a thorough approach for monitoring nonconformities to identify weaknesses in the control system that can be targeted for improvement. ISO 15189 [1] provides strong guidance in this area:

- ***4.9 Identification and control of nonconformities.*** *The laboratory shall have a documented procedure to identify and manage nonconformities in any aspect of the quality management system, including pre-examination, examination or post-examination processes.* Nonconformity is defined as the *"nonfulfillment of a requirement."* More commonly, a nonconformity means an error, an adverse event, an incident, or an occurrence where a customer's requirement for quality is not achieved. The industrial term is defect or defective result. The laboratory shall identify such nonconformities and take actions to control their consequences. The laboratory should identify the responsibility and authority for handling nonconformities, the actions to be taken particularly to halt analytic testing and deal with erroneous test reports when necessary.

- ***4.10 Corrective actions.*** *The laboratory should take corrective action to eliminate causes of nonconformities.* The laboratory should have a procedure for reviewing nonconformities, determining root causes, implementing corrective actions, recording such actions, and monitoring their effectiveness.

- ***4.11 Preventive actions.*** *The laboratory should take preventive action to eliminate the causes of potential nonconformities in order to prevent their occurrence.* While corrective actions are a response to observed nonconformities, preventive actions are based on a review of data and information with the objective of identifying potential causes of nonconformities. This may involve trend analysis of Quality Indicators as well as formal risk analysis to identify possible failure-modes.

- ***4.12 Continual improvement.*** *The laboratory should continually improve the effectiveness of the quality management system, including the pre-examination, examination and post-examination processes...* The laboratory shall monitor the effectiveness of its QMS with the objectives of making improvements in its testing processes as well as the QMS itself. Improvement activities should be prioritized based on risk assessment, action plans should be developed and implemented, and the effectiveness of improvements should be monitored and controlled. *Laboratory management shall ensure that the laboratory participates in continual improvement activities that encompass relevant areas and outcomes of patient care. When the continual improvement programme identifies opportunities for improvement, laboratory management shall address them regardless of where they occur. Laboratory management shall communicate to staff improvement plans and related goals.*

6σQMS Policy. The laboratory shall monitor performance of the total examination process to identify non-conformities and defective results and prioritize problems for corrective action, preventive actions, and quality improvement.

In industry, this monitoring is often performed as part of a Failure Reporting and Corrective Action System, commonly called FRACAS. After performing a FMEA on the design of a product, the performance of the product is then monitored in the field to collect data on the actual failures that occur. That data will lead to actual figures for frequency of occurrence that can be used to provide new estimates of risk based on the real performance of the product, rather than on expected performance figures in the FMEA. FRACAS and FMEA are therefore complementary tools: FMEA is used in the design of a product or process to minimize risks, whereas FRACAS is used to monitor the actual performance and characterize the real risks that are observed.

CLSI EP18 [2] discusses FRACAS, which is defined as follows:

- *Failure Reporting and Corrective Action System (FRACAS) – a process by which failures are identified and analyzed so that corrective actions can be implemented back into the process.*

Those last few words – *back into the process* – are a bit awkward, but their meaning is that improvements are to be made to the process to further mitigate the risks that have been observed. For manufacturers, this means revisiting the risk mitigation options, eliminating the occurrence when possible, adding controls to detect the failures if necessary, and informing customers of these changes and their expected impact. For laboratories, the mitigation strategies are more limited and often focus on optimizing the control mechanisms to improve detection in order to facilitate recovery, or corrective actions.

CLSI EP23A [3] describes post-implementation monitoring of a Risk-Based QC Plan in the context of CAPA (Corrective Actions and Preventive Actions).

> *As part of its quality management system, a laboratory should establish a surveillance system for monitoring the effectiveness of the QCP over time. Unacceptable performance will trigger an investigation to identify the root cause and appropriate modification of the QCP. This surveillance should be part of the CAPA process. In addition, identification of opportunities to reduce acceptable risks even further is part of the CQI program for the laboratory.*

Likewise, ISO 22367 [4] casts risk analysis as a natural and logical part of a laboratory's quality management system and management's responsibility for corrective and preventive actions, e.g., *laboratory management should prepare a plan for investigation and prevention/correction of any non-conformity, error, or incident identified in an FMEA or observed in another way.*

FRACAS and CAPA are similar, but FRACAS seems to extend naturally from FMEA applications, with the primary difference being how occurrence is determined. In the case of FMEA, occurrence is very subjective; for FRACAS, occurrence should be determined from the observed failures under real operating conditions. In that way, FRACAS provides a clearer focus on the monitoring of failures, particularly those failures that have already been identified in the FMEA. Any other failures that are observed would also be included, but the list from the FMEA provides guidance for the type of monitors, or quality indicators, that should be implemented.

6σQMS Process. The laboratory shall identify failures and defective results using data collected from SQC records, peer comparison programs, external PT/EQA programs, and selected Quality Indicators.

Recall that one aspect of risk analysis is to make sure that the analytic testing process performs up to specifications, which is part of *quality by design*. Validation of performance specifications is an early step in the analytical quality management process and should also be an ongoing process after the implementation of the Six Sigma Quality Management System and TQC Plans. Some of the control mechanisms in the TQC Plan provide long-term monitors of performance, rather than short-term indicators of failures. This category includes monthly review of QC data, peer-comparison programs, External Quality Assessment (EQA) and Proficiency Testing (PT), trueness controls, as well as periodic evaluation of operator competency.

SQC. Periodic review allows laboratories to make assessment of precision and observe changes or trends over time. While trends in the mean may also be observed, it is difficult to assign the cause of such changes without additional data or information. If conducted in conjunction with a peer comparison program, changes in the mean may be traced to changes in method bias or instability of the control material itself. In addition, the laboratory review of monthly SQC data should identify the number and types of failures and the effectiveness of the corrective actions.

Peer comparison. Programs typically involve a month's worth of control data to estimate the imprecision and bias of a method relative to a comparative or "peer" method. That time period would generally include a minimum of 20 to 30 control measurements for an analyte in a month and could be considerably higher, which facilitates good estimates of precision, as well as good estimates of bias versus other comparative methods. Such programs are often provided by the manufacturers of control materials to allow individual laboratories to assess their performance against a group of laboratories using the same lot number of control material.

EQA or PT. All US regulatory and accreditation programs require participation in EQA/PT as an external monitor of quality.

Testing surveys occur a few times per year and involve a handful of samples for each event. For example, the US PT requirements are 3 events per year with 5 samples/event for regulated analytes or 2 events per year with 2 samples/event for non-regulated analytes. That translates to a maximum of 5 measurements per event and 15 measurements per year, which limits the reliability of EQA or PT to assess bias. The samples are usually at different concentrations and laboratories are usually limited to making one measurement per sample, which makes it impossible to distinguish systematic and random errors. By taking an average of the differences between the individual samples and their respective means, an estimate of bias can be made, but it is not very reliable.

Quality Indicators. In addition to these measures of performance, there is a need for specific Quality Indicators that address institutional goals for quality, regulatory and accreditation guidelines, as well as public and private agencies that monitor quality in healthcare. Examples of additional indicators are provided by The Joint Commission (TJC) patient safety goals and the College of American Pathologists (CAP) Q-Probes and Q-Trends. Many of these indicators focus on pre-analytic and post-analytic processes, e.g., patient identification, order accuracy, clinical utility and appropriateness of tests, adherence to national practice guidelines, physician satisfaction, and clinical outcomes. CLSI provides guidance for selecting and implementing Quality Indicators in GP35A [6].

6σQMS Procedure. Identification of Quality Indicators to monitor performance of the total examination process.

Here is a starting point for considering the kind of data that should be collected to monitor the failures of a laboratory testing process:

- Specimen and sample conditions
    - Incorrect identification/specimen labeling problems, Number of hemolyzed samples, Number of clotted samples, Number of samples with inadequate volume
- Analyzer problems
    - Number of runs rejected

        - Types of failures, such as Reagent degradation, Calibration, Control degradation, Hardware failure, Software failure, Inadequate maintenance, Operator errors, and Adverse environmental conditions
    - Number of patient error conditions
        - Delta check errors, Correlation check errors, Reportable range problems, Panic values called
    - Instrument flags and error messages
- Turnaround time (TAT)
    - TAT Distributions, TAT limits for 95% of samples, STAT, priority, and routine service
- Customer Complaints
    - Department/source, Specimen/sample problems, Turnaround time, Analytic quality, Other service conditions

Your lab should customize its own QI list. The effectiveness of these monitors will depend on the thoroughness of the data collection and the capabilities for accessing and analyzing that data. Ideally, these data should be collected in the Laboratory's Information System and periodic reports should be provided for review by analysts, quality specialists, managers, and directors.

6σQMS Process. The laboratory shall measure nonconformities as defects per million and express quality on the Sigma scale.

For examination procedures, the methodology on the right side of Figure 14-1 has been employed in earlier chapters. It uses estimates of process variation and predicts the number of defects. This methodology fits naturally for analytical quality because laboratories have information about the variation for each examination in terms of precision and bias. Sigma can then be calculated as (TE_a – Bias)/SD where all terms are in concentration units, or (%TE_a – %Bias)/%CV where all terms are in percent. The calculated Sigma-metric is considered to be a "long-term" sigma because the calculation includes a measure of bias, rather than an assumption that bias may be equivalent to 1.5 SD for "short-term" sigma.

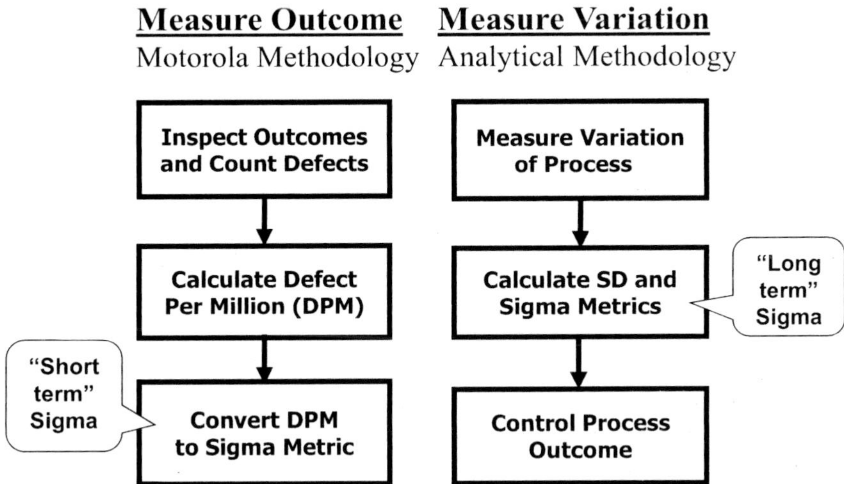

Figure 14-1. Comparison of "counting methodology" and "variation methodology" for determining Sigma.

For pre-examination and post-examination procedures where data on nonconformities can be collected, quality on the Sigma scale can be estimated by following the Motorola counting methodology shown on the left-side of Figure 14-1. Six Sigma was developed and promoted by Motorola for use in manufacturing where a product is inspected to determine whether or not it meets specifications. The quality of the process is determined by counting the non-conformities or defects, calculating Defects Per Million (DPM), then converting DPM to a Sigma-metric by use of a standard DPM/Sigma table (following the Motorola methodology that makes use of a "short-term" sigma that accommodates shifts equivalent to 1.5s). This counting methodology is particularly appropriate for pre-examination and post-examination processes where you can inspect the outcome and count the defects.

6σQMS Procedure. Calculation of sigma quality from DPMs for nonconformities.

Application of the counting methodology for pre-examination and post-examination processes was first described for medical laboratories by Nevelainen and Berte in 2000 [7]. The methodology is based on inspection of outcomes or the review of records where non-conformities can be identified and counted.

Directions for calculation of DPM and conversion to a Sigma metric

1. Identify the performance characteristic that is to be monitored.
2. Specify a quality requirement for conformance.
   a. Requirement should be considered a 95% limit
   b. Consultation with customers may provide an objective requirement
3. Identify data sources or a prospective experimental protocol for collecting information about the characteristics of interest.
4. Identify the nonconformities where the characteristics of interest does not satisfy the requirement that has been defined.
5. Count the number of nonconformities and the total number of opportunities.
6. Calculate % Defects and Defects per Million (DPM)
   a. % Defects = (nonconformities/total opportunities)*100
   b. DPM = (nonconformities/total opportunities)*10^6
7. Use a sigma conversion table to relate DPM to sigma.
   a. Standard practice is to use the column for "short term" sigma
   b. Interpolate between DPM values as necessary to estimate sigma

Example Application: Sigma calculations for Turnaround Times (TAT).

To illustrate the application of "counting defects", let us consider the example of turnaround time (TAT). Assume that the tolerance interval is defined as 1 hour for emergency orders. Data involves recording the appropriate times from origination of orders to return of test results, then inspecting those records and counting the number of defective results, i.e., those TATs that are longer than 1 hour. That number of defects is divided by the total number of records inspected, then expressed as Defects Per Million (DPM). Finally, the DPM/Sigma conversion table shown in Table 14-2 [8] can be used to express quality on the sigma scale.

In Table 14-2, columns 1 and 2 are used when applying the standard Motorola counting methodology. Column 3 considers "centering" and the estimation of bias, rather than assuming biases up to 1.5s. Column 4 represents process "yield", which is related to % of results that are acceptable. A process that produces a 99% yield has a 1% defect rate. In cases where error figures are given in terms of %, it is simpler to calculate 100 minus % errors to provide % Yield to access the table. Finally, column 5 gives Cpk, which is not an enzyme measurement, but rather a measure of "process capability" long used in industry: Cpk can be multiplied by 3 to calculate Sigma.

A process that performs at Six Sigma is considered World Class Quality. Minimum acceptable process performance in industry is 3-sigma. Airline baggage handling is approximately 4-sigma and has actually gotten worse in the last ten years since these benchmarks were first published. Typical business processes are expected to perform at the 4-sigma level.

Table 14-2. Six Sigma Defects-Per-Million Table

DPM	Sigma Short Term	Sigma Long Term	Yield	Cpk
3	6	4.5	99.99966	2
5	5.9	4.4	99.99946	1.97
9	5.8	4.3	99.99915	1.93
13	5.7	4.2	99.9987	1.9
21	5.6	4.1	99.9979	1.87
32	5.5	4	99.9968	1.83
48	5.4	3.9	99.995	1.8
72	5.3	3.9	99.993	1.77
108	5.2	3.7	99.989	1.73
159	5.1	3.6	99.984	1.7
233	5	3.5	99.98	1.67
337	4.9	3.4	99.97	1.63
483	4.8	3.3	99.95	1.6
687	4.7	3.2	99.93	1.57
968	4.6	3.1	99.90	1.53
1,350	4.5	3	99.87	1.5
1,866	4.4	2.9	99.81	1.47
2,555	4.3	2.8	99.74	1.43
3,467	4.2	2.7	99.65	1.4
4.661	4.1	2.6	99.5	1.37
6,210	4	2.5	99.4	1.33
8,198	3.9	2.4	99.2	1.3
10,724	3.8	2.3	98.9	1.27
13,903	3.7	2.2	98.6	1.23
17,864	3.6	2.1	98.2	1.2
22,750	3.5	2	97.7	1.17
28,716	3.4	1.9	97.1	1.13
35,930	3.3	1.8	96.4	1.1
44,565	3.2	1.7	95.5	1.07
54,799	3.1	1.6	94.5	1.03
66,807	3	1.5	93.3	1

DPM	Sigma Short Term	Sigma Long Term	Yield	Cpk
80,757	2.9	1.4	91.9	0.97
96,801	2.8	1.3	90.3	0.93
115,070	2.7	1.2	88.5	0.9
135,666	2.6	1.1	86.4	0.87
158,655	2.5	1	84.1	0.83
184,060	2.4	0.9	81.6	0.8
211,855	2.3	0.8	78.8	0.77
241,964	2.2	0.7	75.8	0.73
274,253	2.1	0.6	72.6	0.7
308,538	2	0.5	69.1	0.67
344,578	1.9	0.4	65.5	0.63
382,089	1.8	0.3	61.8	0.6
420,740	1.7	0.2	57.9	0.57
460,172	1.6	0.1	54.0	0.53
500,000	1.5	0	50.0	0.5
539,828	1.4	-0.1	46.0	0.47
579,260	1.3	-0.2	42.1	0.43
617,911	1.2	-0.3	38.2	0.4
655,422	1.1	-0.4	34.5	0.37
691,462	1	-0.5	30.9	0.33
725,747	0.9	-0.6	27.4	0.30
758,036	0.8	-0.7	24.2	0.27
788,145	0.7	-0.8	21.2	0.23
815,940	0.6	-0.9	18.4	0.20
841,345	0.5	-1	15.9	0.17
864,334	0.4	-1.1	13.6	0.13
884,930	0.3	-1.2	11.5	0.10
903,199	0.2	-1.3	9.7	0.07
919,243	0.1	-1.4	8.1	0.03
933,193	0	-1.5	6.7	0.00

Figure 14-3 shows a comparison of quality in terms of % Acceptable, % Defectives, defects per million (DPM), and Sigma. Laboratories commonly express defects in terms of percent, as shown in the second column. That figure must be multiplied by 10,000 to convert to DPM, as shown in the third column. Then DPM is converted to Sigma using Table 14-2. Find the DPM figure in the first column of the table, then look up the Sigma-metric in the second column. A 5% error rate, which doesn't sound terribly bad to laboratories, corresponds to a Sigma of 3.15, which is not considered very good. A 1% error rate, which usually sounds pretty good, corresponds to a Sigma of 3.95, which borders on what is expected from standard business processes. An error rate of 0.1%, which sounds like excellent performance, corresponds to a sigma of 4.6, which is good, but not yet World Class. To achieve World Class quality, we need to aim for error rates that are better than 0.01%.

%Acceptable	%Defective	DPM	Sigma
90.0%	10.0%	100,000	2.75 s
95.0%	5.0%	50,000	3.15 s
98.0%	2.0%	20,000	3.55 s
99.0%	1.0%	10,000	3.95 s
99.5%	0.5%	5,000	4.15 s
99.9%	0.1%	1,000	4.60 s
99.95%	0.05%	500	4.75 s
99.99%	0.01%	100	5.20 s

Figure 14-3. Relationship between % Acceptable, % Defective, Defects Per Million (DPM) and Sigma.

This counting methodology seems simple, but requires inspection of a high number of "items" to provide a reliable estimate. Guidance for sample size can be provided by calculating the 95% confidence range for estimating sigma for an expected defect rate. For example, if the defect rate is expected to be about 1%, then a sample size of 100 items would provide a 95% range of estimates of sigma from 3.4 to 6.0 sigma. That clearly is not precise enough to be useful.

Increasing sample size to 1,000 items would give a confidence range of 3.65 to 4.1 sigma. That might be sufficient for laboratory applications. To get more exact estimates, a sample size of 10,000 items would assure that a reliable estimate of sigma is obtained between 3.75 to 3.9 sigma. It is also important to recognize that as defect rates get lower, more samples are needed.

Thus, the counting methodology is simple, but requires the inspection of a *lot* of data to provide a reliable estimate.

Measuring quality on the Six Sigma scale provides a better perspective for understanding the quality being achieved by the system. As shown for TAT, an error rate of 0.01% corresponded to a sigma of 5.2. To approach World Class Quality requires less than 0.001% errors, which corresponds to 5.75 sigma. Compare that perspective to today's common thinking in healthcare organizations and medical laboratories, where 5% errors are often considered acceptable and 1% errors thought to be really good performance. However, those levels of errors represent only 3 to 4 sigma quality. Much lower error rates must be achieved to provide truly reliable services.

What's the point?

It is important to recognize that Sigma-metrics can describe the quality of pre- and post-examination processes. The "counting methodology" is simple to apply, but requires significant data to get precise estimates. You need access to a DPM/Sigma table, but that can be found in any Six Sigma textbook as well as online.

The "variation methodology" is uniquely applicable for analytic processes. It is a predictive methodology, which means it assumes that the process remains under stable operation (a reasonable assumption for method validation studies). Sigma-metrics also provide guidance for the selection and design of SQC procedures, which are essential for daily management of quality in a medical laboratory. Thus the reliability of the predicted Sigma depends on providing the appropriate QC to detect unstable performance. Sigma also clarifies priorities for improvements in the laboratory. Low-sigma processes are the best candidates for applications of risk management, as well as quality improvement.

Specific failure modes that show an increased occurrence should be targeted by changes in the TQC Plan. This will involve investigating the root causes and considering the redesign or risk mitigation options. In effect, the data from monitoring failures and measuring performance powers the feedback loop for SQC redesign, the impact of new risk factors, or revised estimates of risks, the TQC strategy, and the TQC Plan.

Fundamental improvements in examination processes often depend on new technology, which might include new analyzers, SQC software, middleware, new LIS programs, new HIS reports, etc. Other mechanisms for short-term improvements may include improving operator checklists and increasing maintenance to reduce occurrence, increasing the frequency of controls and improving the SQC design to improve detection, and improving trouble-shooting guides to support recovery and corrective actions. All of these improvements will require in-service training to maintain and advance the skills of laboratory analysts and operators.

References

1. ISO 15189. Medical laboratories – Requirements for quality and competence. ISO, Geneva, 2012.
2. CLSI EP18A2. Risk Management Techniques to Identify and Control Laboratory Error Sources. Clinical Laboratory Standards Institute, Wayne, PA, 2009.
3. CLSI EP23A. Laboratory Quality Control Based on Risk Management. Clinical Laboratory Standards Institute, Wayne, PA, 2011.
4. ISO/TC 22367. Medical laboratories – Reduction of error through risk management and continual improvement. ISO, Geneva, 2008.
5. CLSI EP15A2(e). User Validation of Performance for Precision and Trueness. Clinical Laboratory Standards Institute, Wayne, PA, 2010.
6. CLSI GP35A. Development and use of quality indicators for process improvement and monitoring of laboratory quality. Clinical Laboratory Standards Institute, Wayne, PA, 2010.
7. Nevelainen D, Berte L, et al. Evaluating laboratory performance on quality indicators with the six sigma scale. Arch Pathol Lab Med 2000;124:516-519.
8. Westgard JO. Six Sigma Quality Design & Control, 2nd ed. Madison, WI:Westgard QC, 2006.

15. Measuring the Uncertainty of Measurements

An important issue in measuring quality is the ISO 15189 [1] guidance to determine measurement uncertainty (MU). The authoritative reference on MU is the *Guide to the expression of uncertainty in measurement*, otherwise known as GUM [2]. The GUM approach usually emphasizes identifying the many factors that contribute to the variation of measurement results, then characterizing the variance of each of those factors and combining those variances to describe the uncertainty in the final test result. This approach is also described as a "bottom up" methodology. In contrast, there is also a "top down" methodology where the estimates of variation come directly from experimental data, such as method validation experiments or routine quality control data. In laboratories it is more practical to implement a "top-down" approach to estimate MU from the laboratory's own performance data. There has been much debate about the proper methodology for determining measurement uncertainty, particularly whether or not to include an estimate of method bias along with method imprecision to express the expected total error of the examination procedure [3].

CLSI also provides guidance in document C51A that was also published in 2012 [4]. In looking at C51A, the bigger half of this 55 page document is devoted to the "bottom-up" methodology, which is appropriate for manufacturers who want to identify and evaluate the many individual factors that contribute to the total variation in order to be able to isolate and reduce individual sources if necessary. For those who are stimulated by pages of mathematical equations, this provides interesting reading. For others who are interested in the simpler "top-down" methodology, it will be useful to focus on section 7 (pages 28-31) and Appendix B (pages 53-55). The "top down" methodology is more suitable for medical laboratories where the interest is mainly to characterize the variation that will be expected in the final test results, which can be directly estimated from QC data.

Review of MU Concepts and Approaches

The most readable discussions of MU are papers by White. As stated by White [5], the basic parameter of MU is the SD. The top-down approach depends primarily on obtaining a reliable and realistic estimate of the method's SD or CV. C51A recommends long-term QC data. This refers to QC results on control materials that are analyzed repeatedly over a long period of time. Typically two or three different control materials are used to monitor performance at critical medical decision concentrations. If these QC results are obtained over a period of several months, they can be expected to reflect the contributions of different lots of reagents, calibrations, different lots of calibrators, analyzer pipetting, temperature stability, sensor stability, different operators, different operating conditions, etc., thus providing a realistic estimate of random error that affects the variability of laboratory measurements. We can debate the number of months, but it would be reasonable to consider 3 to 6 months of QC data as recommended in C24A3 for cumulative control limits [6].

In addition to the variability from random error, there is the possibility of systematic error, or bias. Bias may be estimated by analysis of certified reference materials, comparison of patient results between methods (comparison of methods experiment), or from an External Quality Assessment or Proficiency Testing program. Any estimate of bias has its own inherent uncertainty that depends on the experimental conditions. The uncertainty in the estimate of bias should be included in MU, regardless of whether or not bias is corrected. White has described this in practical terms, as follows [5]:

> *In practice, bias correction and replicate measurements can reduce, but not completely eliminate systematic and random errors, and therefore total error cannot be exactly known. It follows that the true value of a measured quantity cannot be exactly known either. This assumption is fundamental to the MU approach. The MU concept also assumes that if the bias of a procedure is known, then steps are taken to minimize it, e.g., by re-calibration. However, because the bias value cannot be known exactly, an uncertainty will be associated with such a correction. Thus, in the MU concept, a measurement result can comprise two uncertainties (i) that associated with a bias correction (uBias),*

and (ii) the uncertainty due to random effects (imprecision, uImp). Both of these uncertainties are expressed as SDs which, when combined together, provide the combined standard uncertainty for the procedure (uProc).

Correcting for bias. This is the crux of the problem of applying metrological principles in a medical laboratory! The bias of any measurement procedure is supposed to be eliminated when possible, corrected if practical, or ignored if necessary. Clearly, it is preferable to eliminate or correct for bias, but if that is not possible, the ISO and CLSI guidelines *ignore* bias as a factor contributing to the variation of measurement results. This may be acceptable in a single laboratory that employs a single measurement procedure for a test and establishes its own reference ranges and critical medical decision cutoffs, which allows the laboratory to assume that bias is constant, or remains stable, and thus does not cause any variation of test results. Most laboratories do not operate under these simplistic conditions, thus the bias between routine methods and reference methods will contribute to the values observed for test results and may affect their use and interpretation.

HbA1c provides an example of the difficulties in correcting for bias. In spite of national and international efforts at standardizations, CAP surveys show that significant biases still exist between many of the examination subgroups and the "true" values assigned by reference examination procedures. For example, in surveys performed in 2013, for sample GH2-03 with an assigned reference value of 6.07 %Hb, the average absolute subgroup bias was 0.11 %Hb and maximum subgroup bias was 0.27 %Hb (or 4.3%); for sample GH2-01 with an assigned reference value of 7.11 %Hb, the average absolute bias was 0.10 %Hb and the maximum was 0.27 %Hb (or 3.7%); for sample GH2-02 with an assigned reference value of 9.32 %Hb, the average bias was 0.13 %Hb and the maximum was 0.38% (or 3.9%). Thus, biases from 0.1 %Hb to 0.4 %Hb are being observed for examination procedures that have been certified by NGSP as being equivalent.

These observed biases seem small, but Bruns and Boyd [6] have discussed the medical significance of such biases in terms of patient misclassifications in the US population. A bias of 0.1 %Hb at a HbA1c concentration of 6.5 %Hb could result in 0.2 to 1.1 million patients being misclassified, depending on whether the bias is positive or negative; a bias of 0.2 %Hb to 0.3 %Hb could result in 0.4 to 1.9 million misclassifications; a bias of 0.4 %Hb could result in 0.7 to 3.0 million misclassifications; and a bias of 0.5 %Hb could result in 0.9 to 4.7 million misclassifications.

The evidence from HbA1c surveys of harmonized, standardized, certified examination procedures shows that bias cannot be completely eliminated or corrected for physio-chemically complex measurands that are common in medical laboratories, therefore it is necessary to account for the bias in any attempt to characterize the quality of the measurement process [2]. Traditionally, the estimate of Total Error has provided a practical approach for doing this. However, ISO does not recognize the utility of Total Error because it includes a linear contribution from method bias (i.e., bias is added to the 95% or 2*SD estimate of uncertainty). According to strict metrological principles, bias should be eliminated or corrected and therefore *should not exist* in reported test results. If bias can be completely eliminated or corrected, then only random error exists and the estimation of Total Error simplifies to the estimate of random error. If bias cannot be completely corrected or eliminated, then it must be included when characterizing of the expected errors of the final test results.

Unfortunately, C51A does not resolve this issue. The document does recognize the concept of Total Error, but discourages its use for estimating MU:

> *Traditionally, a so-called total error for a measured quantity value is the calculated sum of two terms. The first term, the total systematic error, is based on observations or literature and expressed as the mean of the difference between observed values and the reference or target value. The second term is an estimate of the random measurement variation, ie, the SD of the observed differences multiplied by a coverage factor, according to the desired level of confidence. The sum of the two terms is an upper limit of the total error of a measurement, assuming random error follows a Gaussian distribution.*

If a quantity for which a total error was calculated is used as input to another measurement, the total error has to be separated into its systematic and random components before they can be combined with those of the other input quantities in a measurement model. This lack of transferability is an important drawback of the error model.

The reasoning is that any estimate of MU needs to be "combinable" with other uncertainty components, which is done by squaring the SDs, adding the variances, then extracting the square root as the estimate of combined uncertainty. One application that is discussed in C51A is the need to combine uncertainties to estimate MU for calculated quantities, such as creatinine clearance, glomerular filtration rate, anion gap, etc. Other important applications involve adding the effects of pre-analytic variables, such as sampling variation and individual biologic variation.

Correcting for uncorrected bias. C51A doesn't resolve the issue of what to do about uncorrected bias, except to make reference to a paper by Magnusson and Ellison that examines different ways to treat uncorrected bias in estimates of MU [7]. These authors first examine cases where bias corrections are not possible or not practical, then conclude that there are many situations that require laboratories to incorporate bias in reporting MU.

Routine laboratories are necessarily faced with the problem of treating uncorrected bias. For comparability of measurement results more guidance on bias and bias corrections is needed to help the laboratories in their work and to minimize differences in interpretation arising from different approaches to the treatment of bias. Given an observed bias or other strong reason for suspecting bias, it is misleading to report uncorrected results without reflecting the resulting bias. The options available are then:

1. *Report the result and its uncertainty together with the bias (or the correction) and its uncertainty.*

2. *Report the result with an increased uncertainty interval.*

This first option puts the burden of interpreting the meaning of bias and MU on the consumers of the test results. The second option would be more practical in medical laboratories and the authors evaluated several approaches for increasing the uncertainty interval to include the effect of uncorrected bias.

> *On the basis of current studies, and taking into account testing laboratory needs for a simple and consistent approach with a symmetric interval, we conclude that for most cases with large degrees of freedom, linear addition of a bias term adjusted for exact coverage as described by Synek is to be preferred.*

Therefore, the recommendation is to add the estimate of bias linearly to the expanded combined uncertainty (95% interval) of the observed long term imprecision plus the uncertainty in the estimate of bias. This approach is actually consistent with the way bias is handled in the Total Error model and it can be expected that this estimate of MU will be slightly larger than the Total Error estimate because it includes the uncertainty of the estimate of bias.

C51A "top-down" approach. Long-term QC data should be used in order to include variations from changes in reagent lots, calibration, calibration lots, different operators, routine maintenance, etc. C51A recommends that important factors that contribute to variation be identified and the QC data be subjected to an Analysis of Variance (ANOVA) to estimate the various components of variation. C51A provides an example for creatinine that shows 5 replicates obtained for each of 5 different runs to illustrate the use of ANOVA. This example suggests that one might employ a short protocol, such as recommended in CLSI EP15, for the initial estimates of bias or trueness, imprecision, and measurement uncertainty.

A second example is provided in Appendix B of the document. Those data illustrate triplicate measurements on one control material over a period of 42 runs with multiple operators and 2 different lots of reagents. ANOVA gives an estimate of 6.1% for the measurement CV, which would be multiplied by a coverage factor of 2 to provide an estimate of MU of ± 12.2%. By comparison, simple calculation of the SD from all 126 measurements gives a CV of 5.8% or a MU of 11.6%. The difference between estimates of MU of 12.2% and 11.6% is small and for practical purposes, both of these numbers represent an estimate of 12%. Maybe the simple calculation of the

SD or CV from existing long-term QC data is a reasonable way to get started estimating MU.

The value of these examples is to show there are different ways of estimating MU and the experimental procedures and data calculations need not be overly complicated. For practical applications, it is a matter of working out a clear experimental protocol together with related calculation tools to make estimations of MU doable in busy production laboratories. It remains for those of us in the laboratory to provide those practical protocols and calculation tools.

6σQMS Policy. The laboratory shall evaluate the uncertainty of measurement for each examination procedure where imprecision data are available from stable QC materials.

The 2012 revision of ISO 15189 [3] includes significant changes regarding the laboratory's responsibilities for uncertainty of measurement (MU). The guidance in the previous edition [8] was that *"the laboratory should determine the uncertainty of results, where relevant and possible."* The phrase *"where relevant and possible"* allowed considerable room for argument, first (where relevant) whether physicians really want this information and know what to do with it, and second, (where possible) whether the GUM methodology for determining uncertainty makes it too complicated and impractical to estimate MU in a medical laboratory. Because of this clause, there was considerable debate about whether laboratories should try to estimate MU and whether there were any practical methodologies for doing so.

Section 5.5.1.4 in the 2012 guideline [1] is significantly different:

> *"The laboratory shall determine measurement uncertainty for each measurement procedure in the examination phases used to report measured quantity values on patients' samples. The laboratory shall define the performance requirements for the measurement uncertainty of each measurement procedure and regularly review estimates of measurement uncertainty."*

Remember that in ISO-speak, the word *shall* means the laboratory ***must*** determine measurement uncertainty, not that the laboratory might do this where relevant and possible. In addition, the laboratory shall define performance requirements for measurement uncertainty, i.e., quality requirements for intended use, in order to evaluate whether the observed MU is acceptable.

In addition, the notes provide new guidance on how measurement uncertainty can be determined:

"Note 1. The relevant uncertainty components are those associated with the actual measurement process, commencing with the presentation of the sample to the measurement procedure and ending with the output of the measured value.

"Note 2. Measurement uncertainties may be calculated using quantity values obtained by the measurement of quality control materials under intermediate precision conditions that include as many routine changes as reasonable possible in the standard operation of a measurement procedure, e.g., changes of reagent and calibrator batches, different operators, scheduled instrument maintenance.

"Note 3. Examples of the practical utility of measurement uncertainty estimates include confirmation that patients values meet quality goals set by the laboratory and meaningful comparison of a patient value with a previous value of the same type or with a clinical decision value."

Note 1 clearly limits MU to the analytic phase of the total testing process. Note 2 recommends estimation from routine SQC data over a period of time that includes common changes or process variables that would contribute to MU. Note 3 again brings in the responsibility to define goals for how good a test should be in order to periodically evaluate estimates of MU.

The practical estimation of MU comes down to calculating the SD from SQC data, then multiplying that SD by a factor of 2 to provide a conventional 95% confidence limit for a test result. The SD is known as the *standard measurement uncertainty*, the factor of 2 is called the coverage factor, and the 95% limit or interval is known as the *expanded measurement uncertainty*.

There is no mention of bias in this guidance, not even a mention of the uncertainty in the estimate of bias, which has generally been included in previous recommendations for top-down estimates. Thus, the new ISO 15189 guidance says (1) the laboratory must determine MU and (2) the laboratory can do this with SQC data collected over some extended period of time, not just one month.

6σQMS Process. The laboratory shall determine measurement uncertainty from SQC data obtained under intermediate precision conditions.

Intermediate precision conditions generally means one examination procedure in one laboratory, with changes between reagent lots, calibrator lots, operators, operating conditions, routine maintenance, periodic service, etc. The practical issue is the appropriate time period for collecting and analyzing SQC data. This time period will depend on the particular operating conditions for an individual test or analyzer, such as how often runs are performed, how often operators change, how frequent maintenance is performed, how often there are changes in reagent and calibrator lots, etc. In addition, other factors that should be considered include the the number of measurements needed to obtain a reliable estimate of an SD, the frequency of SQC, and the time period over which data is collected to establish control limits.

- **Number of measurements for reliable estimate of SD.** The reliability of an estimate of the SD can be characterized by the confidence interval for that estimate, which depends on the number of measurements collected. While there is a "rule of thumb" that a minimum of 20 control measurements should be used to calculate an SD for setting control limits, many more are needed to obtain a *reliable* estimate of the SD. For example, if we assume a true standard deviation of 10 units, the 90% confidence interval will range from 7.4 to 15.9 when N=20, i.e., an SD as low as 7.4 could be observed, which is 26% low, or an SD as high as 15.9 could be observed, which is 59% high. For N=100, the confidence interval is 9.0 to 11.3, i.e., the reliability of the estimate of the SD is much better, within approximately 10% of the correct value. Therefore, it's prudent to aim for >100 measurements when estimating MU.

- **SQC frequency.** There is no standard practice for SQC frequency, but many laboratories, globally and in the US, tend to follow the CLIA guideline that a minimum of 2 levels of controls be analyzed per day. High volume laboratories often analyze many more controls per day. On the other hand, US laboratories that have implemented Equivalent Quality Control (EQC) procedures may only be analyzing controls once per week or even once per month. Likewise, the new emerging practice of Risk-based QC Plans may lead to low frequency of SQC, particularly in point-of-care applications. Clearly the practicality of estimating MU from SQC data will depend on having a sufficient number of control measurements to provide a reliable estimate of the SD. A reliable estimate of MU may not be obtainable for unit-use devices used in point-of-care applications, even though knowledge of the quality in these settings is critically important for patient treatment.
- **Cumulative control limits.** Given the difficulty of obtaining a reliable estimate of an SD, C24A3 [5] recommends that laboratories utilize several months data to establish cumulative control limits. For example, if a laboratory analyzes 2 levels of controls per day, then data will be needed over 100 days to provide reliable SDs at the 2 levels. This is the basis for the C24A3 recommendation that laboratories should combine control data from 6 consecutive monthly periods, calculate a cumulative SD, and implement control limits based on that cumulative SD.

While there is no specific ISO guidance for how many control measurements are needed, the estimate of the SD will be more reliable if at least 100 data points are included, which will often require that SQC data be collected over a period of several months. A period of 6 months should be practical in many laboratories and matches the CLSI recommendation for establishing control limits from a cumulative SD obtained from 6 successive months of routine SQC data.

6σQMS Process. The laboratory shall compare estimates of the standard measurement uncertainty to the performance required for intended use of the examination procedure by determination of Sigma-metrics.

Recall that *"the laboratory shall define the performance requirements for the measurement uncertainty of each measurement procedure and regularly review estimates of measurement uncertainty... Examples of the practical utility of measurement uncertainty estimates include confirmation that patients values meet quality goals set by the laboratory and meaningful comparison of a patient value with a previous value of the same type or with a clinical decision value."*

The strategy in a Six Sigma Quality Management System is to compare the observed performance of the examination procedure to the defined quality required for the intended use of the examination. The mechanism for doing this is to determine performance on the sigma scale which takes into account the quality required for intended use and the imprecision and bias observed for the examination procedure. Earlier estimates of imprecision and bias were determined from method validation studies. Now estimates should be made from intermediate-term precision data and bias from EQA or PT surveys.

Regardless of the arguments whether or not to include bias in the estimation of MU, everyone agrees that bias should be monitored along with MU. Given the availability of the Standard Uncertainty (i.e., 1 SD or CV) and the estimate of bias, the sigma quality of an examination can be calculated from the defined Allowable Total Error, as follows:

Sigma = (%TEa - %Bias)/%CV

Thus the laboratory can easily evaluate performance on the sigma scale in order to satisfy the requirement to review performance in relation to quality goals.

It would also be helpful if EQA and PT survey results were presented in a way that demonstrated the sigma performance of examination procedures on a regional, national, or international basis to evaluate the reliability of examinations for evidence-based diagnostic and treatment guidelines. For example, Figure 15-1 displays the mean and range (±2 SD) for a HbA1c survey conducted by the College of American Pathologists and evaluated by the National Glycohemoglobin Standardization Program [9]. This graphical presentation shows that the measurement variation of some examination subgroups exceeds the quality goal of ± 7%. Note that the inner zone represents the NGSP/CAP requirement of 6% that applies in 2014). Also note that the 3rd subgroup from the left should be disregarded due to the interference of the anticoagulant in the survey sample.

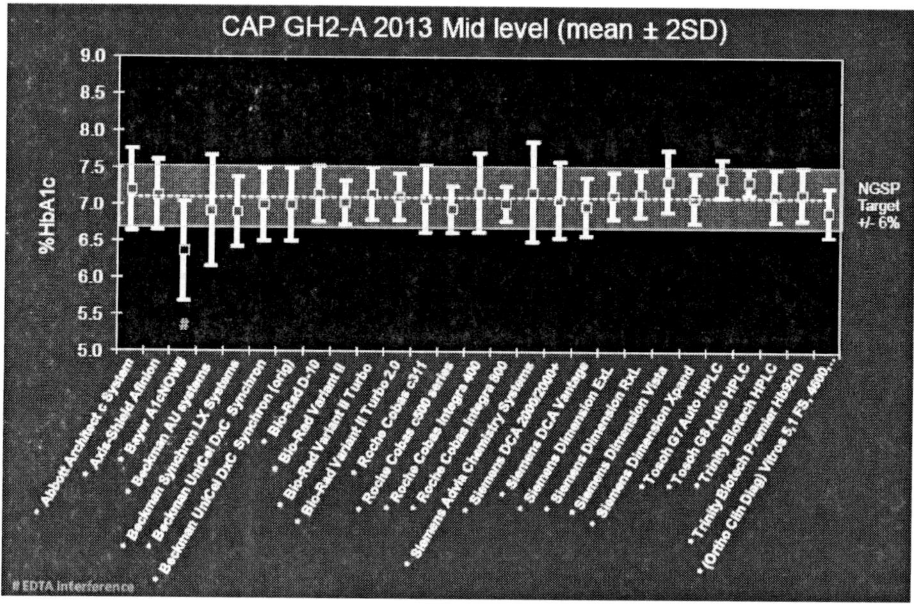

Figure 15-1. Observed mean and range of survey results for 27 HbA1c method subgroups. CAP sample with assigned reference value of 7.11 %Hb. Note that one method subgroup (3rd from left) is affected by anti-coagulant in sample and those results are not included in group calculations.

Figure 15-2 shows these same survey results presented on a Sigma Proficiency Assessment Chart. This chart is prepared for an Allowable Total Error of 7.0%. The y-axis describes the observed bias with a range from +7.0% to -7.0%. The x-axis shows the observed CV with a range from 0% to 7.0%.

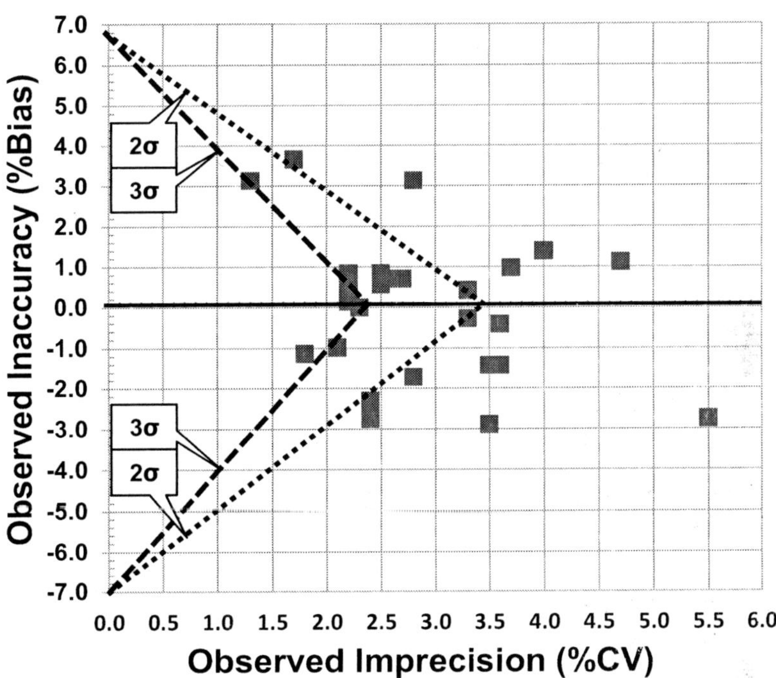

Figure 15-2. Sigma Assessment from Proficiency Testing Data for CAP sample with assigned reference value of 7.11 %Hb. Each data point represents observed mean and observed SD of survey results for a method subgroup. The region above the dashed line represents less than 2-sigma quality. The region below the solid line represents 3 sigma quality or better. Region between the lines represents 2 to 3 sigma quality.

For each examination subgroup, the mean and SD are plotted as operating points where the y-coordinate is equal to the observed %Bias and the x-coordinate equal to the observed %CV. The dashed lines represents 3-sigma performance and the dotted lines 2-sigma performance. Examination subgroups outside the dotted lines achieve less than 2-sigma performance, those between the lines from 2- to 3- sigma, and those with the dashed lines better than 3-sigma performance. Most method subgroups show performance less than 3-sigma!

What's the point?

Estimates of intermediate-term precision and ongoing bias are the keys to providing realistic estimates of the performance and reliability of routine examination procedures. There will be different sources for those estimates of random and systematic errors at different times in the life-cycle of a testing process. For estimating bias from CRMs, comparison studies, EQA or PT results, it will be necessary to work out the calculations to estimate both bias and the uncertainty of the estimate of bias. Depending on the design of QC protocols, it may be possible to employ simple calculations of the SD or CV, or it may be useful to employ ANOVA calculations. The CLSI C51A guideline allows medical laboratories the flexibility to employ various "top-down" designs for estimating MU and the 2012 edition of ISO 15189 also adopts that approach.

The ISO standard identifies a simple and practical methodology using SQC data obtained under "intermediate precision conditions", i.e., a single laboratory and measurement principle, but with the changes in routine operating conditions (operations, reagent lots, calibrator lots, etc.). The laboratory should calculate a mid-term SD and utilize this estimate to express the standard uncertainty, then multiply by a coverage factor of 2 to express an expanded measurement uncertainty (95% confidence limit or interval).

Laboratories should also compare estimates of the Standard Uncertainty (1 SD) and the bias observed in EQA and PT surveys to the quality required for intended use by calculation of Sigma-metrics for each examination procedure. A graphical presentation is possible using Sigma Proficiency Assessment Charts.

None of this actually applies to US laboratories that operate under the CLIA regulations, rather than ISO15189 accreditation. Nonetheless, US laboratories should consider how to implement a methodology for determining MU because that will be part of the global standard of practice for quality management in medical laboratories.

References

1. ISO 15189:2012. Medical laboratories – Requirements for quality and competence. 3rd ed. International Organization for Standards, Geneva, Switzerland, 2012.

2. GUM. Guide to expression of uncertainty in measurement. ISO, Geneva, 1995.

3. Westgard JO. Managing quality vs. measuring uncertainty in the medical laboratory. Clin Chem Lab Med 2010;48:31-40.

4. CLSI C51A. Expression of Measurement Uncertainty in Laboratory Medicine. Clinical and Laboratory Standards Organization. Wayne, PA 2012.

5. White GH. Basics of estimating measurement uncertainty. Clin Biochem Rev 2008;29:S53-S60.

6. Bruns DE, Boyd JC. Few Point-of-Care Hemoglobin A1c assay methods meet clinical needs. Clin Chem 2010;56:4-6.

7. CLSI C24A3. Statistical Quality Control for Quantitative Measurement Procedures: Principles and Definitions. Clinical and Laboratory Standards Institute, Wayne, PA, 2006.

8. Magnusson B, Ellison SLR. Treatment of uncorrected measurement bias in uncertainty estimation for chemical measurements. Anal Bioanal Chem 2008;390:201-213.

9. ISO 15189:2007. Medical laboratories – Requirements for quality and competence. 2nd ed. International Organization for Standards, Geneva, Switzerland, 2007.

10. NGSP website, www.ngsp.org, accessed September 24, 2013.

16. Managing Quality in the Real World – ISO, CLIA, CLSI, and YOU

In this book, we have discussed the guidance from ISO, CLIA, and CLSI for the implementation of Quality Management Systems (QMS). In our assessment, each offers useful guidance, but not the complete answer. There is a need to provide a more *quantitative* quality management system in medical laboratories today! That creates a real problem for you and your laboratory because there is no single guidance that provides the right QMS. The consequence is that YOU must be the final arbitrator and advocate for developing and implementing the right QMS! We believe that a scientific approach based on Deming's Plan-Do-Check-Act cycle (PDCA) and Six Sigma concepts and principles provides the additional guidance that is needed. Quality can become both measurable and manageable by implementing a Six Sigma QMS.

ISO. The strength of ISO 15189 guidance is that it provides a comprehensive overview and organization of both management and technical requirements, plus identifies important requirements for assuring the quality of testing processes (define intended use, validate that methods fulfill requirements for intended use, design QC procedures to verify attainment of the intended quality of results). The shortcoming is a lack of details, the "how to do it" part that we have attempted to describe in this book.

The approach we recommend for implementing a QMS starts with ISO management requirements as the first phase and ISO technical requirements as the second phase. This doesn't necessarily mean the two phases should be entirely sequential, only that management requirements must be considered first to ensure commitment and leadership from the top of your organization. We recommend that a laboratory first form a Management Planning Team and later a Technical Planning Team that will work in parallel. The advantage of these two groups is that they minimize the time for implementation, utilize the scientific expertise of the laboratory analysts and supervisors, and achieve more widespread buy-in throughout the laboratory.

CLIA. US laboratories face the difficult choice of settling for compliance with the CLIA regulations or striving for improved management systems by following ISO 15189. Both CAP and A2LA now offer accreditation for both CLIA and ISO 15189, which we hope will stimulate US laboratories to aim higher and implement improved quality management practices. One important consideration is that A2LA is accredited by ILAC, which means A2LA accreditation has world-wide acceptance. If your customers or operations are global, ILAC accreditation is attractive. CAP-ISO 15189 accreditation focuses on the ISO management requirements while technical requirements are addressed under CLIA accreditation. That means some ISO technical requirements, such as traceability and measurement uncertainty, are not addressed by CAP-ISO 15189 accreditation. Nonetheless, for US laboratories, ISO0-CAP 15189 provides a path from compliance to excellence.

While CLIA may have established high standards for laboratory performance when introduced in the early 1990s, CLIA has not kept pace with improvements in quality management practices in the last two decades, nor with laboratory needs and practices for improving QC. Under CLIA today, QC really means "quality compliance" to minimal requirements. CLIA's shortcomings can be traced to the lack of implementation of the review of manufacturers' recommended QC procedures, the so-called "QC clearance" provision of the original CLIA Final Rule. That problem led to CLIA's establishment of a minimum QC requirement of 2 levels per day that was supposed to provide *temporary* guidance, but in fact became a permanent "default" minimum practice. Even that minimum practice was found to be too much for point-of-care testing, which then led to the implementation of so-called "Equivalent" QC procedures that reduced daily QC to weekly or even monthly QC. Problems with reduced QC frequency regulations in turn led to today's Individualized Quality Control Plans (IQCP) based on risk management, which leads to qualitative and subjective QC practices. IQCP, in effect, means "any QC will do." As a result, CLIA quality standards now represent minimal levels of compliance, rather than practices for excellence. For this reason, we encourage US laboratories to take more interest in the ISO 15189 guidelines and accreditation by A2LA or CAP.

CLSI. During the last decade, CLSI has emerged as a partner for CMS to address CLIA shortcomings. CLSI has developed practice guidelines for QMS in the form of Quality System Essentials (QSEs) for healthcare organizations, as well as specific guidelines for medical laboratories. CMS has attempted to integrate QMS ideas into the CLIA regulations, but the success of that integration has been limited by the regulatory structure of the CLIA Final Rule. CLSI is also working with CMS on the application of risk management principles, particularly for the implementation of risk-based QC Plans (called QCP by CLSI and IQCP by CMS/CLIA).

In principle, the CLSI consensus process should lead to objective guidelines for standardizing laboratory practices, but in practice industry and the government exert more influence than the professional sector and that may in turn compromise the CLSI standards. This is particularly evident for risk-based QC Plans that depend on the performance of manufacturer's controls. Laboratories need information from the manufacturers risk studies to evaluate the detection capabilities of a manufacturer's controls, but that information is not readily available, even though CLSI developed a draft guideline that specified the information that should be provided (EP22P – Presentation of a Manufacturer's Risk Mitigation Information for Users of *In Vitro* Diagnostic Devices). Manufacturers withdrew their support for that guideline and disbanded the committee. Those actions have left laboratories in the position of having to request risk information from manufacturers, but manufacturers are under no obligation to provide any. That experience reveals that "politics" still play an important role in CLSI activities and that laboratory professionals need to carefully assess the merit of each CLSI guideline.

YOU. Your understanding of quality management practices is still the key to effective quality management in your laboratory. We hope that this book has helped you understand the merits of the available guidance, plus the benefits of a data-driven quality system that embodies Deming's principles and Six Sigma. The foundation of this approach is the scientific method as described in Deming's PDCA cycle and the quantitative techniques for measuring quality on the Sigma Scale and managing quality on the basis of the Sigma performance observed for laboratory testing processes. While we have focused the Six Sigma application on the analytical testing process, or the examination process, we have also illustrated how the Sigma concepts can be applied to pre-analytic and post-analytic processes. Your knowledge and understanding of these concepts, principles, and metrics will allow you to tailor the development of Quality Management Systems to meet the specific needs of your laboratory. You can then plan the implementation of the right QMS for your laboratory.

Your basic plan for implementing a Six Sigma QMS should consider the following:

1. Commit to implementation of a quantitative quality management process as part of the laboratory's strategic plan for improvement of processes and services.
2. Establish quality policies, processes, and procedures to implement a Six Sigma Quality System as part of the laboratory's ISO 15189 accreditation process or as part of implementing the CLSI Quality System Essentials.
3. Assign responsibility for organizing the QMS activities to someone who has competencies to plan, implement, monitor, and improve the Six Sigma QMS.
4. Train key supervisors, analytic system specialists, and analysts to understand the ISO 15189 technical requirements and Six Sigma concepts, metrics, and application tools.
5. Define quality goals, objectives, and requirements for intended use for each laboratory examination.
6. Select examination procedures on the basis of traceability and the expected analytic performance. Estimate the sigma capability from manufacturer's data for performance claims or, when available, from independent method validation studies.
7. Validate analytical performance of new examination procedures against the defined quality requirements. Utilize a Method Decision Chart to determine the Sigma-metric from the performance data collected in your laboratory and judge acceptability.

8. Formulate a Total Quality Control strategy on the basis of your observed sigma to provide an appropriate balance between SQC, manufacturer's recommended controls, and regulatory/accreditation requirements.

9. Select SQC procedures on the basis of the quality required for a test and the precision and bias observed for the examination procedure. Utilize a Sigma SQC Selection Tool or Chart of Operating Specifications to select appropriate control rules and the total number of control measurements needed to detect medically important errors.

10. Optimize risk-based Total Quality Control Plans for individual tests and analytic systems to provide control mechanisms that are effective for expected failure modes. Add controls to monitor pre-examination and post-examination processes to those needed for the examination process.

11. Estimate measurement uncertainty from intermediate-term SQC data and evaluate against defined quality goals.

12. Estimate ongoing bias from PT or EQA programs. Use this estimate of bias, along with the intermediate estimate of precision, to calculate and monitor the sigma quality of your processes. For visual assessment, use the Sigma Proficiency Assessment chart.

13. Identify issues and prioritize improvements that are needed to satisfy requirements for intended use. Employ carefully selected Quality Indicators that monitor the total examination process. Determine nonconformities in terms of defect rates (or frequency of errors) and evaluate on the sigma scale. When possible, use risk management tools to identify potential failure modes that are unique to the particular examination process.

14. Review yearly the quality goals for intended use, the quality achieved, the TQC Plan, and the plan for improvements.

This just happens to work out to 14 points and reminds us again of the importance of Deming's original 14 points (as discussed in Chapter 4), which set out the principles, philosophy, and values that are the keys to effective quality management. Quality should be an organizational value. Management commitment is required to achieve quality. Quality must be measured in order to be managed. Problems are caused by bad processes, not bad people. Process improvements are the key to improving quality. Well-trained people are the critical and enduring resource for continuous improvement of quality. That means YOU!

17. Improving Quality in the Real World

Editor's note: about Gabriel Migiliarino

In the last 6 years, Gabriel Migliarino and his consulting service have taken more than a dozen laboratories through the ISO 15189 accreditation process, in Argentina, Chile, the Dominican Republic, Mexico, Panama and Uruguay.

As a Quality Management System consultant, Dr. Migliarino has useful insights to share with us. Even though the resource and logistical environment of US hospitals are often far better than those of labs in Latin and South America, there are many common challenges and deficits that face labs all over the world.

We know Dr. Migliarino best from his collaboration with us in the translation projects sponsored by the Wallace Coulter Foundation. Dr. Migliarino delivers training in Latin and South America about verification of measurement procedures and internal statistical quality control. This workshop is delivered in 5 different countries in the area per year and has an estimated total duration of five years.

Experiences from the field

Gabriel Migliarino, PhD
Evangelina Hernandez, MS

Introduction

Each laboratory takes its own individual path towards Quality Management Systems accreditation but many share the same weaknesses and concerns during the journey.

In Latin and South America, scientists have not received a lot of education on "management." When laboratories seek accreditation, this is a new concept – to "manage quality" – for the laboratory. As mentioned on Chapter 5, the accreditation project comprises three stages: management requirements, technical requirements and accreditation.

What happens generally with the accreditation process in the Latin and South American region? The second stage, particularly the application of technical requirements (5.5 Analytical Procedures, 5.6 Quality Assurance of Analytical Results), often moves forward before the first stage (management requirements). Why? Applying technical requirements involves the area of operations where most laboratory scientists are more comfortable and more interested in making improvements. Most scientists are already working on the technical parts of measuring, monitoring, and improving quality. But "managing quality" is something new to them.

The Starting Point : Management Requirements

For most laboratories, starting the process of accreditation for Quality Management Systems, applying the management requirements of ISO 15189:2012 [1] standard moves forward slowly and with great difficulty.

Below we list the management requirements that generally present the most difficulty to our clients:

1. Documents
2. Quality Policy and Objectives
3. Nonconformities and corrective actions
4. Indicators

1. Documents. How to organize them.

Generally, the documents system has a basic common structure as shown on Figure 1.

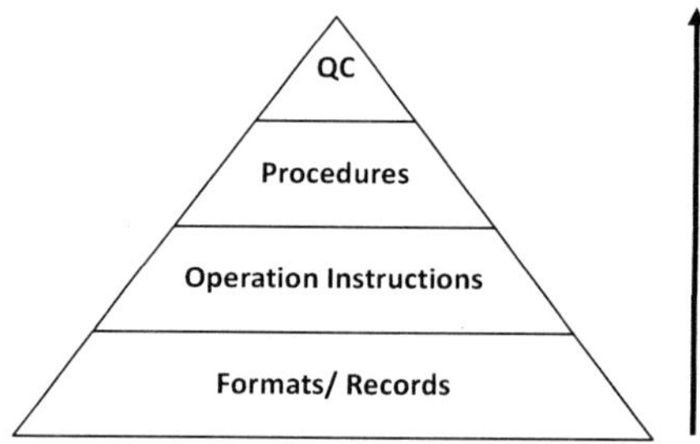

Figure 17-1 Document Pyramid

Quality Manual

The Quality Manual is the "Big Daddy" of all the documents in the Quality Management System and is therefore of crucial importance. Its function is to express the policies (intentions) of the company to comply with the regulatory requirements and criteria of the accreditation entity.

What we observe

Many times, the Quality Manual is a complex document, difficult to read and understand. Other times it is an almost exact copy of the ISO 15189:2012 standard, so generic and repetitive of the official requirements, it loses all usefulness for the laboratory.

What we recommend

Labs should focus on the idea that the Quality Manual is the foundation for the entire Quality Management System. If this is true, the Quality Manual must be as clear as possible. It has to concisely express the will of the laboratory to comply with the regulatory requirements, provide a guide to the documented procedures, and explain the activities to implement.

Other documents

The documents of the Quality Management System must show traceability, in the sense indicated by Figure 1. Namely, each document must have its "father/reference document" which enables tracing every procedure back to its foundation in the Quality Manual.

What we observe

We find many "orphan" documents, fatherless, and, consequently, not traceable to any part of the Quality Manual. It is most common to find forms and records that are controlled but without documentary traceability.

What we recommend

The first step is to identify all the procedures in the Quality Manual. Then, for instructions and forms, we suggest generating a coding system that indicates the origin of each document. The codes enable the "traceability" of the procedures back to the references in the Quality Manual.

2. Quality Policy and Objectives. How to present them.

The Quality Policy reflects the laboratory's intentions concerning quality and is the reference framework to establish the Quality Objectives.

What we observe

Generally, we find Quality Policies are too complex and difficult to understand. Concerning Quality Objectives, they show several weaknesses, among them:

a. They are not coherent with the Quality Policy.
b. They are not concrete or measurable.
c. Sometimes they are not realistic or achievable, sometimes they are too easy (not ambitious).
d. They are not planned and lack follow-up.
e. They are not communicated to staff.

What we recommend

To establish a Quality Policy appropriate to the organization, it should be short and clear. It should be kept in mind that it must be communicated and understood within the organization; any member of the organization should be able to explain it.

To define coherent quality objectives, they should be SMART: Specific, Measurable, Achievable, Realistic and on Time.

Objectives must align with procedures, not only the operative procedures (pre-analytical, analytical and post-analytical) but also supportive (staff management, services and supplies management, among others). Remember that managing a system, and consequently its procedures, implies that you have established Quality Objectives.

Manage objectives according to the following stages:

1. Establish objectives.
2. Develop the general plan: scope, time frame, costs, specifications, risks.
3. Develop the resources plan: staff, materials, equipment, funding.
4. Implement: organization, communication, leadership, decision-making, problem-solving, monitoring, corrective actions.
5. Review: final evaluation, lessons learnt.

3. Nonconformities. Corrective Actions. How to identify and manage them.

The laboratory must have a procedure to identify and manage nonconformities on any aspect of the Quality Management System. The most common sequence, though not the only one, to treat nonconformities is as follows:

Stage 1. Identification of the nonconformity.
Stage 2. Immediate action.
Stage 3. Analysis of the root cause.
Stage 4. Corrective action.
Stage 5. Verification of the corrective action efficacy.

What we observe

There are several weaknesses that often occur.

1. Some nonconformities are not recorded in the system. According to our experience, we see see mainly four causes.
    a. Implementation of models centered on finding a culprit, not a root cause.
    b. Failure to identify nonconformities. In the absence of data, the staff doesn't even know a nonconformity has occurred.
    c. Notification and recording systems so complex and unwieldy that they are not used by the staff, so nonconformities are not recorded.
    d. Lack of confidence in the usefulness of the nonconformities management system (a consequence of causes 2 and 3 below).

2. Extensive delays in analysis of the information.
3. The root cause cannot be identified, the corrective action is not appropriate and the same errors occur over and over.
4. The lab is not capable of effectively taking action. Well-intentioned but inadequate corrective actions are unable to resolve the root cause.

What we recommend

Work with all the staff on the culture of identifying and responding to nonconformities. From the QMS perspective, the main responsibility of errors are attributed to the design, the organization and the system functions. Staff are not blamed for errors. It's the system and the management who bear responsibility.

- Generate an easy, quick recording system that captures the minimal information necessary for nonconformity management. Many labs implement a simple record of daily events to improve error notification. All staff record undesirable situations of daily operation without having to decide if it is or is not a nonconformity. The Quality Team reviews these records and determines if the event is or not a nonconformity.
- Establish the responsibility for the follow-up of non-conformities.
- Train the staff in root cause analysis and on methods to verify the efficacy of the actions taken.
- Assemble multidisciplinary teams for the analysis of causes and determination of corrective actions when nonconformities are complex.
- Notify the staff of improvements for the analysis of non-conformities.

4. Quality Indicators.

Quality Indicators are a measure of the level at which a set of inherent characteristics comply with requirements. Quality Indicators may be used for many reasons:

- To monitor a specific function, normally stable.
- To monitor complex procedures involving many entries or multiple activity sequences.
- To monitor the efficacy of planned improvements on operations.
- To explore risks.

What we observe

Below, some weaknesses associated with ineffective and inefficient Quality Indicators are described:

1. Indicators with implementation or design errors generating confusing or erroneous information.

2. Indicators correctly designed but with impractical results because the laboratory does not devote the necessary resources to the collection of data.

3. Indicators correctly designed but without the correct follow-up. The indicator is chronically out of specification and there is no evidence of corrective action.

4. Indicators that are very stable but do not enable continuous improvement.

What we recommend

Associate the measuring procedure of the indicators to a PDCA Cycle (Deming Plan-Do-Check-Act Cycle).

PLAN. The specific Quality Indicators must be defined.

We recommend starting with a few key indicators.

Below we enumerate questions that may be useful to select indicators:

- Does it monitor a critical procedure?
- Does it monitor a complex procedure?
- Does it monitor a highly automated system?
- Is it applied to an area of known vulnerability or subject to repetitive problems?
- Is it applied to an area subject to improvement where it is necessary to verify the efficacy of the action taken?

DO. It comprises the following activities:

1. Definition of purpose, scope and authority.
2. Development of the strategy for the collection and analysis of data.
3. Establishment of objectives and thresholds of action.

CHECK. An indicator is implemented during a test period.

Below we enumerate questions that may be useful to determine the final implementation of the Quality Indicator:

- Is the indicator objective?
- Is the indicator specific?
- Is the indicator achievable?

ACT. We detail possible actions:

1. Monitor.
2. Discontinue the indicator.
3. Implement an immediate action.
4. Investigate the root cause.
5. Implement a corrective action.
6. Develop an improvement strategy.
7. Modify the objective or the action threshold.
8. Report to the interested parties.

Part 2: Technical Requirements

Introduction

When clinical laboratories implement accreditation standards, the technical requirements are a great challenge. It is often assumed that the manufacture assures the analytical quality of the measurement procedure and that it is not the laboratory's responsibility. This belief leads to a gap between current practices and the required practices of a QMS.

Starting point: Technical Requirements

All laboratories have a different starting point. The most significant difference lies in the fact that some laboratories already have a Quality Management System, while other laboratories do not. The existence of a "mature" Quality Management System enables faster implementation of the management requirements. However, we have noticed that both labs with and without existing Quality Management Systems have weaknesses at the level of technical requirements:

1. Equipment qualification
2. Quality Requirements (according to the intended use of each measurement procedure)
3. Verification and/or validation of performance measurement procedures.
4. Internal Statistical Quality Control Planning
5. Implementation and monitoring of the planned Internal Statistical Quality Control
6. Analysis and monitoring of the results of the participation in External Quality Control Assessment Schemes and/or Proficiency Testing Schemes
7. Estimation of measurement uncertainty
8. Monitoring the performance of the measurement procedures

Approach these points at the beginning of implementation, consider the requirements for appropriate application and identify the observed gaps in different laboratories.

1. Equipment qualification

Supplier selection: As the laboratory considers new analytical platforms, they must identify the critical aspects of performance that will be assessed during the selection process. The laboratory must establish the intended use of the equipment and define the appropriate functional and operational specifications. Of course, a balance must be struck between the ideal and the available, taking into account economic and practical issues.

What we observe

As mentioned before, some laboratories already have a Quality Management System. In this case, it is highly probable that those labs also already have a list of qualified suppliers. It may also occur that at the time they commence their search, they must re-evaluate and grade one or more potential suppliers.

In many countries, the large manufacturers work with distributors, which may make it more difficult to obtain the necessary information to make an informed decision.

It is true that when a laboratory applies for accreditation most of the equipment, if not all, is already installed and functioning; thus laboratories need to consider these policies more for future installations, not for their currently installed equipment.

Equipment qualification: It is a recorded process by which the appropriate installation and operation of the equipment is verified. That is to say, the laboratory must assure that the instrument was installed in an appropriate way, as established by the manufacturer, and that it is in working conditions also as established by the manufacturer (manual of operation).

There are different stages during equipment qualification:

a. Installation Qualification

b. Operation Qualification

c. Performance Qualification

a. Installation Qualification

At this stage it must be established that the instrument has been received as it was designed and specified, that it is adequately installed and that it is appropriate for its operation.

b. Operation Qualification

At this stage it must demonstrated that the instrument functions according to operational specifications (calibration/verification of critical points).

c. Performance Qualification

At this stage it must be demonstrated that the instrument works according to the adequate specifications of routine operation (performance with materials similar to routine samples).

What we observe

The most common problem is that the laboratory lacks the documentation that their instruments were correctly installed.

As a rule, the suppliers who were assessed qualify their instruments at the time of installation. The critical issue is documentation. The only record that laboratories generally keep is the technical service order which says that the instrument has been correctly installed. The laboratory must have documentation and records of the different stages of equipment qualification. Therefore, immediate action is required to document the appropriate installation of the equipment (by itself, the technical service order is not enough).

Many times we try to fill in the missing information by working with manufacturers and /or distributors, although this is not always possible. This is a temporary problem, however. While it is a difficulty to document the current instruments in the lab, these problems can be avoided in the future.

It is important that the laboratory requires the equipment supplier to provide all the needed documentation and records to prove that installation was correct. In fact, this issue should influence even the selection of the supplier.

It is recommended that the Quality Manager together with the professional responsible for the testing section monitor the qualification process and ensure that proper documentation and records have been received before the supplier finishes installation.

Not all the news is bad. There are manufacturers and distributors who offer all the documentation and records generated throughout the different stages of equipment qualification. This information should be highly appreciated by the laboratories and it is also another critical issue to be considered at the time of selecting new equipment.

We have worked hard on this issue during each laboratory accreditation that we have completed, providing practical training and establishing effective channels of communication with manufacturers, distributors and laboratories.

2. Quality

This topic was covered earlier in chapter 9 ("Defining Quality"). It was clearly expressed that each laboratory must consider the intended use of the measurement procedures and choose a quality requirement for each one of them. It is important that each measurement procedure relies on a quality requirement.

What we observe

Our experience working with laboratories in many different countries is that most laboratories do not specify quality requirements for measurement procedures.

In this issue the gap is large and critical as quality requirements (selected according to the intended use of the measurement procedures) are of extreme importance in the technical requirements implementation process: making decisions about the clinical use of the results, designing the internal quality control, assessing the reports of the external quality assessment schemes and/or proficiency testing schemes, and monitoring the measurement procedures periodically (e.g. using the Sigma-metric).

Although the gap is significant, the solution is simple and its implementation is swift. We always start by training the laboratory staff at the bench level, those responsible for each testing section, Quality Managers and Laboratory Managers, to understand the need for quality requirements. We present different alternatives, criteria and sources for quality requirements.

During the first stage of implementation many laboratories select CLIA (Clinical Laboratory Improvement Amendments) quality requirements for measurement procedures for clinical chemistry, hematology and hemostasis, and RCPA (The Royal College of Pathologists of Australasia) quality requirements for hormones, oncology markers and immunology.

Laboratories generally need to choose their quality goals by consensus; the process may at times be complicated, since there are several criteria sources available.

Once the quality requirements are established, we make sure that they are known by all parties, accepted by the managers and easily available in the working areas.

3. Verification and/or validation of performance measurement procedures.

In the introduction we mentioned that many laboratories believe that the analytical quality of the measurement procedures is assured by the manufacturers.

When we start an accreditation project, we work hard to dispel this myth. Most of the time we find that laboratories have done nothing about quality requirements, and they have also not bothered to either verify or validate their methods.

Evaluating a measurement procedure implies determining its errors through the use of statistical tools (protocols). Once the magnitude of each type of error is known we compare it with the performance specifications declared by the manufacturer in their manual or package insert (measurement procedure verification) or we compare the magnitude of the different kinds of errors with a specification or quality requirement (measurement procedure validation). There is a summary of what has been presented in the following Figure (Figure 17-2). Review "5.5 Analytical procedures" in chapter 3 for more detail.

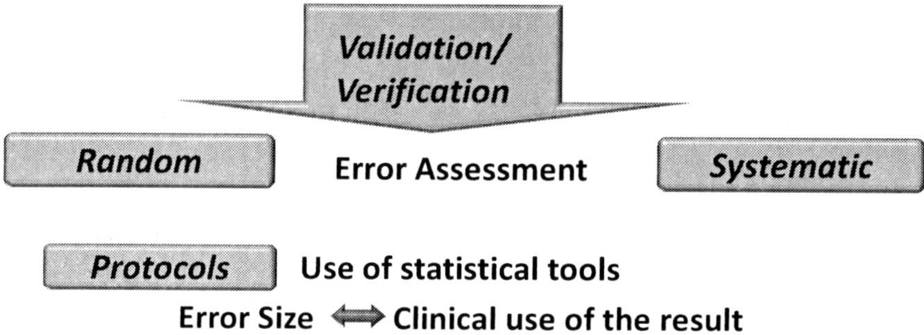

Figure 17-2: Scheme which defines in a simple way the objective of measurement procedures assessment.

It is important to associate the analytical concept related to each type of error and identify the corresponding statistics (Figure 17-3).

Type of Error	Related Concept	Statistics
Random	*Precision*	*CV, SD, Variance*
Systematic	*Trueness*	*Mean, Bias*
Total	*Accuracy*	*Total Error*

Figure 17-3: Type of error, related concept and statistics.

Laboratories should know when it is appropriate to validate or verify a measurement procedure (Figure 17-4).

In many cases, method verification is sufficient; however, we strongly advise that once the initial verification of critical performance parameters has been completed, the laboratory integrates the information to estimate the Total Error of the measurement procedure and assess if the performance is acceptable according to the quality requirement selected in accordance with the intended use of the measurement procedure (see the "Method Decision Chart" in chapter 11).

Sigma-metrics can also be used to judge the performance of the measurement procedure once the initial verification has been finished (see the "OPSpecs Chart" in chapter 12).

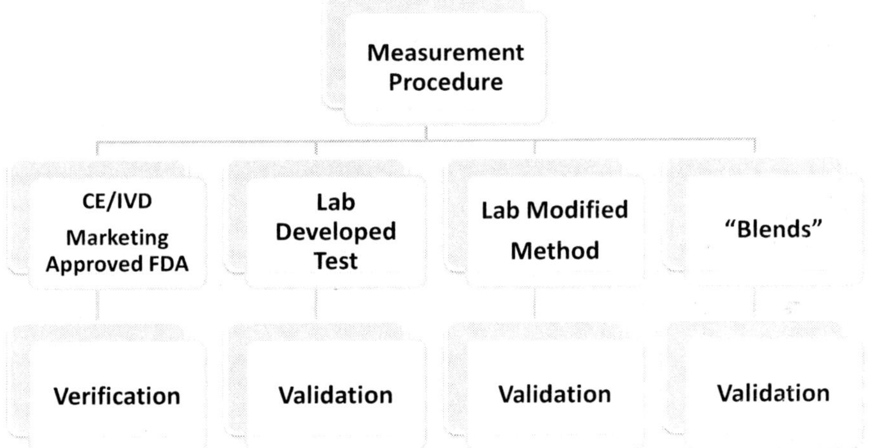

Figure 17-4: Decision Figure to define when to verify or validate a measurement procedure.

We emphasize issues related to method verification. The laboratory must identify the critical performance parameters which should be verified. In order to do this, the laboratory must know the regulation requirements and /or standards (Figure 17-5).

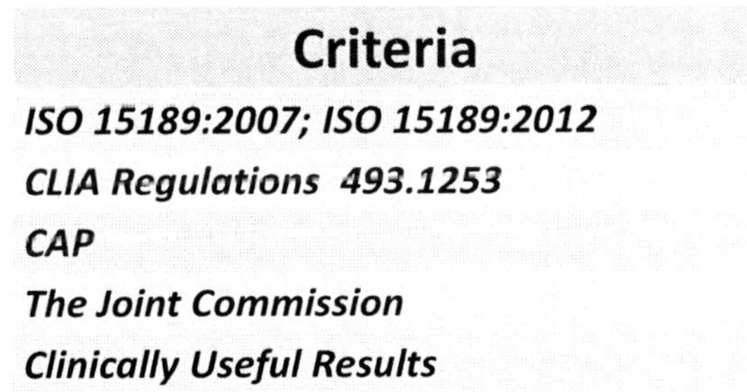

Figure 17-5: Different regulatory adn accreditation criteria

Despite the variety of requirements, there is consensus about many of the critical performance parameters which should be verified for quantitative and qualitative measurements procedures. The following Figure (Figure 17-6) shows the framework for quantitative measurement procedures.

Quantitative Measurement Procedure	
Development Parameter	**CLSI Guideline (Protocol)**
Accuracy in repetition conditions	EP 15- A2 [2]
Accuracy in intermediate accuracy conditions	EP 15- A2 [2]
Veracity	EP 15- A2 [2]
Analytical Range (linearity)	EP 06-A [3]
Quantification Limit (when applies)	EP 17-A2 [4]
Reference Interval (when applies)	EP 28-A3C (before C 28-A3c) [5]

Figure 17-6: Quantitative measurements procedures

CLSI provides guidelines for validation and verification which are widely disseminated. Although these guidelines are very useful, they are not the only ones available. There are other tools which can be applied, some of them simpler, others more complex.

Here is the framework for qualitative measurement procedures (Figure 17-7).

Qualitative Measurement Procedure	
Development Parameter	**CLSI Guideline (Protocol)**
Accuracy in repetition conditions	EP 15- A2 [2]
Accuracy in intermediate accuracy conditions	EP 15- A2 [2]
Diagnostic Sensitivity	EP 12-A2 [6]
Diagnostic Specificity	EP 12-A2 [6]

Figure 17-7: Qualitative measurements procedures

What we observe

As we have mentioned before, method validation and verification is not performed frequently in the laboratories. When labs reach this stage of implementation, they have already established the quality requirements and clearly defined the scope of the accreditation. When we begin this stage of the project, we train all the parties involved, starting with the EP 15A2 protocol.

We emphasize that this assessment is most of the time performed on tests and instruments which are already installed and routinely operating in the laboratory, except in rare cases when the accreditation process coincides with the installation of a new analytical system. It is essential to plan the needs prior to the implementation of the guideline. The appropriate materials should be selected, ensuring the correct interpretation of the statistics. The staff in charge of processing the routine samples should be responsible for selecting the materials for verification. It is important that they perform the validation in the midst of routine operation conditions. This EP15 guideline enables the laboratory to verify precision under repeatability conditions, precision under intermediate precision conditions, and trueness. We do NOT suggest running all three protocols simultaneously, nor do we recommend verifying all methods in the laboratory at once. In general, we work with each different laboratory section in turn. The initial interpretation of the results is completed with the staff of each lab section, or with the supervisors or staff in charge of those sections, and the Quality Manager. They all should be able to understand and interpret the results.

We have identified the following problems in the use of the EP15 guideline:

- Selection of correct materials to work with precision and trueness.
- Interpretation of the information provided by the manufacturers in their manuals or package inserts.
- Interpretation of the results through the use of worksheets.
- Equipment with repeatability problems due to inappropriate or lack of service.
- Problems with trueness trial-runs caused by incorrect interpretation of the measurement procedure traceability.

We emphasize that this protocol is a verification tool. We strongly encourage laboratories to use the data generated by the EP 15A2 protocols (Bias, CV) together with the quality requirement selected for the measurement procedure, to judge the clinical use of the test using the concept of Total Error (see "OPSpecs Chart" in chapter 12).

In this way, the laboratory assures that the performance observed meets the performance claimed by the manufacturer (published in the package insert and/or manual) and also show that the performance fulfills the selected quality requirement according to the intended use of the test.

At this stage of implementation, the staff is usually deeply interested and involved in the process and can identify improvement opportunities. It is probable that corrections can be made and the EP 15A2 protocol for some methods is repeated after implementing the improvements (e.g. maintenance or parts replacement).

Next, we recommend that laboratories use the EP06A guideline to establish the reportable range (or linearity).

We have found the same problem in most laboratories. Manufacturers and/or distributors do not usually register commercial materials for linearity. There is progress, however. Recently, we have noticed improvement related to the necessary materials for the area of hematology, as several manufacturers and /or distributors are providing these products. It used to be a complex chore for the laboratories to prepare linearity materials for hematology.

In the rest of testing sections, the laboratory must work carefully and exert considerable effort to obtain high concentration samples. Labs must seek out and secure patient samples with values closest to the high end of the range claimed by the manufacturer.

Once again, accurate training is essential for all staff. The protocol of equidistant concentrations should be explained clearly and all the technical and operational details implied in its use. (Figure 17-8)

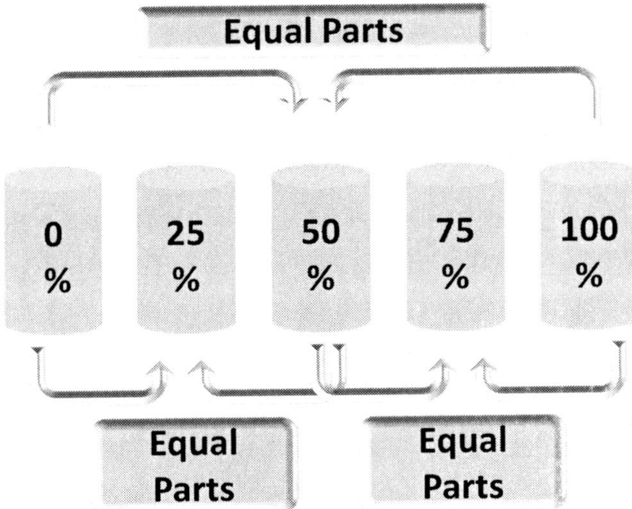

Figure 17-8: Protocol of equidistant concentrations

The critical issues of the use of EP6 are:

- Selection of the high concentration sample
- Selection of diluent or low concentration sample
- Volumetric material
- Volume of the dilutions
- Homogeneity of the dilutions
- Availability of software

During training we ensure that all staff understands the concepts of clinical linearity and statistical linearity.

The dilutions are processed in triplicate and a graph (Figure 17-9) of assigned concentrations ("X" axis) against observed concentrations ("Y" axis) is prepared.

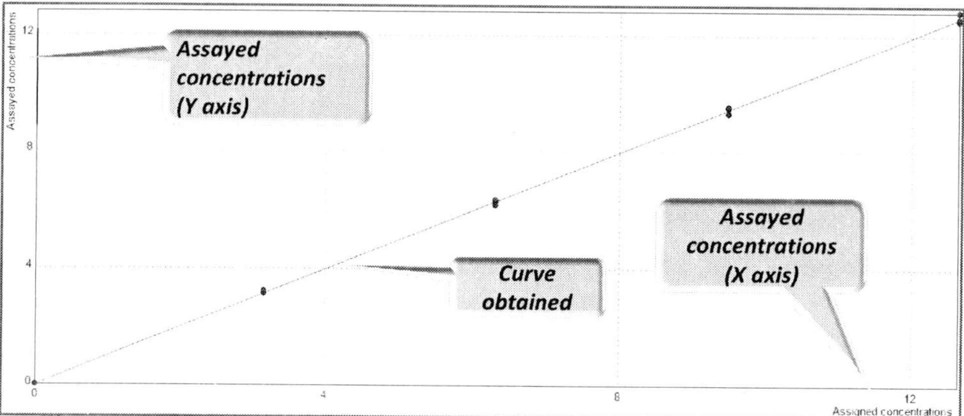

Figure 17-9: Graphic obtained through a linearity protocol implementing the equidistant concentrations scheme.

It is essential that all parties understand that a measurement procedure may not be statistically linear and yet can be clinically linear. The method will be statistically linear only if the equation obtained through the traced points is based on an equation of order 1. Otherwise, (equations obtained through order 2, 3 or 4) clinical linearity should be assessed. If a measurement procedure is to be clinically linear, the non-linearity error should not exceed 50% of the selected quality requirement (Figure 17-10)

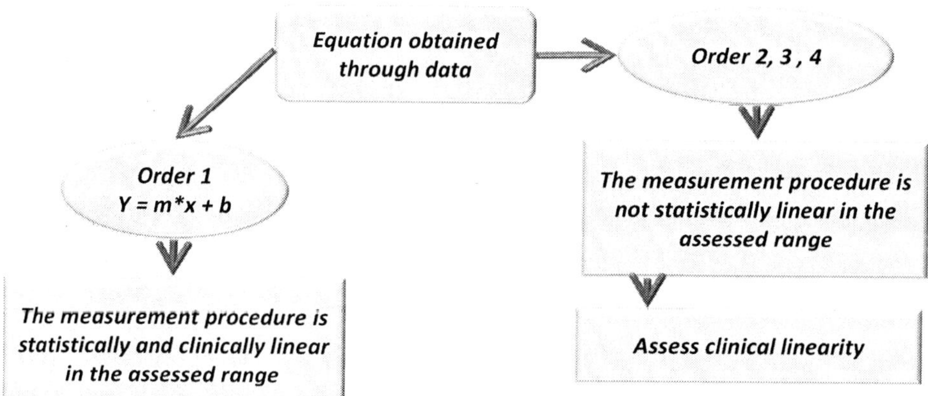

Figure 17-10: Statistical and clinical linearity assessment

The following Figure (Figure 17-11) summarizes the possible results for reportable range assessment

Equation	Statistically linear	Non linearity error	Clinically linear
Order 1	*Yes*	*0 (zero)*	*Yes √*
Order 2, 3 or 4	*No*	*Higher than 50 % TEa*	*No*
Order 2, 3 or 4	*No*	*Lower than 50 % TEa*	*Yes √*

Figure 17-11: Assessment of results for an analytical range verification protocol (linearity) through the implementation of an equidistant concentrations scheme.

We stress the fact that getting the high concentration sample is the biggest challenge facing the implementation of this guideline. Also, choosing an inappropriate diluent or low concentration sample may cause difficulties.

If the quantification limit of the assessed measurement procedure is relatively high, then working with diluents is not advisable. We suggest working with a high concentration sample (as close as possible to the highest limit of the range claimed by the manufacturer) and a low concentration sample (barely above the quantification limit declared by the manufacturer). Sodium is a clear example of this situation.

Due to matrix and test run design, labs frequently use the "zero" concentration calibrator as diluent together with a high concentration sample (as close as possible to the high end of the range declared by the manufacturer) for many hormones and oncology markers.

Generally, there are no international regulations – as there are in the USA – that require reportable range verification and/or periodic calibration verification. However, those laboratories with international accreditations choose to carry out calibration verifications at least once a year.

Verification of quantification limit is not usually done in the laboratories in the area due to high cost and the complexity of the statistical analysis. The protocol proposed in the last version of the EP17 guideline from CLSI (EP 17A2) brings a simpler approach. This assessment is only required by some accreditation organizations; therefore labs usually avoid it. It does apply to methods which have critical concentrations – representing medical decision levels – in the low end of the measuring interval.

The use of the EP17 guideline applies to certain hormones (e.g. TSH), oncology markers and certain cardiac markers (e.g. troponin).

The limiting factors of the protocol proposed in the first version of the EP17A1 guideline were:

- Economic (required 100 to 140 determinations)
- Time (duration of protocol: 20 days)
- Data analysis (need for software)
- Training
- Handling of dilutions
- Limitation of equipment to offer reading data

Due to these limitations, this protocol was rarely applied.

The new CLSI guideline EP17A2 proposes a simpler protocol for quantification limit verification, in a shorter time period and with fewer samples. It could be completed within 4 to 5 days, running about 50 samples, with a very easy statistical analysis.

Finally, it is important that laboratories verify their reference intervals. This task is always done at the end of the verification process.

As usual, we begin by training all parties. Then we ask the laboratories to revise their test reports and make sure that the current reference intervals are the correct ones. Usually, we find that laboratories have reference intervals selected for methods which are no longer in use or have already been replaced but are still loaded in their LIS systems. Many times the new measurement procedures employ a different measurement principle and have different traceability. Therefore, the old reference intervals are no longer valid.

This initial assessment of the reference intervals in use provides the laboratory with many opportunities for improvement. Once the laboratory assures that the reference intervals are appropriate, it should proceed with its verification.

The statistical tool to be used for the reference intervals verification (EP 28A3C "before C28A3c") is very simple. During the training in reference intervals, we offer a questionnaire taken from the CLSI guideline for the selection of healthy individuals which provide several exclusion criteria (Figure 17-12).

Alcohol consumption	*Breastfeeding*
Transfusion	*Obesity*
High blood pressure	*Occupation*
Drug abuse	*Oral contraceptives*
Drugs prescriptions	*Pregnancy*
Genetic factors	*Surgery*
Recent hospitalization	*Tobacco consumption*
Recent disease	*Vitamin abuse*

Figure 17-12: Exclusion criteria for Reference intevals

Twenty healthy individuals are needed for the verification of a reference interval. The following Figure establishes the acceptability criteria (Figure 17-13):

Amount of individuals off reference interval proposed over twenty evaluated individuals	Percentage	Conclusion / Action
≤ 2	*< 10 %*	*Proposed interval verified*
From 3 to 4	*From 15 to 20 %*	*Assay twenty new healthy individuals*
≥ 5	*≥ 25 %*	*Establish reference interval*

Figure 17-13: Reference intervals verification criteria

Laboratories quickly find out that most of their reference intervals are partitioned by sex, by age or other criteria. Should laboratories select twenty healthy individuals for each partition? The answer is no! They should select the majority population partition and verify it.

However, in cases where the reference intervals are only partitioned by sex, we suggest that laboratories verify both the intervals with twenty male adults and twenty female adults. Once the majority reference interval has been verified, it is considered that the rest of the population partitions are also verified.

It is relatively simple for outpatient laboratories to obtain twenty healthy individuals. This is not so simple for hospital laboratories as most of the patients are affected by a disease or are excluded due to the criteria presented in Figure 17-12. For these laboratories, we advise them to ask for help from the blood bank to obtain twenty healthy individuals.

In most of our projects, we have not had any inconvenience with laboratories adopting this guideline and the results are highly beneficial.

4. Planning Internal Statistic Quality Control

In Chapters 6 and 7, particularly on Chapter 8, the requirements for the internal statistical quality control (SQC) were introduced. In addition, the book *Basic QC Practices*[7] details the rationale and theory on planning the internal statistical quality control and good practices on statistical quality control. It is essential to recognize the need to plan an internal quality control for each test, taking into account the quality requirement and the current performance of the method. Figure 17-14 and 17-15 present explanations of elements in designing IQC and the sources for specifications.

Quality Requirements	• Taking into account the intended use of the measuring procedure
Random Error	• Precision (Imprecision) • CV; Standard Deviaton
Systematic Error	• Accuracy • Bias

Figure 17-14. Elements in Designing Internal Quality Control (IQC)

Quality Requirements	• Web sites • Bibliography
Random Error	• Validation/Verification • Interlaboraty Schemes • Internal Statistic Quality Control
Systematic Error	• Validation/Verification • Interlaboraty Schemes • External Quality Control • Internal Statistic Quality Control

Figure 17-15. Sources of Specifications and Data for Design of Internal Quality Control

Using the Six Sigma (Sigma Performance and Critical Systematic Error), IQC can be designed effectively. There are different tools (software or manual graphics) available to carry out this task.

What we observe

In many laboratories the current internal quality control is arbitrary and the planning is non-existent. It is very common that laboratories analyze controls at two levels (or three levels for hematology and immunology) once a day for the different tests. Further, it is commonplace that labs use only the 1_{2s} rule with their Levey-Jennings control charts. Worse still, this 2 SD specification seldom represents the *actual* performance of the laboratory method. It is easy to see that this type of system is arbitrary, corrupted by errors, and incapable of detecting clinically significant errors. More frequently, this type of IQC leads to high false rejections. Clearly, this situation is not aligned with the appropriate design of internal statistic quality control.

When we encounter laboratories with these problems, we build upon elements that will ease the work. Consider that at this stage the laboratory has already complied with:

- Selecting the Quality Requirements taking into account the intended use of the measuring procedure.
- Verifying and/or validating its measuring procedures (it knows its "CV" random error and its "Bias" systematic error).

It is essential that everyone is trained. In this case, we make our training "hands on" and use the data obtained during the initial verification of the methods together with the quality requirements already selected. In this way, the laboratories are working with their own data and can immediately apply the new concepts. While a laboratory may run hundreds of tests, only three to four different QC procedures for internal quality controls are usually recommended, taking into account the Sigma Performance of each evaluated measuring procedure (see Figure 17-16).

Sigma	Performance
$\sigma < 2$	*Unacceptable, not valid as routine measuring procedure.*
$2 \leq \sigma < 3$	*Marginal, a quality improvement scheme must be applied.*
$3 \leq \sigma < 4$	*Poor, it will need an quality control procedure with more than one anlytical run (R) and multiple measurements per run (N).*
$4 \leq \sigma < 5$	*Good, the clinical utility of the results is assured by multiple rules.*
$5 \leq \sigma < 6$	*Very Good, the clinical utility of the results is assured by a single rule.*
$\sigma > 6$	*Excellent!!!!!!*

Figure 17-16: Sigma Performance and Internal Statistic Quality Control

Customized IQC requires system support in the laboratory. Depending on the laboratory and its resources there are different alternatives:

- Using the QC software of the individual instruments (as long as they are updated and allow the selection of control rules).
- Using specific quality control software to implement the laboratory QC.
- Using software offered by the quality control material providers (many times offered with participation in EQA schemes or peer group comparison programs).
- Using the QC module of the laboratory LIS system as long as it allows the individual selection of rules.
- Using the QC module of software aimed at the follow up of the samples as long as it allows the individual selection of rules.

Laboratories applying for accreditation often run a great number of tests. To achieve accreditation means that manual implementing of internal quality control procedures would be too complex.

We have encountered resistance by some laboratories against the application of IQC procedures that require running controls several times a day (more than one analytical run (R) with several controls per run (high N)). When test performance is poor, IQC design results in an increase in the costs and complexity.

Accreditation standards, and quite simply good laboratory practice, indicate that if controls are out of range, samples should be retained, problems analyzed, corrective actions taken and then the patient samples reanalyzed.

Cost analysis demonstrates quickly that the expense associated with the repetition of patient samples (not only economically) is much higher than the cost resulting from segmenting the day into more than one analytical run for the methods with inferior performance (running more controls more frequently). In fact, the new version of the ISO 15189:2012 [1] standard clearly refers to this situation (5.6.2.3 Data of the quality control).

5. Implementation of Customized Internal Quality Control

As mentioned earlier, laboratories generally perform internal quality control in an arbitrary way. We strongly recommend consulting *Basic QC Practices* [7] where the reader will find rational instructions on the design of internal quality control and good practices on interpretation of statistical quality control procedures.

Basically we train laboratories to embrace the correct way to implement internal quality control generated by the initial planning, always remembering that the control charts must represent the current performance of the laboratory.

What we observe

Whenever we undertake an accreditation project we find the laboratory does perform some kind of internal quality control. However, what they perform rarely emerged from an objective, scientific approach to designing statistical quality control.

An initial inspection of the typical internal statistical quality control reveals issues that deserve immediate attention.

The critical points are:

- Selection of control material
- Treatment of control material
- Mean and standard deviation assigned to the control charts
- Blanket application of a single rule for internal quality control
- Actions taken against out of control situations

Again training is essential to achieve short term improvements. We deliver training on best practices for internal quality control together with training on design and planning of QC procedures.

Substantial improvements are always achieved by standardizing the treatment of the control material. We frequently see inconsistencies in the treatment, storage and handling of control materials.

Due to cost and availability issues, lyophilized controls are frequently used in areas lacking a reliable logistical chain. The following figure (Figure 17-17) highlights the critical aspects to achieve a correct standardization on the treatment of this type of material.

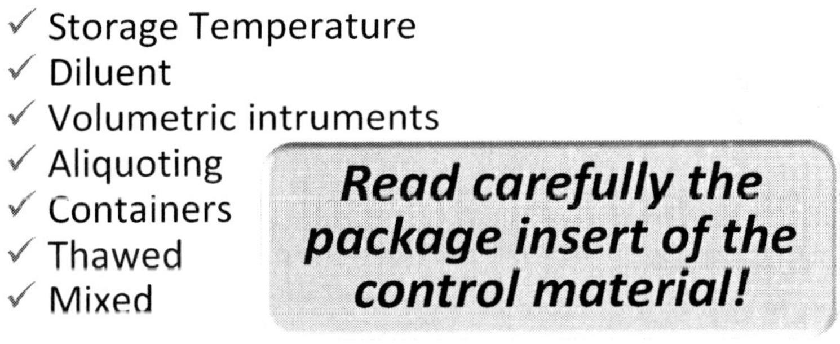

Figure 17-17: Critical aspects for the correct treatment of the control material

We have also found many instances where laboratories use control charts that do not represent the actual performance of the method. This error is of great importance. If the control chart doesn't reflect true performance, it can't detect true changes in the method.

Control charts are frequently found with assigned means and standard deviations that do not represent the actual performance of the laboratory method (for instance, mean and standard deviation taken from the package inserts offered by the providers of the control materials). Usually, the laboratory implements a quality control system based on the principles shown on the following figure (Figure 17-18).

Basis of Internal Quality Control

✓ *Select the appropriate control materials.*
✓ *Treat control materials correctly.*
✓ *Establish mean and standard deviation for the values obtained under stable conditions.*
✓ *Generate the control limits.*
✓ *Compare daily results with the ones expected in stable conditions.*
✓ *Identify unusual situations which may represent unstable performance.*

Figure 17-18: Basis of the Internal Statistical Quality Control

Once the control charts are correctly designed and able to detect the clinically significant errors (i.e. a high probability of error detection) and able to reduce the generation of unnecessary rejections (i.e. a low probability of false rejections), laboratories apply the QC procedures with the following characteristics:

- Number of Analytical Runs (R)
- Number of control measuring per analytical run (N)
- Control rule/s

The most frequent issues found and targeted for eradication in training are:

- Inappropriate treatment of the control materials.
- Control charts with incorrectly assigned mean and standard deviation.
- Arbitrary application of quality control procedures.
- Facing an out-of-control situation, responding with a repeat of controls immediately (without carrying out any investigation).
- Automatic repetition of controls with a new control aliquot (without carrying out any investigation).
- Ignoring out-of-control situations.
- Refusal to repeat patient samples when out-of-control situations occur.
- Repeat controls (without corrective measures in the middle) until obtaining a control valid result.
- Omitted deviations.
- Serious lack of information in the action logs related to the internal statistical quality control.
- Confusion over corrective actions (lack of clear guidance to solve problems).

Although there is a big gap, important changes can be achieved through careful training and awareness-building. Once the laboratory understands the dynamic of the internal quality control it stops being a hassle. Properly designed QC procedures are a true ally, enabling the detection and correction of errors before they impact on the clinical utility of the test results.

6. Analysis and follow up of the participation on Schemes of External Quality Assessments (EQA) and/or Proficiency Testing (PT).

Many times, though not always, we find that laboratories in the area participate in schemes of external quality assessment (EQA). Local, regional and international schemes are available.

We strongly encourage reviewing Chapter 13 to understand the participation and treatment of the data resulting from the analysis of schemes reports on the external quality assessments (EQA) and/or Proficiency testing schemes (PT).

There is a guideline available from CLSI (GP27A2 "Using Proficiency Testing to Improve the Clinical Laboratory; Approved Guideline—Second Edition")[8] providing recommendations on how to use data from EQA/PT for the continuous improvement at the laboratory.

What we observe

It is worth mentioning the results of our recent experiences involving several countries. Before a large audience, consisting of members from private and public laboratories with different levels of complexity, we asked how many of them participated of external quality assessment programs. The response was alarming; the participation percentages were extremely low.

In general, laboratories facing accreditation do participate in EQA and/or PT. Nevertheless, we have detected severe deficiencies on the treatment and interpretation of the reports generated by this type of schemes.

The common practice of laboratories receiving the reports is to check if there is any exclusion and if everything appears correct, it is archived on the corresponding folder.

If there is an excluded result, the laboratories try to see what might have happened. These may be random attempts, not standardized and rarely registered.

Once more, hands-on training is essential.

The first aim is to generate awareness on the utility of the EQA/PT reports. We make it known that much information can be obtained from not only the rejected results, but also the acceptable results. It is important to get laboratories to analyze the results of the last surveys together with previous surveys, looking for deviations or tendencies which could be gradually unfolding without having a clinical impact yet (Figure 17-19).

We encourage laboratories to change from a reactive attitude to a proactive, preventive attitude with these reports.

At this stage of the implementation we propose alternatives so the laboratories can estimate their method bias from a set of surveys.

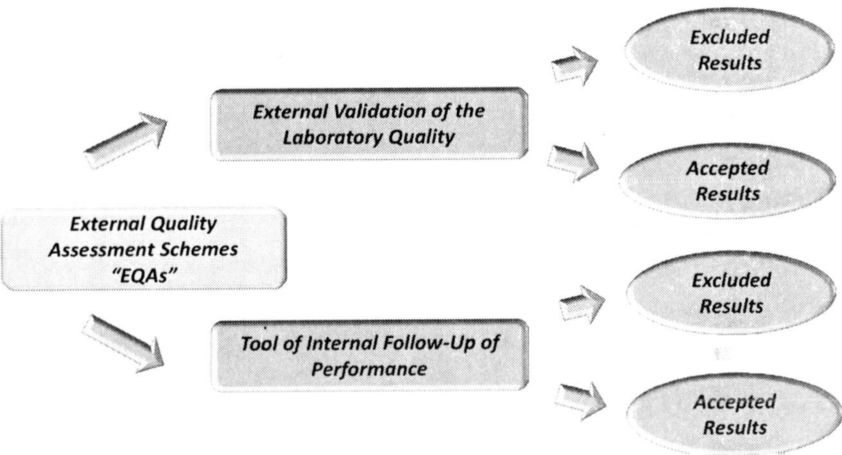

Figure 17-19: Analysis of EQAs results

This bias estimate is renewed with each new arrival of an EQA/PT reports; this bias estimate enables the laboratory to get a periodic estimate of the systematic error. That, along with the random error estimate provided by the internal statistical quality control, allows laboratories to continuously monitor method performance over time.

At this stage, the laboratory again uses the selected quality requirement to assess the clinical utility of the results. To achieve this, the laboratory must comprehend the concepts of "bias" and "measurement error" very clearly and understand the difference between them. We recommend reviewing these two concepts of the VIM (International vocabulary of metrology — Basic and general concepts and associated terms JCGM 200:2008) [9].

Laboratories can compare the results of the individual surveys against the quality requirement established according to the intended use of the measuring procedure. The "measuring error" (generally estimated aas a % of an individual survey) must be lower than the selected quality requirement.

When laboratories estimate the measuring procedure bias (generally %) starting from a set of surveys, it must be lower than 50% (or 25%) of the selected quality requirement (presumably from the quality requirement assigned to the systematic error).

When laboratories evaluate results of the last survey with previous surveys, they abandon their reactive attitude and adopt a preventive attitude, frequently detecting deviations and tendencies earlier than they would have, errors that have not yet impacted the clinical utility of results but will do so in the future if there is no action.

Another newly instilled behavior is the event log. Results excluded according to different criteria (scheme provider and/or by the laboratory) are treated as nonconformities. We must work this aspect many times with laboratories.

7. Estimation of measurement uncertainty on measuring procedures

Chapter 15 discusses "Measuring the Uncertainty of Measurements" and is completely devoted to the development of this subject with different points of view and focuses. Therefore, we will not go deeper into the theory.

What we observe

Laboratories seeking accreditation according to the ISO 15189:2007 [10] standard had to adopt new practices to estimate the uncertainty of the measuring procedures. In the 2007 version of the standard, ISO only required this when it was "relevant and practical."

When we work with laboratories seeking ISO 15189 accreditation, we explain the MU concepts and present the different calculation models so the laboratories can decide which model to apply.

This implies the estimation of uncertainty of the quantitative measuring procedures. No laboratory we have worked with applied the model of the "Guide to the Expression of Uncertainty in Measurement (GUM) [11]. They all used approximation models including the following elements:

- Uncertainty component associated to the random error
- Bias (not usually corrected at the clinical laboratory)
- Uncertainty component associated to the bias estimation

The component associated with the random error (on all models of approximation) is always taken from the data of the internal quality control of the laboratory itself (intermediate precision conditions) of a period not shorter than 6 months.

The source of the bias and the uncertainty associated to the estimation of the bias come from different resources depending on the chosen model. The applied models use two different data resources for the uncertainty component associated to the systematic error:

- Data obtained from the participation on schemes of pair group comparison or inter-laboratory schemes.
- Data coming from the participation on External Quality Assessments Schemes (EQA) and/or Proficiency Testing Schemes (PT).

The applied models enable a periodic estimation of the measurement uncertainty. In no case are variables of pre-analytical or post-analytical phases taken into account.

Another relevant point is the fact that laboratories only *estimate* the uncertainty because the ISO 15189 standard compels them to, but they seldom make practical use of the data or compare them with a requirement to evaluate acceptability. They only keep them available in case inspectors request the data. They are not obliged to report the measurement uncertainties with the patient's test results.

It is a fact that clinicians receiving results, in most cases, are not able to interpret the concept of measurement uncertainty and in case MU was reported accompanying the results, it would probably cause great confusion.

Another relevant fact is that the uncertainty estimations are only required of laboratories at the moment of the accreditation audit or follow up by the corresponding accreditation agency.

In summary, laboratories facing ISO accreditation will estimate the measurement uncertainty for their audits, but they generally operate using the concept of Total Error and monitor method performance using the Sigma-metric.

The new version of the ISO 15189:2012 Standard [1] (see Chapter 15) deals with the measurement uncertainty in a more practical way and the reader may observe that what is requested does not differ greatly from what accredited laboratories in the area have been doing all along.

As time goes by, the concept of MU will probably take root and its application may become potentially useful to the clinical laboratory.

8. Follow-up Performance Measuring Procedure

By this stage of the accreditation process, laboratories are highly trained, have an accurate grasp of the concepts developed above, and count on all necessary elements to interpret the performance of their methods. Much of the performance follow-up data can be used to formulate indicators of the analytical quality for the Quality Management System.

What we observe

All the laboratories applying for accreditation must carry out periodic assessments of their method performance. In general, labs review their performance monthly. We may start with training to show the different alternatives. Laboratories are obliged to participate on External Quality Assessment Schemes (EQA) and/or Proficiency Testing Schemes (PT). At the same time, many of them participate in peer group comparison or interlaboratory programs.

To carry out a performance assessment it is necessary to access data on the random error and the systematic error of the measuring procedure during the considered period.

The most classical follow-up schemes are:

a. Random error: Internal Statistical Quality Control (CV%).
   Systematic error: External Quality Assessment Schemes and/or Proficiency Testing Schemes (Bias %).

b. Random error: Schemes of peer group comparison or interlaboratory (CV%).
   Systematic error: Schemes of peer group comparison or interlaboratory (Bias %).

Independently from the model chosen by the laboratory, the CV % and Bias % are then compared with the selected quality requirement according to the intended use.

Again, new alternatives arise:

- Total Error (see Figure 17-20)
- Sigma Performance (see Figure 17-21)

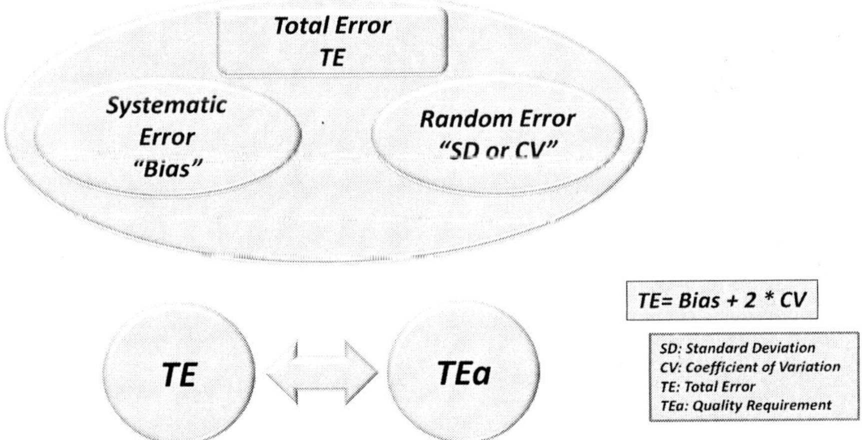

Figure 17-20: Concept of Total Error

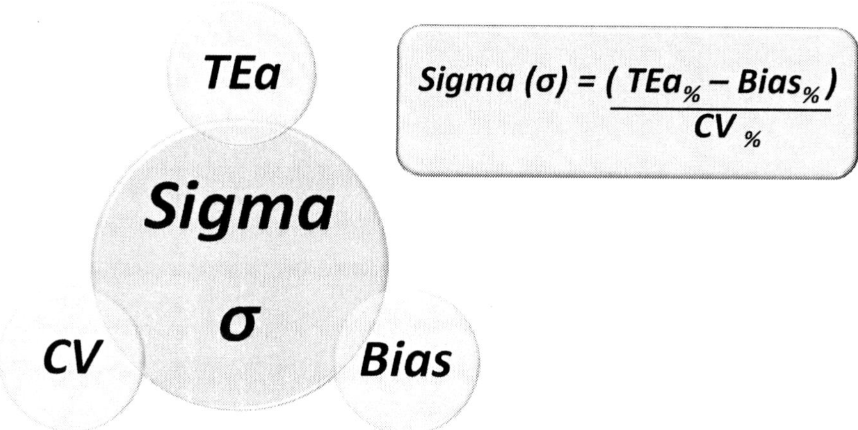

Figure 17-20: Concept of Sigma Performance

What's the point?

When laboratories seek accreditation, most of them find a large gap at the analytical quality level. The assumption that the analytical quality is assured by the manufacturers or vendors is deeply rooted.

A clear plan following a logical order of implementation and hands-on, down-to-earth training is essential to achieve improvement.

It is important to stress that laboratories working on this type of implementation construct a continuous improvement cycle. They must identify a permanent structure or process that will help them identify improvement opportunities and ensure the utility of the clinical results.

This continuous improvement cycle is fundamental to implement and maintain a lasting Quality Management System.

References

1. ISO 15189:2012. Medical laboratories – Requirements for quality and competence. 3rd ed. International Organization for Standards, Geneva, Switzerland, 2012.

2. CLSI EP 15A2. User Verification of Performance for Precision and Trueness. CLSI, Wayne, PA 2005.

3. CLSI EP 06A. Evaluation of the Linearity of Quantitative Measurement Procedures: A Statistical Approach. CLSI, Wayne, PA 2003.

4. CLSI EP 17A2. Evaluation of Detection Capability for Clinical Laboratory Measurement Procedures; Approved Guideline—Second Edition. CLSI, Wayne, PA 2012.

5. CLSI EP 28A3C (Formerly C 28-A3c). Defining, Establishing, and Verifying Reference Intervals in the Clinical Laboratory; Approved Guideline - Third Edition. CLSI, Wayne, PA 2010.

6. CLSI EP 12A2. User Protocol for Evaluation of Qualitative Test Performance; Approved Guideline - Second Edition. CLSI, Wayne, PA 2008.

7. Westgard JO. Basic QC Practices - Wallace Coulter Edition. Madison WI: Westgard QC, Inc., 2013.

8. CLSI GP 27A2. Using Proficiency Testing to Improve the Clinical Laboratory; Approved Guideline—Second Edition. CLSI, Wayne, PA 2007.

9. VIM. International vocabulary of metrology Basic and general concepts and associated terms JCGM 200:2008

10. ISO 15189:2007. Medical laboratories – Requirements for quality and competence. 2nd ed. International Organization for Standards, Geneva, Switzerland, 2007

11. GUM. Guide to expression of uncertainty in measurement. ISO, Geneva, 1995.

Index

ISO 15189 sections

A

B

C

N

O

P